The Madness of John Terrell

TRUE CRIME HISTORY

The Madness of John Terrell

Revenge and Insanity on Trial in the Heartland

Stephen Terrell

The Kent State University Press   *Kent, Ohio*

To my parents,

MARTHA LOUISE BREWER TERRELL

and

THOMAS ORVILLE TERRELL

for the rich legacy of family stories they,

and my more than forty aunts and uncles,

passed down.

Just not this one, of which they never spoke.

Melvin Wolfe was a mean, nasty, cheating son of a bitch and the handsomest man I ever saw—right up to the day my pa put a shotgun against his head and blew his brains all over Doc Saunders's office. Blew him straight to hell. Guess he blew the rest of our lives to hell, too.

LUCY TERRELL JOHNSON, 1958

Contents

Acknowledgments

This book could not have been written without the assistance, advice, and encouragement of so many people. Primary among them is Janis Thornton. A wonderful author in her own right, she took time to give her thoughts on early drafts and revisions, insights on the publishing process, and most importantly, continuing encouragement even when my own confidence ebbed.

I want to thank my friends Mike King, Keith Roysdon, and Ted Waggoner, and the Speed City Sisters in Crime Critique Group who gave their comments on early drafts. Their advice helped craft the final shape of this book.

Libraries are far more than books on shelves. Over the more than three years of research on this project, many librarians provided invaluable assistance. Specifically, I want to thank the librarians at Wells County Public Library in Bluffton, Indiana; Bracken Library at Ball State University; Indiana State Library; and Marion Public Library. They guided my research in ways that allowed me to find materials I would never have located on my own. At a time when librarians face unprecedented challenges, they have been staunch defenders of the First Amendment. And long before Google, librarians helped us all find answers to those seemingly unanswerable questions.

A special thank-you to the staff at the Indiana State Archives. They found the twenty-five-hundred-page transcript of John Terrell's trial, the papers of Gov. Winfield T. Durbin, and the single sheet of paper concerning my great-uncle that remained from the papers of the East Haven Asylum. They also exhibited unending patience and courtesy as I spent two weeks, my iPhone in hand, scanning each page of the fragile transcript.

The Randolph County Historical Society provided background information dating back to the first Terrell to step foot in Indiana and remarkable insight into life in frontier Indiana. The Wells County Historical Society pointed the way to the sites where the Bluffton Grand Opera House (now a parking lot) and the old Wells County Jail (now the Wells County Public Library) used to stand.

I owe an enormous debt of gratitude to the staff of the Wells County Circuit Court, Clerk, Auditor, and Recorder; Randolph County Auditor and Recorder; and Huntington County Clerk. To a person, those who work in those government offices were friendly, courteous, and helpful in digging through records more than a century old.

Thanks to the Wells County Land Title Company for tracking down the property records that confirmed the location of the house (still standing) where John Terrell and his family lived when the events in this book took place.

Of course, I owe much to modern technology. Without the ability to conduct internet searches and the existence of websites such as Ancestry.com, Newspapers.com, NewspaperArchive.com, and other similar sites, much of what I discovered in this book would be lost to history.

Finally, my undying gratitude and thanks to Susan Wadsworth-Booth, director of Kent State University Press; Kat Saunders, associate editor; and the entire staff at Kent State University Press. Without their talents and tireless efforts, this book would never have reached your hands, and my dreams of writing this book would never have been fully fulfilled.

Stephen Terrell
April 24, 2024

Prologue

In the early months of the pandemic, and recently retired, I used my suddenly available free time to work on my family tree, something I had dabbled with over the years but never investigated in depth. Modern online tools made the task much easier.

I found newspaper searches for obituaries and death notices invaluable in uncovering family history. They frequently provide information about where the person lived or his or her occupation. Sometimes such notices contained difficult-to-find information such as names of married daughters, their husbands, and grandchildren.

I began my search with a head start. Dozens of family stories had been passed down through the years at reunions and holiday gatherings. I knew that my great-grandfather, William Wesley Terrell, had the largest headstone in Union Cemetery where so many of my relatives were buried. He was a land-wealthy farmer and preacher of the gospel, and he and my great-grandmother, Mary Ann Thornburg, had eleven children, including my grandfather, William Ulysses Grant Terrell.

What I did not know until my ancestry search was that Mary was William's second wife. His first wife was Rebecca Thornburg, Mary's first cousin. William and Rebecca had two children, Josephine, born in 1850, and John Wesley, born in 1852 and the focus of this book. Rebecca died not long after John's birth, and William remarried about eighteen months later.

I knew nothing of John except his birth and death dates. So, I set out to find more. As I searched, I found a sometimes-troubled family that in many aspects resembled William Faulkner's star-crossed Compson family of Yoknapatawpha County.

My first step was to use an online database of historical newspapers. I typed a search for "John Wesley Terrell," the date of his death, and searched Indiana newspapers, looking for an obituary. The first result left me staring slack-jawed at my computer screen.

JOHN W. TERRELL SUCCOMBS HERE
Wells County Man Who Murdered Son-in-Law,
Dies at Home of Daughter

Death of John Terrell Marks Close of
Noted Criminal Case

With the death at 9 o'clock this morning of John W. Terrell, 63, at the home of a daughter, Mrs. Lucy Terrell Johnson, in Muncie, Ind., there was written the final chapter in one of the most noted criminal cases in Wells County and the state of Indiana, a case in which John Terrell, in 1903, shot and killed his son-in-law Melvin Wolfe.[1]

A quick scan of several newspapers of the time revealed that my great-grandfather's eldest son was not just a murderer, but one of the most infamous criminals in turn-of-the-century Indiana.

More than three years of research followed. I found hundreds of newspaper stories about the shooting, the trial, and the aftermath, including a front-page article in the *New York Times*. In the Indiana State Archives I found, untouched for more than a century, the twenty-five-hundred-page trial transcript, as well as orders from Indiana governor Winfield Durbin. There were also records in various county offices, historical societies, local and state libraries, and cemeteries.

The records told a remarkable story of love, money, lust, abuse, betrayal, rage, violence, murder, and insanity.

What follows is the story of John Terrell, a hardworking farmer who became perhaps the wealthiest man in Wells County, Indiana, when oil was discovered on his farm in the early 1890s. But wealth did not bring good fortune.

This story is told as narrative nonfiction. The extensive testimony and news stories provided details and much of the actual dialogue. I've used citations to indicate when dialogue was documented in a court transcript or another source. When not accompanied by a citation, I've used fictional dialogue consistent with known facts, reflecting the diction of the time period and the characters' individual voices and personalities as I've come to understand them through their testimony, newspaper accounts, and historical records.

Part I

Wealth and Misfortune

Oil is the excrement of the devil.

PEREZ ALFONZO

Revenge is an act of passion;
vengeance is an act of justice.

SAMUEL JOHNSON

1

Ambush on a Sunday Afternoon

July 12, 1903

A dust cloud rose from behind the two buggies, each with their tops down, headed south along Bluffton-Camden Pike.[1] Single horses drew the carriages along at a four-beat ambling gait. Now nearing 6 P.M., the searing afternoon heat had passed its zenith. The sun, now tinged with red, was lowering in the western sky. It was perfect for a Sunday sweetheart's buggy ride.

Clarence Turner, a rough-hewn farmer, held the reins of the lead carriage. Rosa Dowling, a rather dour, petite young woman, sat close against him. Twenty yards behind was the buggy driven by Melvin Wolfe, dressed in his dark Sunday suit. Seated too close for propriety, mainly since Melvin was still legally a married man, was his nineteen-year-old stepsister Della Reed. A buxom brunette, her posture was held erect by the whalebone stitched into her corset.

Melvin leaned toward Della. "We're coming up on old man Terrell's place," he said, a mischievous glint in his eye. "Let's have some fun."

"Mel, you'll get us all in trouble," Della said, covering her mouth politely to conceal her conspiratorial laugh.

"He's such a cabbage head," Mel said. "Let's steam him up a little."

Mel eased back on the reins, slowing the horse to a walk, and guided it toward the left edge of the gravel road. A weather-worn man in late middle age was carrying a bale of hay toward the barn. Six feet tall and sinewy, he wore a sweat-stained undershirt, denim bib overalls, and a scuffed pair of dirt-covered work boots. Two toddlers played in the dust only a few feet from where he worked.

5

Melvin drew the carriage nearly even with the man. Then, with a wink toward Della, he yelled, "Hold up the little bastard. I want to see it."

John W. Terrell dropped the hay bale and glared at the passersby. Melvin let loose with a hearty laugh and gave the horse a flip on the reins. The horse immediately responded by breaking into a trot.

Della put a playful elbow into Mel's ribs. "Oh, Mel, you're awful."

A mile down the road, Clarence slowed the lead carriage, then turned it around to face the direction from which he had just come. Melvin pulled in the reins, bringing his buggy to a halt next to Clarence.

"Time to head back," Clarence said.

"Not yet," Della protested.

"I'd like to keep going as much as you, maybe more," Clarence said, nodding toward Rosa, who was snuggled tight against him. "But I still got to feed and water the stock and get the cows in the barn before nightfall. It's more than five miles back to Melvin's place. It'll take me an hour to get back there, drop off Rosa, then get home to do my chores."

Melvin looked toward Della and gave a begrudging nod. He urged the horse in a big half circle and again fell behind Clarence's rig. The horses resumed the easy four-beat gait, retracing the path traveled only minutes before.

Della turned toward Melvin. "Mel, is there some way we can avoid the Terrell place? The way you yelled at him, he looked perty upset."

"That old man don't worry me none. He's nothing but a milksop. If you're scared, you can scoot up closer to me. And I got something you can hold on to."

Della's mouth opened, feigning shock. She pulled her arms tight against her breasts. "Why I never."

"You sure did," Melvin said, throwing his head back in a laugh.

Della stuck out her tongue, unfolded her arms, and scooted across the seat board against Melvin.

A half mile up the road, they approached John W. Terrell's farm. No one was visible around the house or in the barn lot on the opposite side of the road.

"Melvin, can't you speed up a little 'til we get by Terrell's place?"

"Aw, I'm just having fun. That old man ain't nothing to worry about."

Della saw a movement of the weeds in the ditch on Melvin's side of the road. Then she saw the glint of metal catching the late-afternoon sun.

John Terrell stood from where he was concealed among buckhorn, goldenrod, and thistle, revealing himself and the double-barrel shotgun he held in his hands. Still wearing his grimy undershirt and overalls, he was no more than eight feet from Melvin's buggy. The first blast went off before John raised the gun level, scattering the shot in a cloud of dust, gravel, and steel pellets.

The horse startled and reared, its front legs pawing at the air. Melvin pulled tight on the reins, trying to maintain control. Terrell cursed at his misfire. He took careful aim, then squeezed the trigger again.

This time Terrell did not miss. The blast hit Melvin with the impact of a mule kick. The air went out of Melvin so fast that he could not even yell.

Melvin looked down. His right leg was bent at an unnatural angle between his hip and knee. Countless holes perforated his trousers, spewing a river of red. He had seen that much blood only when slaughtering hogs. His leg would not move. Melvin knew shock was holding back the pain. He had seen that when hunting. But he knew the pain would come soon.

Della gulped in a deep breath, screamed, then screamed again. The horse reared again and took off at a gallop. Melvin could do nothing but look at his leg. Della grabbed the reins from where they had fallen from Melvin's hands. She pulled back enough to regain control of the horse but not so much that she slowed its pace.

Melvin was only vaguely aware of Della and her actions. The pain began to work through the shock and into Mel's consciousness. It was like nothing he had ever felt, not even when, as a boy, he got his foot caught under a fully loaded corn wagon. Holy Jesus! He never knew anything could hurt that bad.

"Mel!" Della screamed breathlessly. "Oh, God, Mel. Hold on. I'll get you to the doctor. Just hold on."

A guttural groan was Mel's only response. He fell hard against her, his face already turning ashen. Their carriage flew by Clarence and Rosa at a dead run. Della did not see their startled looks.

John Terrell watched the speeding buggy disappear down the road. He broke his shotgun open and pulled two more cartridges from a pocket on his overalls. He loaded them in the breach, then snapped the gun closed as he walked into his barn. His son-in-law's bay horse was waiting, still in its harness from the ride home from a family dinner an hour earlier. It was a plow horse to use in the field, but now John had another purpose in mind.

Mumbling to himself, John led the horse from the barn and hitched it to his buggy. His pale-blue eyes bulged and face flushed, John climbed into the buggy. With one hand holding the reins and the other hoisting the shotgun above his head, John gave a yell, and the horse took off at full gallop.

Dust clouds still hung in the air from where Melvin Wolfe's buggy had passed only minutes before. John drove his horse forward at a fearsome pace, heading toward the bustling town of Petroleum and the event that would forever change his life and the lives of everyone connected with him.

2

Raining Money

Spring 1892

Located thirty miles south of Fort Wayne, Wells County, Indiana, is a rural area of flat rich farm ground and game-rich woods. In the late nineteenth century, it was an area of farms and small towns that were not much more than crossroads with a general store and a church. More than a century later, not much has changed except for running water, electricity, cars, the internet, and national chain stores that have driven out most of the local merchants. An occasional rusted pump dots the landscape, the only remaining sign of the oil boom that swept the county beginning in 1889 until the wells began drying up after 1906.[1]

John Wesley Terrell, then twenty-seven, moved to Wells County with his family in 1880.[2] They moved with John's widowed and childless great-uncle, seventy-seven-year-old Drummond Terrell, who had raised John from the time he was two years old. In February 1880, Drummond sold his land in Randolph County and purchased a quarter section in southern Wells County near the hamlet of Nottingham. Within four months, Drummond conveyed 120 acres to John, and six months later, he conveyed the remaining forty acres.[3]

Farming was backbreaking work in late-nineteenth-century Indiana. Men guiding teams of horses or mules attached to moldboard plows provided the only power for plowing, taking two weeks of twelve-hour days to break the ground in a forty-acre field. Provided it didn't rain.

In the spring of 1892, thirty-nine-year-old John Terrell was, for the most part, indistinguishable from other farmers in Wells County. Like so many others, he worked from before sunrise to after sunset to support his family—raising cash crops and livestock and carefully managing his accounts to the penny. His wife Catherine tended to the vegetable garden, cooking and keeping house, but epilepsy and pernicious anemia plagued her throughout her life. Fortunately, their four children were old enough to help around the house and farm and did not need much attention: Sarah, known to everyone as Sally, at fourteen, was the oldest. Lucinda, whom everyone shortened to Cinda, was one year younger. Mary Lucy, never called anything but Lucy, was ten. The youngest was the only son, Jake, age six.

But in spring 1892, John's life and the lives of his family changed in an instant.

John was plowing a twenty-acre stretch not far from the railroad line that ran through the eastern part of his land. The long-sleeve work shirt under his overalls was drenched with sweat and dirt. He pulled the team to a stop and grabbed the water jug that hung off the plow frame, taking a long drink.

A hundred yards distance, standing stark and black against the spring sky like a giant spider, was a wooden derrick where Frank Brown and his two-man crew were drilling. In the three years since the first well hit oil about eight miles north of John's farm, derricks had sprouted across Wells County like some new crop. John, his shoulders aching from a week of constant plowing, decided to check the progress of the well. He left the two-horse team where it stood and walked toward the tower.

As John drew closer, the consistent "Clang! Clang! Clang!" of steel pounding on steel grew louder. A large big-bellied man in worn overalls and a battered straw hat turned and, noticing John, waved. He stepped off the wooden rig where he had been giving orders to two men in ragged shirts covered with dirt and grime and walked to meet John.

"How d'you do, John," he said, spitting a long stream of reddish-brown tobacco into the soil and rubbing it into the dirt with his boot. "What brings you over here?"

John took off his straw work hat and wiped sweat from his thinning hair with the sleeve of his work shirt. "Thought I'd come over and see how the well's doing, Frank."

Frank Brown shook hands with John then turned so that he and John were side by side, looking up at the derrick. "We're down about nine hundred feet, I reckon," Frank said.

"How far you gotta go down to know if you're gonna hit something?"

"The average 'round here is about nine hundred feet, so if we're going to hit something, we should be getting close."[4]

John nodded but didn't speak. The two men stood silent, listening to the sharp rhythmic pounding of steel on steel as pipe was forced deeper and deeper into the earth.

John felt it first. A rumbling came up from the soil.

"Hey, boss!" one of the men yelled from the derrick. "Something's going on."

Frank's eyes widened. "This may be it," he said to John, then turned and trotted back toward the derrick.

John heard the horses behind him. First one horse, then the other started making noises, their nostrils flared. Then the horses bolted, turning and running across the field, the plow bouncing behind them. John knew that the horses wouldn't leave the field; he could retrieve them later. He kept his focus on the derrick.

Frank and his two workers grabbed wrenches and scurried around the wellhead. Then came the sound—a rumbling rushing sound. Pipes hummed. Bolts popped. Timbers creaked.

A black liquid column shot out of the earth, up the forty-foot wooden structure and thirty feet beyond. Oil fell like a summer storm, coating the derrick, equipment, and men. Whoops and hollers cut through the roar of the gushing oil. The oil workers, already covered in oil, grabbed oversized wrenches and went to work capping the well, careful not to ignite the oil stream.

Frank ran over to John, oil covering his face and arms and dripping from his clothes. "There's your answer, John!" he shouted. "You got yourself an oil well."

"Looks pretty, Frank. But ain't that wasting money?"

Frank gave a hearty laugh and shook his head. "We'll get it capped. But don't you worry. We'll put this land's tit in a wringer and get out every drop of oil we can."

John nodded. "So, when you gonna drill the next one?"

3

The Vandergriff Boys

1895

In the three years following the discovery of oil on John's farm, he became a wealthy man. Three oil wells were already producing on his farm, which he had expanded by fifty-five acres,[1] and a fourth well was in the works. By May 1896, six oil wells were producing on John's farm.[2]

The Vandergriff brothers arrived on the Terrell farm early in 1895, hired by Frank Brown to work in the oil field. From Van Buren in neighboring Grant County, they were lean, strong, and handsome with well-defined muscles. And young. Joseph was twenty-five and Ben was only eighteen.

When the Vandergriff brothers came to work in the Terrell oil field, John's oldest daughter, Sally, was seventeen, and his middle daughter, Cinda, was sixteen. The girls were tall, good-looking, and becoming young women with a burning desire to leave the farm.

Cinda first saw the brothers, naked to the waist, covered with oil and dirt as she took lunch to her father as he worked the fields. It wasn't long before Cinda caught the eye of the youngest brother, Ben.

That entire summer and fall, Cinda took every opportunity to sneak away from the house and find Ben, spending a few minutes with him behind the pump house, stealing kisses when no one was watching. By October, they were going for buggy rides.

Neither John nor Catherine was excited about an oil field worker wooing their sixteen-year-old daughter. Roughnecks were known as ruffians, hellraisers, and men of low morals. But they did not interfere.

That December, with her mother's consent, Cinda invited Ben to Christmas dinner with her family. The family sat around the large dining room table where Catherine and her three daughters placed a meal of ham, biscuits, canned corn and beans, boiled potatoes, and both pumpkin and sugar cream pies.

Even though both John's father and grandfather were hellfire and brimstone preachers, there was no grace. John wasn't a believer, something rare in the Bible Belt country of rural Indiana. Instead, he pronounced the Bible as "a bunch of hooey" and preachers as charlatans who kept trying to stick their hands in other men's pockets. But despite his beliefs, he tolerated a Christmas tree and decorations, and an exchange of gifts.

"I have something to say," John announced as Catherine passed enormous pieces of pie around the table to finish Christmas dinner. "Ma and me decided we're gonna move into town."

"You selling the farm?" Sally asked.

"Nope. I ain't selling nothing. But I got enough money. We're gonna try town living for a change."

"What town we moving to?" Lucy asked.

"Bluffton," he said, naming the Wells County seat. "It's only ten miles up the road. I can still work the farms and keep an eye on my property."

"You gotta house picked out?" Lucy, the youngest, asked.

"It's a grand two-story brick house on West Cherry Street. It's even got indoor plumbing. Your ma likes that."[3]

A hubbub circulated the table about the wonders of indoor plumbing and the prospect of no more winter trips to the privy. When the conversation subsided, Cinda cleared her throat to get everyone's attention.

"I got something, too." When everyone's attention was on her, she continued. "Me and Ben are getting married."

Neither John nor Catherine shared their daughter's joy. Cinda had just turned seventeen, and her older sister, Sally, had not yet married. Worse, she was marrying an oil field roughneck. Catherine would have been much happier if her daughters married farmers or shopkeepers.

John grunted. "I ain't paying for no church wedding," he said. "You can go down to the courthouse and get married."

And on Monday, January 13, 1896, that's what Cinda and Ben did.[4]

Two months after Cinda's wedding, John moved his family—his wife Catherine, daughters Sally and Lucy, and son Jake—into a two-story federalist-style home on West Cherry Street in the county seat of Bluffton.

John rose early most days to travel nearly a dozen miles to the farm. Once a week, sometimes twice, he stayed in Bluffton, tending to his expanding business portfolio. John purchased property with his oil money, including a business building in Bluffton and a stable in the newly platted and aptly named town of Petroleum, both of which he leased out.[5] He bought several farmhouses, renting them mostly to hired farm laborers. He became known as one of the best resources in the county for small loans between $100 and $200, each done with a formal note and security agreement. Anyone who fell behind would quickly hear from John's lawyer.[6]

Cinda and Ben moved into a small house that John owned not far from the village of Nottingham. He let Cinda and Ben stay there rent-free until they got on their feet.[7]

Perhaps with the encouragement of her younger sister, Sally began courting Ben's older brother, Joseph. On January 3, 1897, Sally, now twenty, married Joseph Vandergriff in a simple civil ceremony.[8]

At first, the couple lived with Joseph's parents in Van Buren in Grant County. But after about eight weeks, they moved onto the George Gerhard farm near Warren in Huntington County, where Joseph got a job drilling a new well.[9]

Wedded bliss wasn't in the future for the Terrell sisters. Thanks to the Vandergriff brothers, their worlds soon collapsed.

1897

There was no real honeymoon for Sally. Joseph started mistreating his new wife shortly after they moved to Warren. After work, he often stayed late at the local tavern, leaving Sally at home with no money and little food in the house. When he did come home, he had few good words to say to her, cursing and sometimes striking her.

Just over six months after their wedding, Joseph packed a bag with his clothes and all the money he could find and left. Sally was alone, without food, and penniless except for five dollars hidden in a shoe.

The next day, Sally returned to her parents' home on West Cherry Street in downtown Bluffton. "He was just awful," she told her parents. "He yelled at me, hit me, beat me. He never gave me money to buy food. Then yesterday he says, 'I've had enough of you,' and he packed his bags and left."

"Don't you worry none," Catherine said. "You can stay here as long as you need to."

John stood. "I knew them goddamn well drillers weren't no good. Ain't no need staying married to a man like that."[10]

That night, Sally shared Lucy's room, lost in tears. Through the next few days, John paced, wringing his hands and mumbling. He didn't talk. He didn't eat. He didn't sleep.

In late September, Joseph showed up at the Terrell house. He had a new job in the oil country in Pennsylvania. He begged Sally to come back to him. After a week of persistence, Joseph convinced Sally. On the last day of September, she and Joseph caught a train and settled in Oil City, Pennsylvania.

Three weeks after Sally left with Joseph, Cinda showed up at the door of the West Cherry Street home. Catherine saw Cinda's trunk sitting on the street, and her heart sank.

"He hit me and was mean to me," Cinda said, tears running down her cheeks. "He said he couldn't keep me, and he got in our wagon and just left."

Catherine put her arm around her daughter and led her into the house. "Them Vandergriff boys ain't worth spit," she said.

John returned home from his usual Saturday routine of conducting business at the bank and his lawyer's office. He found Cinda sitting in the parlor with her mother. He comprehended the news before anyone said a word.

"He left me," Cinda said to John.

John sat down as Cinda told her story.

"He was just mean to me. He'd come home and hit me and yell at me. And that horse you gave me? Ben sold it and kept the money." Cinda paused, then added, "He even had the nerve to accuse me of messing around behind his back with his brother."

"Sally's husband?" Catherine exclaimed.

"Not him. His younger brother, Bill. He's just a boy. Only about fifteen. I ain't done nothing with him but talk."

John remained silent, wringing his hands.

Cinda looked up, tears streaming down her face. "And the worst part is I'm gonna have his baby."

In Pennsylvania, the renewed bliss between Sally and Joseph did not last. Joseph resumed going to local taverns, spending all his wages on whiskey and card games. Worse, he became violent, and Sally had nothing to do but sit on her bed and cry for hours at a time. By Thanksgiving, Joseph was gone, taking all the money in the house.

Sally pawned her new bedroom suite for fifteen dollars, packed her clothes, and bought a train ticket for Fort Wayne.[11] From there, she caught the interurban to Bluffton. By Sunday afternoon, she sat in the parlor of the West Cherry Street home, telling her story that differed little from Cinda's. John sat in his overstuffed chair, saying nothing as tears rolled down his face.

A month after Sally returned home, she realized she was pregnant. As the New Year approached, John and Catherine found themselves with two pregnant daughters in their house, both of whom had been abandoned by their husbands.

. . .

Cinda's pregnancy was difficult. In late April 1898, she went into labor. The family summoned a doctor, but there was little he could do. The baby, a boy, was stillborn. The doctor considered himself lucky to have saved Cinda's life.

Ben didn't try to visit his wife. When the doctor sent him a bill for his services, Ben refused to pay it. Neither did he pay for the cemetery plot or tombstone.

So, John did. He paid the doctor's bill, picked out a plot in the cemetery, and paid all the funeral expenses for his hours-old grandson.[12]

Sally's pregnancy was less eventful. On June 27, 1898, she gave birth to a healthy baby girl she named Georgia Elliott Vandergriff.[13]

It was not long before John began talking about moving away from their troubles—moving back to the farm. Little did he know that his family's greatest ordeal lay in front of them.

4

The Cad of Wells County

By 1901, the calamity in the Terrell household caused by the Vandergriff brothers was beginning to subside. The previous year, John Terrell sold his West Cherry Street property and moved his family back to the farm in Nottingham Township just over a mile south of Petroleum.

John's two oldest daughters, Sally and Cinda, were now both divorced.[1] Sally's baby, Georgia, was three years old. Sally was courting twenty-nine-year-old John Schott. Like her first husband, he was an oil pumper she met while working on her father's oil wells. But unlike the Vandergriffs, he was from a local farming family and still helped his father with farming.[2] John and Catherine were leery of any more oil workers in the family, but they soon felt more comfortable with John Schott than they ever did with either of the Vandergriffs.

Cinda was also courting a local man, William Books. He lived on the Warner family farm, where he worked year-round as a farm laborer, and talked of his plans to buy their farm. John and Catherine were comfortable with a farm worker as a prospective son-in-law.[3]

Oil was still flowing, and John's businesses were doing well. He now owned three farms, two in Nottingham Township and one in Jackson Township.[4] He continued renting houses and business properties and lending money. John was talking with several businessmen in the southern part of Wells County about forming a bank in Petroleum.[5]

. . .

On a breezy Sunday afternoon in June, John sat on a cane-back chair in the shade on the front porch of his house. He dozed off after dinner but was now awake, knowing he would soon have to get up to feed the livestock.

A black buggy with its top down pulled to a stop just outside the white fence in front of the Terrell farmhouse. Two men got out and headed toward the porch. John recognized the tall man wearing overalls and a white cotton shirt as sixty-four-year-old William Faulkner, a farmer who lived about two miles east of the Terrell farm. The other man, taller and younger, wore a black suit with a summer straw hat.

They each shouted a greeting as they approached, but John stayed silent. The two men stepped onto the porch and held out their hands. As they did, Faulkner spoke, a jovial grin across his face. "John, this is Reverend Leonard Denny."

John leaned forward in his chair just enough to reach the outstretched hands, but he did not offer the men a seat. "What can I do you for?"

Faulkner continued, undeterred by John's cool response. "Reverend Denny here is from over in Blackford County, but he's been preaching some right powerful sermons around here. A bunch of us think he's truly a man who has the spirit in him, and we'd like to build him a church over in Domestic. If we do, he'll come here and be the preacher."

The preacher spoke up. "I prayed on it, Brother John, and the Lord told me that this is what I should do—spread the Word to these parts."

John smirked. "I got me three half brothers, and best I recollect, you ain't one of 'em."

For an instant, the smile disappeared off the preacher's face, but he promptly pasted it back on.

Faulkner continued. "Now John, I know your daddy and granddaddy both were preachers of the gospels. You have been blessed by God with the riches that come from this farm land and the oil underneath it. We're sure you want to give back to God to show thanks for his blessings and help build his new house of worship."

John leaned back in his chair. "That oil was down in the ground, and I had to hire men to find it and pump it out. It weren't no gift."

The preacher spoke up. "Now surely, Mr. Terrell, you must know that oil was created by the hand of God when he created the Earth."

John smirked. "I don't believe in all that mumbo jumbo. You ever read Robert Ingersoll?"

"You don't mean that atheist heathen?"[6]

"I do. And I'd advise you to read it, too. In my opinion, preachers ain't nothing but storytellers trying to get into people's pockets, and you ain't getting in mine."

"John!" Faulkner interrupted. "Don't speak that way to the Reverend Denny. He's a good man full of the spirit."

John leaned his head back. "Well, you the ones who come here wanting to pick my pocket. I didn't ask you up here."

"Well I never." With that, Faulkner took the preacher's arm and left.[7]

Lucy Terrell, now nineteen, was the youngest and, by any objective observer's account, the most beautiful of John's three daughters. She was tall and shapely, with smooth features and piercing blue eyes. For the past several years, local boys had tried to woo her without success. Her sisters' experience with the Vandergriff brothers left Lucy cautious.

Melvin Wolfe considered Lucy's rejection of other boys as a challenge.

Christened Leo Melvin Wolfe, he was the youngest son of a prominent farmer, livestock breeder, and oilman who lived on a large farm two miles east of Petroleum.[8] His mother, Hanna Wolfe, died on Melvin's seventh birthday.[9] Two years later, his father, Jacob, traveled to Pennsylvania, where he was introduced to and married a widow, Mary Reed. Mary brought with her a daughter from her prior marriage, Della Reed, who was three years younger than Melvin.[10]

Lucy knew Melvin from occasional meetings at the general store in Petroleum or seeing him at church socials. Even though John Terrell was not a believer in either the Bible or religion, he did not prohibit his family from attending social gatherings at area churches.

Lucy also was aware of Melvin from the gossip about him and sixteen-year-old Chloa Blair. The past fall, the story scorched through the south end of the county like an August grass fire. Chloa Blair was pregnant, and Melvin Wolfe was the daddy.

Melvin and Chloa Blair never married. Melvin's father, Jacob, paid off the Blair family debts in exchange for an agreement not to bring a bastardy charge against Melvin or insisting that the couple be married. The rumors were confirmed when Gladys Mae Wolfe was born on February 27, 1901.[11]

The whole episode had little impact on Melvin. He was out and about, flirting with girls and attending every cakewalk, square dance, and ice cream social between Bluffton and Pennville.

At the community Fourth of July celebration in Petroleum, Melvin walked up behind Lucy. "Miss Lucy, aren't you looking beautiful this fine summer day."

Lucy turned. Melvin stood in front of her, tall with a devilishly handsome face and deep brown eyes. His black hair was parted sharply down the middle. Despite the ninety-degree heat, Melvin looked cool as a fall day.

"Why Melvin Wolfe, I'm surprised you'd show your face here today. Where's that baby of yours?"

"She ain't my baby. Chloa got together with some farmhand her daddy hired, and she tried to pin it all on me 'cause my daddy has some money."

"That's not what I heard."

"Well, that's what happened. So, like I said, you are looking truly fine today. Did you bring anything to the picnic, or did your momma make everything?"

"I can cook. I made a buttermilk cake for the cakewalk. But you can't have any unless you win it."

"I might do that just to see if that cake is as sweet as you."

Lucy swatted at Melvin with the fan in her hand, but she could feel herself blushing.

Oil money that flowed into Nottingham Township paid for a firework display in Petroleum that exceeded anything that area farmers had ever seen. Lucy stood near the stable her father owned, watching red, white, and silver fireballs explode in the night sky. Clouds of acrid smoke drifted across the town on a gentle breeze.

Lucy felt a hot breath on the back of her neck. She turned quickly and immediately was kissed on the lips before she even knew it was Melvin Wolfe. Lucy pulled back and reflexively started to slap Melvin. But he grabbed Lucy's wrist before she could bring her arm forward.

"Don't tell me you've never been kissed before."

Lucy felt herself blush and was thankful for the darkness. "I've been kissed. Lots of times."

Melvin smiled. "Some Sunday afternoon, you and me are gonna go on a buggy ride. How about this Sunday? I'll stop by your house about 4 P.M."

Before Lucy could answer, Melvin disappeared around the corner of the stable.

True to his word, Melvin showed up at the Terrell farm the following Sunday afternoon. As the summer wore on, Melvin and Lucy were seen together more often, taking buggy rides, attending church socials, or taking walks. In their private moments away from prying eyes, Melvin pushed the limits of gentlemanly courtship. His kisses lasted longer, and his hands roamed to private places. Lucy would pull away, but Melvin persisted.

During the first week of September, Lucy's oldest sister, twenty-three-year-old Sally, remarried, this time to John Schott.[12] Sally and John moved into a small farmhouse, leaving Sally's three-year-old daughter Georgia with John and Catherine. That was her new husband's only condition on the marriage. He didn't want to raise someone else's child.

Only eight days later, on September 12, Cinda married Will Books.[13]

The following weekend, in a barn where he first tried to seduce Lucy, Mel tried again. After weeks of Melvin's pleading, demands, cajoling, begging, and repeated promises of undying love and marriage, Lucy gave in.

Eight weeks later, Lucy was certain of the worst. She was pregnant.

5

He Promised

"You promised me!" Lucy's voice was more pleading than demanding, more heartbroken than enraged, more desperate than lovelorn.

Mel stood along the path in the woods not far from the Wolfe farm, his wool coat pulled tight, his hands shoved in his pockets. It was a path he and Lucy had walked often through late summer and autumn, watching the sugar maple leaves change from green to orange to fiery red and finally drying to a dull brown. Now, on an overcast mid-November day, nearly all the leaves had fallen.

"I did no such thing," Mel finally said. "I never said we was engaged or that I was going to marry you."

"You did so!" Tears rolled down Lucy's cheeks. The cold cut through her, not from the icy wind but from the hatred on Mel's face.

"Never did. You're just trying to trap me like Chloa tried. But I ain't gonna be trapped. It ain't my baby."

"Mel, I ain't been with no one else."

"Sure you have. I bet you been with plenty. Hell, I bet you even been with that old daddy of yours."

"That's awful. You can't say that about me or about my pa. You know you told me that we was gonna get married and that's the only reason I let you have your way."[1]

"Well, I ain't gonna marry you. I ain't gonna pay for no baby. And I ain't gonna stay here and argue with you no more."

Mel brushed by Lucy, giving her a small shove out of the way. He tromped through the brambles toward the Wolfe house.

Lucy turned and walked across a fallow field to where her father's big bay Percheron stood, hitched to a farm wagon. She climbed into the driver's seat and broke into wailing sobs. The horse looked back, then without a command, began walking. It knew the way home.

It took several days before Lucy worked up the courage to tell her parents. One evening after supper, Lucy went into the parlor where John sat in his favorite chair, reading a newspaper, and Catherine sat on the davenport, knitting.

"I need to talk with you about something," Lucy announced, then sat on the hickory rocker that her father built a few years earlier. John put down his newspaper and Catherine dropped her knitting in her lap. They sat, waiting for Lucy to speak. After several long moments, John said, "Well, get on with it. What did you want to say?"

"I'm gonna have a baby." Lucy let the words out all at once.

Catherine gave a short gasp, her hand going to her mouth.

After a long moment, John spoke up, his voice gruff.

"I suppose that Wolfe boy is the daddy."

Lucy looked down at her lap.

"Well, is he?"

"Yes, Pa. He told me we was going to get married."

"It was a goddamn stupid thing for you to do. Didn't you learn nothing from your sisters?" After a moment, John added, "You're just going to have to marry him and make do the best you can."

"He said it ain't his and he ain't gonna marry me."[2]

With that, Lucy burst into tears. Catherine patted the davenport cushion. "Come here, dear," she said. Lucy got up and sat near Catherine. She buried her head on her mother's shoulder and sobbed.

John waited until the sobs had stopped before he spoke again. "Well, is the baby his or ain't it?"

Lucy looked up sharply, anger flashing across her face. "Of course it's his. He's the only man I been with."

John rose from his chair, then began mumbling and pacing across the parlor floor. Long minutes passed. Finally, John turned and faced Lucy.

"That boy's gonna have to make it right."

"What you gonna do, Pa?"

"I'm gonna have a talk with Jacob about his boy. Either that boy's gonna marry you or I'll set my lawyer and the prosecutor loose on him."

Jacob Wolfe owned a 160-acre farm two miles east of Petroleum.[3] Nearing sixty, Jacob was a successful farmer who was well respected in his community, known for breeding quality livestock. In 1899, a producing oil well was drilled on his farm.[4]

Two days after Lucy told her family of her pregnancy, John Terrell drove to Bluffton with Lucy to meet with Jacob Wolfe at the office of John's lawyer, Levi Mock.

John didn't waste any time getting down to business. "My girl here, Lucy, is gonna have a baby. Your boy Melvin is the daddy. He promised Lucy that he was gonna marry her. That's how she ended up this way. Now he says he ain't gonna marry her."

Jacob rubbed his chin. A long moment passed.

"You sure it's my boy's?"

Lucy spoke up, her voice soft and uncertain. "It's his. He told me he was gonna marry me. Then when I told him I was in the family way, he said he wasn't."

"I'm goddamn sure your boy is the daddy," John said.

Jacob, a strong church-going man, took offense. "No need for blaspheming."

"My girl ain't been laying with any other man," John said. "And this ain't the first time for your boy. He got that Blair girl in trouble. But he ain't getting out of this one. He's gonna marry my girl or I'm gonna sic the law on him. That's all there is to it."

Jacob nodded. "If the boy did this, he's gonna make it right."

John stood. "You talk with him and let me know. I'll give him a week. If he ain't married her by then, I'm gonna go down to the prosecutor's office and make sure he's charged with bastardy. He already ruined one girl's reputation. He ain't gonna ruin my daughter's."

"I'll talk with him," Jacob said. "I'll get word to you."

John left without saying more.[5]

Ten days later, on Wednesday, November 20, Melvin Wolfe and Lucy Terrell met at the Wells County Courthouse. Mel was dressed in a black wool suit with a high-collared shirt and wide striped tie. Lucy wore a white cotton dress with a high lace neck and gathered sleeves. It was too light for the season, but it was the best dress she owned.

In the presence of John and Catherine Terrell, and Jacob and Mary Wolfe, a justice of the peace performed the ceremony, which took less than five minutes. No one smiled. They did not kiss, and when they walked out of the courthouse, they did not hold hands.

Lucy Terrell was now Mrs. Melvin Wolfe, and Mel Wolfe, known as a ladies' man, a scoundrel, and a cad, was now a married man.

At the bottom of the courthouse steps, Lucy hesitated for a moment before following Mel to his buggy. John brought two bags to Mel's carriage containing all of Lucy's clothes. Without a word, he threw the bags in the back of the buggy and walked away.

Mel flipped the reins and the horse started off toward Lucy's new home—the Wolfe house.

6

Wolfe's Den

January–May 1902

The first few weeks at the Wolfe house seemed to go well for Lucy.[1] She and Mel shared a second-floor bedroom. Maybe it was because Mel was trying to make the best of the situation or maybe because he had such easy access to sex, but he was treating Lucy, if not with loving tenderness, at least with gentle indulgence.

Lucy quickly realized that while Jacob Wolfe was the patriarch and owned the farm, Mary Wolfe, Mel's stepmother, ran the house. She was stern, never smiled, and assigned Lucy chores in clipped commands. Lucy tried to fit in and did the chores as best she could, but her efforts never satisfied Mary.

As Christmas approached, the attitudes within the Wolfe house became noticeably cooler toward Lucy. Whether it was because Lucy's girlish figure was disappearing with her advancing pregnancy, or because the novelty of convenient sex was wearing off, or because the reality of marriage was fully taking hold, Mel's tone with Lucy became impatient and harsh.

There were no presents for Lucy under the Wolfe Christmas tree. Sitting in the parlor Christmas morning among the Wolfes, Lucy missed the warmth of her own family. "Mel, I'd like to visit my sister today. Can you take me over there so we can visit a while?"

Lucy heard a grunt from Mary. "Your daddy don't even believe in Jesus. I heard him say it. What does Christmas mean to you?"

"I want to see my family," Lucy said.

"Well, I ain't taking you," Mel said from across the room. "You wanna go, you can walk. It ain't much more than two miles to Petroleum. That's where she lives, ain't it?"

Lucy felt tears welling up, but she refused to cry in front of Mary or Melvin. Lucy went upstairs and dressed in her warmest clothes. She left the house without saying good-bye to anyone and began her walk to her sister Cinda's house in Petroleum.

That evening after supper, Cinda's husband, Will Books, brought Lucy back to the Wolfes' house in his covered buggy. Mel wasn't there.

"He's gone to church," Mary said. "And he took Della."

After the New Year, the Wolfes' coldness toward Lucy became palpable. There were no pleasant words for her—not from Mel, not from his stepsister Della, and certainly not from his stepmother Mary. Jacob wasn't abusive, but he never intervened to stop the mistreatment.

Morning sickness came in waves for Lucy, sapping her energy. But her confinement to bed made her even more of a target. "Get up!" Mel would yell at her before leaving the room in the morning. "There ain't nothing wrong with you except being lazy. You don't work here, you don't eat."

Minutes later, there would be pounding on the door. Mary would walk in, her voice rough as sandpaper. "I'd be ashamed if I were you, being so lazy. Now get up. You got chores to do. And if you don't get 'em done, you ain't eating at our table. Why don't you just go back to your home?"

The words stung. Lucy forced herself up, then dashed for the chamber pot in which she emptied whatever remained in her stomach. With the sour taste of vomit still lingering in her mouth, she dressed and made her way downstairs on wobbly legs to begin work.

Lucy didn't fully share in the food on the Wolfes' table. Mel's stepmother divided up whatever had been prepared for the meal among the family. Lucy's plate had half portions and her serving of meat was largely fat and gristle. Lucy would look at Mary, who sneered back, daring Lucy to say a word.

Lucy tried to make up for her lack of food on her weekly visits to the Terrell farm. She told the family she was always hungry and how she was being mistreated. She met with sympathetic ears, but there was little the family could do except send some extra food back when Lucy returned to her new home.

On a late January evening, shortly after Lucy had gone to bed, Mel burst into the room. She could smell the alcohol as soon as he entered. He was still wearing his boots. His eyes blazed with nothing but hatred. He thrust his hand into a pocket in his overalls. He pulled out a handful of bills and threw them on the bed next to Lucy.

"There," he said. "I went to town today. That's what the doctor will charge to do an operation on you."

Lucy was stunned speechless.

"Take it!" he yelled. "Ma can give you a ride into town. Then she can take you back to your home and your ma can take care of you."

When Lucy spoke, her voice was thin and halting. "You . . . you want me to get rid of the baby? That's what you want?"

"That's the money for it right there. And that's all you're getting out of me. I paid for one kid, and I ain't paying for another."

"We're married, Mel."

"That weren't no real wedding. You ain't no real wife. You should just go home. I think a damned sight more of Chloa Blair than I do you."

Lucy could barely get words out through her sobs. "I'm having your baby."

"That kid don't belong to me. It belongs to your old gray-headed daddy."

Lucy pulled her pillow into her face and screamed. She heard Mel stomp out of the room and the door slam behind him. She cried uncontrollably until exhaustion overtook her, and she fell into a fitful sleep.

Mel didn't return to the room that night. When he returned the next night, he put a quilt on the floor to sleep. He never again slept in the same bed with her.

By April, spring was sweeping across Indiana with blooming daffodils and crocuses, yards filled with dandelions, and blooming dogwoods and crabapple trees. Everything signaled rebirth. New life.

But for Lucy, life was as dreary and bleak and cold as midwinter. Words in the household were even more harsh. Nearly daily, Mel's stepmother would tell Lucy she should leave and go back to her own family. Sometimes she said so in front of Mel. He would just look at Lucy with a sneer, biting at his lips. He never said anything in Lucy's defense. Most nights, Mel did not even make an appearance in their bedroom, and never was he in her bed. No one ever asked Lucy how she was feeling or expressed any concern.

One evening during the second week in April, with Lucy now more than six months pregnant, Lucy heard Mel outside her door talking with Della. Lucy walked to the door, turned the knob, and pulled it open. The door slammed shut.

She tried to pull the door back open but could tell someone, likely Mel, was holding it closed. She grabbed the knob with both hands, and bracing her legs against the doorframe, pulled as hard as she could. The door opened just wide enough that she could see Mel with his hand holding tight on the doorknob. The knob slipped out of Lucy's hands and the door slammed shut again.

"What's going on out there? Who you talking to?"

"It's none of your damned business," Mel yelled back.

"Who you talking to?"

"Go back to bed and shut up. You ain't going nowhere."

Lucy heard a giggle. She wasn't sure, but it sounded like Mel's stepsister, Della.

"Going? Where you going? Who you going with?"

"Ain't none of your business where I'm going or with who. You ain't going."

Lucy threw herself on the bed. She was only twenty, but felt she felt like her life was over. Mel didn't want her or the baby. She knew that. He was going to abandon her just like he did Chloa Blair. And there was nothing she could do about it.

Lucy sobbed uncontrollably. There were not enough tears in the world.

Before 1909, opium and morphine were legal in the United States. With no Food and Drug Administration, no prescription was required. Estimates were that at the turn of the century, as many as one in two hundred people in the United States were addicted to opiates in one form or another.[2]

Among the most common substances sold by pharmacists was laudanum, a tincture of opium dissolved in pure alcohol. Laudanum dated back to the eighteenth century. It was taken by Benjamin Franklin for gallstone pain and given to Alexander Hamilton as he lay dying after his duel with Aaron Burr.[3]

Before the wide availability of aspirin, invented only five years earlier, laudanum was the miracle drug. By 1900, male doctors were prescribing laudanum for upset stomach and as a sleep aid. It was given to women for menstrual cramps, diseases of "nervous character," and for morning sickness. It was even given to babies with their mother's milk to help them sleep.[4]

As Lucy lay on her bed sobbing in great gasps, she saw the bottle of laudanum on the dresser. The bottle held about eight ounces when full. It was hard to see through the dark glass, but Lucy thought it was nearly full. The doctor had told her to take only one teaspoon when needed but no more than twice a day. He warned that more could be dangerous, particularly to a pregnant woman.

Lucy sat up, staring at the bottle for several minutes. No one wanted her. No one wanted her baby. Her life was shattered, without hope of redemption or happiness.

Lucy reached out and grabbed the bottle. She pulled out the cork and put it to her lips. She paused, tears falling in rivers down her cheeks. Then she upended the bottle and swallowed its contents in two big gulps. It was bitter and harsh as it went down. She coughed once but kept the liquid down.

Lucy lay back. Within minutes she could feel the effects of the opium and alcohol. As drowsiness overtook her, Lucy's last thoughts were that she hoped she would not wake up.

The next morning, Lucy did not make an appearance at the breakfast table. Mel, who spent the night sleeping on the chesterfield, was sent to retrieve his wife. He found her sprawled out on the bed, the empty laudanum bottle on her chest. He stood for a long moment, watching Lucy closely. Finally, he saw her chest rise.

Mel stepped outside the room and yelled for Mary. When she didn't respond, Mel yelled again. Finally, after Mel's third bellow, Mary made her appearance.

"What is wrong with you, Mel?"

Mel said nothing but stepped back and pointed into the bedroom. Mary walked by her stepson and looked in. She gave a small gasp and her hand went to her mouth. "How much laudanum was in that bottle?"

"I don't know. The doctor gave it to her a week or two ago."

"Damn fool girl. She's stupider than a hog. Don't she know you can't take a whole bottle of that? It can kill you."

Mel spoke, his voice quiet and more unsure than Mary had ever heard it. "I think that's what she was trying to do."

"Stupid girl," Mary repeated. "Well, she's breathing. I'll bring up a cool cloth, but there ain't much we can do other than that." As she left the room, Mary added, "Stupid girl. She needs to leave."

Even though there were two physicians less than two miles away, no one suggested going for a doctor.

For many Indiana farmers, May 10 marked the beginning of planting season. But for Lucy, it was just another day of despair. She was now more than seven months pregnant. The weight of the pregnancy was causing constant backaches and extreme fatigue. Mel had not bought any more laudanum for her, so she had nothing to relieve the constant pain or to help her sleep.

In her optimistic moments, she thought that once the baby was born, and Mel and his family saw the child, their attitudes would change. No one could hate a little baby, could they? And if they took to the baby, maybe Lucy would be accepted into the family.

But those thoughts were only fleeting. In her heart, she knew that the baby would not change anything. Maybe it would be best to go back home to have the baby. She decided to talk with Mel about it. But he was out working the fields with his father and older brother, getting them ready for planting.

It was near sundown when Mel and Jacob came home. They washed up and had supper. It was Saturday night, so as had become his habit, Mel headed into Petroleum, where Lucy knew he would find some whiskey and maybe a card game. The talk with Mel would have to wait until Sunday.

Near midnight, Lucy awoke. She kept her eyes closed, but knew Mel was in the room. She could smell the whiskey on him, and heard him getting out of his overalls and into his night clothes. She hoped to feel him slide into the bed next to her, but he had not done that in months. Instead, she heard his bare feet shuffle across the floor, the door opened, then latched behind him.

Without the aid of the laudanum, Lucy could not get back to sleep. She lay in the dark of the room, staring wide-eyed at the shadows illuminated by a half moon coming through the window. Later, whether ten minutes or two hours she couldn't tell, she heard noises. It sounded like voices, but she could not make out any words.

Lucy eased out of bed, her feet sliding into her slippers. She pulled her robe from a chair back and wrapped it around her, then silently walked to the door. Definitely there were voices. Male and female voices.

Lucy opened the door as quietly as she could. The sounds were from across the hall. From Della's room. Lucy stepped across the hall and grabbed the doorknob. She threw the door open.

There in the bed were Della and Mel, the blankets undulating, their voices filled with sounds but not words. Della saw Lucy first.

"It's her," Della said, pushing up on Mel. He kept moving but Della persisted. "It's her. It's Lucy. She's in the room."

Mel pulled up and turned. Even in the dim light of the room, Lucy could see a smile cross his face. "Well, if it ain't my wife. Come on over here."

Lucy stood still, not speaking.

Mel jumped up from the bed, not bothering to cover himself. He grabbed one of Lucy's arms with his calloused hand and pulled her toward the bed. Della put her hand to her mouth to stifle her laughs.

Mel sat on the edge of the bed, pulling Lucy with him. She tried to pull back, but Mel was too strong. As she was propelled forward, Mel's other hand went behind Lucy and firmly grabbed the back of her head. He forced her head down into his private parts.

"Put it in your mouth," he commanded.

"No!"

"Come on. You've done it before. Put it in your mouth."

Lucy felt herself being forced down. She could smell the sweatiness of his manhood and the odor of the interrupted sex.

"I won't. I won't," she said through clenched teeth.

Mel raised his hand from her neck then pounded on her back, great thumps that jarred her entire body.

"You push me down there, and I'll bite it. I swear I will."

Mel laughed, then let go of Lucy.

Lucy screamed, then slammed the door behind her as she went back to her room.

With the first sunlight on Sunday morning, Lucy was up, packing her clothes. Seven months pregnant and without any sleep, Lucy's anger could only overcome so much of her fatigue. Pausing when she couldn't continue any longer, it took her nearly two hours to get her bags packed. By the time she went downstairs, dragging her bags behind her, Lucy could tell that the Wolfe family was in the dining room eating breakfast. Even though it was a Sunday, Jacob and Melvin soon would head out to the fields. A fair-weather Sunday couldn't be wasted during planting seasons.

Lucy did not want anyone to see her. She quietly opened the door, dragged her bags outside, then eased the door shut behind her. The day was bright with only a few puffy clouds leisurely drifting across the sky. There was a bit of chill in the morning air, good weather for the long walk.

It was more than four miles home. Before she was pregnant, she could make that walk in an hour. But now, seven months pregnant, on an empty stomach, with no sleep and toting two heavy bags, Lucy figured it would take all of her energy to make the two-mile walk to her sister's house in Petroleum. From there, Cinda's husband could take her the rest of the way in his buggy. With luck, she would get home by dinnertime.

Lucy started the walk. By the time she reached the sheep shed, no more than a quarter mile from the house, she could go no further. Her legs quivered and could no longer support her. Lucy simply collapsed onto the dirt road. She was crying, but there were no tears. She had none. They were all used up.

Jacob spotted her as he was leaving for the fields in his wagon. Without saying anything, he lifted Lucy into the wagon and took her back to the house. "Go up to your room," Jacob directed, without the harshness in his voice she had grown used to. "You wait up there. When we come back for dinner, I'll have Melvin take you home."

Lucy stayed in her room until after noon when Mel opened the door. "My folks said you got to go home. Now get your stuff."

"My bags are downstairs."

"Well, get moving."

Lucy's bags were waiting on the front porch. Mel didn't offer to carry them, so Lucy picked them up. One at a time, she was able to lift them into the back of the wagon. Then she climbed up to the seat. Mel got up in the wagon, too, but kept as far from Lucy as he could get.

He hurried the two horses pulling along at a trot, not concerning himself with making the ride smooth because of Lucy's condition. Twenty minutes later, he pulled his wagon into the barn lot next to the Terrell farmhouse. No one was outside.

"Get out." Mel's voice was filled with anger.

Lucy turned to ease herself down. As she made her first hesitant step, Mel again yelled, "Get out!" and shoved Lucy, who lost her balance and fell to the ground, landing hard on her back.

While she lay in the dirt, Mel reached behind him and threw the bags onto the ground. One of the bags opened, sending Lucy's clothes flying.

Without another word, Mel sharply turned the wagon, shouted to the horses, and took off as fast as he could, leaving a plume of dust rising behind him.

Seven months pregnant, emotionally in tatters, Lucy was home.

7

Fraudulent Marriage

The Terrell family was seated around the table for a Sunday dinner when Lucy walked into the dining room without saying a word. Everyone looked up, stunned to see her.

"Oh, Lucy," Catherine said, "We weren't expecting you. You look so tired. Sit down here, and I'll fix you a plate."

"I'm home," Lucy said.

"Well, we can see that," Cinda responded.

"I'm home for good. Mel and his folks told me I couldn't stay there no more. Mel brought me home and shoved me out of his buggy. He threw my clothes all over the barn lot. They don't want me back."

Lucy's brother Jake, who was only a week away from his eighteenth birthday, was the first to respond. "That son of a bitch. Let me go find him, and I'll give him a good thumping."

Cinda got up, put her arm around her sister, and guided her to a chair. Catherine put a glass of water, a plate, and utensils on the table. Lucy gulped down the water, but she made no effort to put food on her plate.

John spoke his first words since Lucy walked in. "Jake, you go out and gather up Lucy's clothes from outside. You take 'em up to her old room. That's where she's staying now."

Jake took one last bite of chicken, then headed out.

"Tell us what happened?" Cinda said, her voice filled with concern.[1]

Lucy sat silent for a long moment before she spoke. Her voice quivered as she told the story of her time at the Wolfe house, from Mel offering her money to get an abortion to finding him in bed with his stepsister. When she finished, no one spoke.

At the head of the table, John's face was crimson. He pushed his chair back, got up, and walked across the room and into the pantry, closing the door behind him. Through the door, everyone could hear the sound of sobs.[2]

John isolated himself in the pantry for nearly thirty minutes, not speaking to anyone. When he finally opened the door and walked out, Catherine, Cinda, and Lucy had moved to the front parlor. The women discussed how they would make room for Lucy and the new baby.

John entered the room and began rapidly pacing, rubbing his hands as he walked, never saying a word. Finally, after long minutes of pacing, John went to the door, grabbed his bowler from the hat tree, and left.

When he returned nearly two hours later, the women were still sitting in the parlor. He walked to Lucy and stood over her. "First thing tomorrow, we're going into town. I'm taking you to my lawyer."

Located on the second floor of a building in the shadow of the Wells County Courthouse, Mock & Sons, with three lawyers, was the second-largest and most prestigious law firm in Wells County. Sixty-two-year-old Levi Mock was the law firm's patriarch. He stood well over six feet, six inches tall—some newspaper accounts placed him at six feet, ten inches—and weighed more than two hundred sixty pounds, as best anyone could measure.[3] In an era where the average man was five feet, seven inches tall, Levi towered over everyone. He had a long unkempt beard and a full head of unruly white hair that remained unkempt even when in court. But despite his unusual appearance, his command of the law and his overpowering presence in the courtroom were unsurpassed. Two of his sons, George and John, were following in his sizable footsteps.

Levi had handled John Terrell's legal affairs since he struck oil a decade earlier, drafting contracts, leases, notes, and mortgages for John's various business dealings and filing lawsuits when people didn't make good on their obligations.[4] As a result, not many clients in Wells County produced more law firm business than John Terrell. But Levi was getting older; consequently, he passed some of John's business along to his sons, particularly George, who seemed to work well with John.

George was six feet, two inches, making him the second-tallest lawyer in the county. He was slender with a narrow face and brown hair that fell in a curl over his right eye. Both he and his older brother John had already demon-strated that they inherited much of their father's legal acumen.

Levi was surprised when John walked into his office and even more sur-prised when he saw his client's youngest and very pregnant daughter. "John, what a surprise to see you. And is this Lucy?"

"It is," John said, not bothering with a greeting. "We got some business for you."

"Well, have a seat, and tell me what I can do for you."

"You can sue that son of a bitch Melvin Wolfe," John said sharply before even taking a seat. He turned to his daughter. "Lucy, tell Mr. Mock what hap-pened with you and Wolfe."

Lucy took a seat. She folded her hands across her lap and looked down, not speaking.

"Tell him, girl," John said.

Levi sat in a worn brown leather chair behind his oversized desk. He spoke to Lucy in his soothing, baritone voice. With a giant frame and his white hair and beard, some clients—and some jurors—seemed to mistake his deep, reso-nant voice for the voice of God. "Now, Miss Lucy, don't be afraid. What you tell me stays with me. Sit back, take your time, and tell me about you and Melvin Wolfe."

"He's my husband," Lucy started, her voice so soft that Levi had to lean for-ward to hear her. "I'm having his baby."

"Well, that's good, isn't it?"

"No," Lucy said. "He don't want it. He don't want me."

Levi nodded. "Just start at the beginning and tell me everything."

Lucy did. She took her time, her voice becoming louder as she told the story of meeting Melvin, of how he convinced her to yield to him because they were going to be married, then how when she became pregnant, Melvin wanted nothing to do with her.

Levi kept his full attention on Lucy. He did not interrupt with questions. Only when she finished did Levi speak. "That's awful. Unfortunately for you, the law doesn't allow you to get divorced right now because you're with child. That would raise questions about the legitimacy of the child, and the law doesn't allow that."

"Well, ain't there something you can do," John said, his tone irate. "He can't get away with this."

"I think we can do something," Levi said, keeping his tone soothing. "Why don't you and Lucy eat lunch at one of the restaurants here in town and do some shopping or visiting. I'm going to talk with George. I'll get him to do some research and draft a petition to the court. You come back about four o'clock, and I should have something for you to look over."

At precisely four o'clock, John and Lucy returned to the lawyer's office. The firm's secretary showed John and Lucy into George Mock's office. He handed them a document.

"Read that," George said. "If it's accurate, then Lucy can sign it, and I'll file it with the court."

Lucy and John began reading.

COMPLAINT FOR FRAUDULENT MARRIAGE[5]

The plaintiff complains of the defendant and says:

That the relatrix Lucy Wolfe was, on the 20th day of November 1901, pregnant with a bastard child, and the defendant was and is the father of said child and on said day was liable to a prosecution in bastardy for the support of said child.

That on said day, the defendant fraudulently entered into the marriage with the relatrix with the intent thereby to escape and avoid being prosecuted for bastardy, for the support of said child;

That the defendant has, ever since said marriage failed to make reasonable provisions for the support of said relatrix;

That the defendant furnished no place for the relatrix to live other than at the house of his father and stepmother, and while she was so residing at said house, the defendant cruelly and inhumanly mistreated the relatrix in this: that not withstanding the said relatrix was pregnant and in poor health, the defendant without just cause drove her from said house, and the relatrix was compelled to go home to her parents to live. That with the knowledge and consent of the defendant, the defendant's said stepmother ordered the relatrix to leave said house, and when not in a fit condition physically to do so, the relatrix was compelled to walk several miles to her sisters;

That while living at said home, the relatrix was treated so contemptuously by the defendant that she was rendered sick, thereby all her life was rendered miserable. That on the 11th day of May 1902, the defendant drove the relatrix from said house, has abandoned her, and declares that he will never live with or support the relatrix.

That she will be delivered of said child about the last day of June 1902.

Wherefore the plaintiff demands judgment against the defendant for One Thousand Dollars and for all other proper relief.

Said relatrix, Lucy Wolfe, swears that the subject matter set forth in the foregoing complaint are true in substance and fact.

Lucy finished reading the Complaint. Then, without making any changes, she signed it. The next day, George walked one block to the courthouse, where he filed the Complaint with the Wells County Circuit Court clerk. A jury trial was set for September 11.

On July 11, two months to the day after Melvin Wolfe threw her out of the house, Lucy gave birth at home to a healthy baby girl. Lucy named her Mabel Marie Wolfe.[6] As with the two babies born to his older daughters, John paid the doctor's bill for the birth of Mabel.[7]

Two months later, on Thursday, September 11, Lucy and Melvin walked into the circuit court for a jury trial on Lucy's claim for fraudulent marriage.

Shortly after 10 A.M. on Thursday, September 11, Wells County Circuit Court judge Edwin C. Vaughn called the court to order to hear Lucy's case against Melvin for fraudulent marriage. Vaughn was the antithesis of Levi Mock— short, slender, and impeccably groomed. He was handsome with graying hair, deep-set eyes, and a full mustache. For the past decade, Judge Vaughn ruled his court as a benevolent fiefdom. Lawyers generally liked his friendly approach but were wary of his iron fist when someone crossed him.

It took less than an hour to seat a jury of twelve men. George Mock led Lucy step by step through her testimony. It was embarrassing for Lucy to speak of such things in front of a jury of twelve men, all strangers. But as the day wore on, she became more comfortable talking about her relationship with Melvin and her pregnancy. She then told the jury about living at the Wolfes' home and how she was mistreated and eventually thrown out of the house. She concluded by speaking about the birth of her baby, Mabel Marie Wolfe.

Melvin's lawyer was Charles Sturgis, a young man developing a reputation for his courtroom style, so much so that a year later he would be representing Lucy's father. But on this day, he attacked Lucy's credibility and her virtue. When Lucy stepped down from the witness stand, after an hour of cross-examination, George Mock rested his case. She was his only witness.

Charles Sturgis called Melvin Wolfe to the witness stand. He denied ever having promised Lucy he would marry her and denied that he was the father of Lucy's baby. On cross-examination, Melvin continued to deny that he fathered either Lucy's baby or Chloa Blair's child, although he admitted that his father had paid money to Chloa.

It was approaching five o'clock when testimony concluded. Judge Vaughn dismissed the jury for the day and told the lawyers to have their closing arguments ready first thing in the morning.

The next day, the lawyers gave their closing arguments and Judge Vaughn instructed the jury. In less than fifteen minutes, the jury returned its verdict.

> We, the jury, find for the plaintiff and against the defendant. We, the jury, find that the plaintiff is entitled to recover a penalty in the sum of 500 Dollars. Milton Davis, foreman.[8]

The total was only half of what Lucy sought, but it was partial vindication for all Melvin had put her through. Lucy smiled for the first time since she walked into the courtroom.

Melvin and his father stormed out of the courtroom. On their way out of the courthouse, Jacob Wolfe stopped by the clerk's office and signed a replevin to guarantee payment of the judgment. Melvin seethed as he walked down the steps leaving the building.[9]

"Them Terrells is gonna pay," he said to his father through clenched teeth. "They gonna wish they never crossed me."

8

"Bye, Oh, Baby"

In turn-of-the-century rural Indiana, fall was harvest time. Even for farmers who were fortunate enough to strike oil, like John Terrell, harvest was the most crucial time of the year for their financial well-being. Work started before sunrise, tending livestock. Then, once the sun was up, the farmers and all the hired hands they could afford were in the fields, using horse-drawn reapers, threshers, and combines. The work was hard. Days were long. There was no time to waste on grudges.

Throughout the fall, Melvin Wolfe's anger toward the Terrell family simmered, but the demands of the fall harvest took priority. Meanwhile, Lucy spent her days at the Terrell home taking care of the new baby and helping her mother, whose health problems worsened. It was not until the spring of 1903, some six months after they last saw each other in the Wells County Courthouse, that Lucy again saw Melvin.

Sally and her husband, John Schott, had their first child, Inez, less than a month after Mabel was born. By April 1903, both babies were old enough for their mothers to take them to town. So, on a warm Saturday afternoon, Lucy and Sally made their first trip to Petroleum in months. They sent word ahead and met up with their friend, Ida Dickason, wife of Dr. John Dickason, at Oliver's Restaurant and Produce Store.

"Your babies are so cute," Ida said as they sat at one of the eight tables in the restaurant. "And they're getting so big. Won't be no time until they're walking."

"Mabel just turned nine months," Lucy said. "She's walking around things already. I 'spect she'll be walking on her own by the end of the month."

"Nine months! Where does the time go?"

The conversation continued, talking about the babies, Catherine Terrell's health, and what was going on with people they knew. While finishing their meal, Ida looked out the window and saw a buggy pull up with Melvin Wolfe at the reins. Sitting next to him was his stepsister, Della Reed.

"Don't look up, Lucy, but Melvin just pulled his rig up outside. Della is with him."

"I don't care nothin' about him. I got much a right to be here as he does."

Sally patted Lucy on her shoulder for reassurance.

"But he's been saying such awful things about you and your family," Ida said. "Spreading just awful lies." Ida looked around the restaurant, then leaned forward, her voice only a whisper. "I heard him telling a bunch of men that he ain't Mabel's daddy, that she's your pa's baby."

"Nobody believes him," Sally said.

"'Course not," Ida said.

"Well, I don't care," said Lucy. "I know the truth. Now can you watch Mabel for a minute? I promised Ma I'd bring her back some bananas."

Lucy left the table just as Mel walked in. Lucy picked out a bunch of bananas and walked to where Mrs. Oliver was standing at the cash register. Mel rushed in front of Lucy, shoving her so that she nearly lost her balance. He slammed two cans of peaches on the counter. "I feel like I wanna eat some peaches today," he said, putting a quarter down next to the cans.

Mrs. Oliver looked back at Lucy, embarrassed. Lucy shook her head. Mrs. Oliver picked up the quarter and rang it up on the register. Mel threw his shoulders back and sauntered out of the restaurant. Before the door closed behind him, Mel let out a full-throated laugh.

As he stepped into his buggy, Lucy heard him yell at Della, "Well, I saw my bastard." They both laughed as Mel laid the whip to the horse, and the buggy took off.[1]

Mrs. Oliver looked up at Lucy with sad eyes. "I'm sorry, dear. I didn't know what to do. Are you okay?"

"I'm fine, Mrs. Oliver. Just let me pay for the bananas."

With spring, farm families around Wells County were out and about more, making trips to the feed and seed store for supplies; the general store for six-penny nails, fence posts, and wire; and the blacksmith's shop to mend tools and shoe workhorses. This occasioned more contact between Mel and members of the Terrell family.

Several times, John or his family members crossed paths with Melvin while traveling area roads. Mel would pull his rig toward the center of the road, forcing the Terrell buggy or wagon to the edge and sometimes even into a roadside ditch.[2] On one occasion, Mel's stepsister, Della Reed, was in the buggy with him. Mel ran the Terrell wagon off the road, and as he passed, he made a face at Lucy, drawing taunting laughs from Della.[3]

In late spring, John and Lucy were returning from a trip into Bluffton. As they headed south on the Bluffton-Camden Pike, a wagon approached from the opposite direction. John could see the erect figure of Melvin Wolfe at the reins. When they were within fifty feet, Mel pulled the reins to move the wagon to the left and onto John's side of the road. John tried to speed up his two-horse team to get by Mel, but it was too late. John could not stay on the road without being hit by the oncoming wagon. He pulled right, and the buggy wheels left the road and slipped into a side ditch. John pulled tight on the reins to stop the buggy before it tipped.

As Mel went by, he stuck out his tongue at Lucy, then bellowed out, "Cocksucker!"[4] The word hung in the air as Melvin broke out in a wicked laugh and headed down the road.

John sat in silence, looking straight ahead. Lucy buried her head in her hands and began to sob.

They sat for several minutes. The only sound was a light wind across the fields and Lucy's gentle sobbing. Finally, John flicked the reins, and the horses pulled the buggy back onto the road and toward Petroleum. The rest of the ride home, John said nothing.

As spring rolled into summer, Mel seemed to make a habit of riding by the Terrell farm, making faces or shouting taunts at whoever was on the front porch. On one occasion as he passed the Terrell house when Lucy was on the front porch, Mel made an obscene gesture by putting his thumb to his nose and wiggling his fingers, the equivalent of a raised middle finger in modern times but perhaps even more obscene.[5]

In the last week of June, he approached the Terrell house on horseback, pulling another pony behind him. As he got near the Terrell property, he dismounted and started walking the horses. Lucy was getting water from the barnyard well. Nearby, John and his son Jake worked with pitchforks and shovels, loading a manure spreader.

They heard Mel singing "Bye, Oh, Baby," a popular lullaby of the day. The words were loving, but neither Mel's voice nor his tone was soothing.[6]

Bye, oh! Bye, oh! Baby dear![7]
Sleep, while mother watches near
Into dreamland, hie away;

. . .

Jake threw down his pitchfork and started toward Mel, but as he did, Mel pulled back his coat to reveal his revolver. Lucy grabbed Jake by the arm as he started by. "Don't cause no more trouble." Behind them, John glared at Mel but said nothing.

Mel laughed, mounted his horse, and trotted away, pulling the pony along with him.

On Friday, July 10, nineteen-year-old Jake Terrell took what had become a familiar road to the George Kirkwood farm. Jake and Minnie Kirkwood had been courting for long enough that most people thought they would soon be married. Minnie climbed into Jake's carriage and headed toward Witmer's Store in Petroleum, where they could get Minnie's favorite summer treat—ice cream.

The store was crowded when Jake and Minnie arrived, but they quickly found a seat at one of the small wooden tables topped with red-and-white checkered tablecloths. The couple chatted and savored their treat. Jake knew he would get a kiss on the lips as his reward.

As they were finishing, Jake saw Mel Wolfe walk in, followed by Cliff Shakley, a brawny laborer on the Wolfe oil wells. Both wore go-to-town suits. They were boisterous, making their voices heard above everyone else as they entered.

"Why there's Jake Terrell," Mel bellowed. "Surprised his old pa let him out by hisself."

"Ignore him," Minnie said. "I'm done. Let's just go. It's cooled off outside. We can take a nice ride."

Jake turned and looked sharply at Mel, but he did not say anything. Instead, he stood and put money on the table to pay for the ice cream. "Let's go. We can take that ride."

Mel turned toward Cliff and whispered something to him. Then, as Jake and Minnie headed toward the door, Cliff took a giant step and banged into Jake, knocking him off balance. Only his outstretched arm against the counter kept Jake from falling.

"Better watch your step," Cliff said.

Mel and Cliff broke out in guffaws, then forced their way outside past Jake and a line of people waiting for ice cream.

Jake and Minnie stepped out onto the board sidewalk. Mel and Cliff blocked the way to Jake's rig, standing side by side.

"Going somewhere?" Mel said with a smirk.

"Yeah," Cliff joined in. "Going somewhere?"

Minnie pushed her way in front of Jake and walked within inches of the two men. "You think you're such a big man," Minnie said, her nostrils flaring with rage. "Everybody knows you're the daddy of two babies, and you ain't taking care of neither of them. In my opinion, that don't make you nothing but a low-down scoundrel."

Cliff stepped forward and, in an instant, slapped Minnie hard across her cheek. "You ain't no better than his whore of a sister," Cliff said, nodding toward Jake.

Jake moved toward Cliff, but immediately Mel pulled back his jacket and revealed a revolver in his waistband. Mel moved his right hand onto the gun handle. "Be careful, boy."

Minnie turned, grabbing Jake by both arms and pushing him back. "It's okay, Jake. Don't give him no excuses. Let's cross the street and take the long way to the wagon."

Jake glared, anger turning his face red even in the dark. But Minnie pushed harder. Eventually, he turned with her and walked across the street, leaving Mel and Cliff puffed up like banty roosters.[8]

Saturday nights were busy in 1903 Petroleum, Indiana. Although it was less than a decade old, Petroleum was the commercial and social center of southern Wells County, surpassing the older towns of Reifsburg, Keystone, and Domestic. There was a post office, Witmer's Grocery Store, Oliver's Restaurant, a barber shop, a livery stable, a general store, and offices for two young doctors, Dr. John F. Dickason, forty-two, and Dr. Jesse E. Saunders, thirty-three. On Saturday night, you could get a meal or a haircut until 10 P.M., meet and socialize with friends, maybe listen to a local fiddle player, or even find a bit of whiskey or a backroom card game.

On Saturday, July 11, 1903, John Terrell got into his buggy a little before 10 P.M. and headed into Petroleum. Earlier that day, Jake had told his father about his run-in with Melvin Wolfe the night before and how Cliff Shakley slapped Minnie Kirkwood. "You did the right thing, boy," was all John said.[9]

Now John was headed into town for a different reason.[10] He had forgotten that Bert Stookey had asked John to bring his shotgun into town. There was a wedding that day, and some menfolk were planning a belling, a raucous, rowdy clanging of bells, whistles, pots, and pans accompanied by hoots, hollers, and shotgun blasts outside the room where the newlyweds were spending their first married night.

John didn't participate in such nonsense but agreed to provide his shotgun. He parked his buggy near the barber shop but left his gun in the rig when he walked in. Even after 10 P.M., the shop was still busy, mostly with men talking, sharing stories and jokes. Bert Stookey wasn't among the men in the shop.

John said nothing. When he saw Stookey wasn't present, he exited the shop and walked a short distance to the house of his friend, Dr. John Dickason.

"John, it's good to see you," Dickason said when he answered the knock at his door. "What brings you here this late?"

"I brought my gun Stookey wanted to borrow for the belling, but I can't find him."

"Oh, that's over. Boys decided to do it early."

"So, it's all done?"

"Yep. Gave the couple quite a cheering on, but it's all over now. Come in and sit a spell. How's your misses doing? I know she ain't been feeling too well."

John took a seat in the Dickasons' parlor. They talked about Mrs. Terrell's health, how the crops were doing, how John's livestock was handling the heat, and whether the corn was "knee high by the Fourth of July." It was nearly 11 P.M. when John left the Dickason home and headed to his buggy.

A few boys were hanging out nearby, but the shotgun was still sitting on the buggy seat where John had left it. He climbed in and headed the horse south toward home.

The next day, his world would change forever.

9

"God Damn the Man That Comes between Me and Wolfe"

Sunday, July 12, 1903, was a special day for the Terrell family. Sally, the oldest Terrell daughter, planned a surprise birthday party for her husband, John Schott. The family and a few friends gathered at John and Sally's house near Nottingham not long after eleven o'clock.[1] The women put the final touches on dinner, and Sally baked a burnt-sugar cake, her husband's favorite.

John Terrell suffered a headache all morning but dressed in his suit and starched cotton shirt and collar.[2] John, Catherine, Lucy, one-year-old Mabel, and five-year-old Georgia, Sally's daughter from her first marriage, loaded into the carriage for the short trip to Sally and John Schott's house.

Everyone gathered around the table. John Terrell sat at one end and, as always, said little. Despite his headache, he seemed in a good mood. Everyone was in a good mood except Cinda. The middle sister picked at her food, eating little. Even when John Schott cut his cake and pieces were handed around the table, Cinda kept her eyes downcast.

"What's eating at you, Cinda?" Sally finally asked across the table. "You coming down with the grippe or something?"

Cinda put down her fork and looked up. "It's that damn Melvin Wolfe."

Will, Cinda's husband, spoke up. "Can't you let it go? It's John's birthday. We don't want to spoil it."

"What did he do now?" Lucy asked, dread in her voice.

"He run us off the road," Cinda said. "We was on our way over here this morning, and here he come in his fancy buggy. When we got up near him, he come across the road and run us out in the side ditch and pretty near upset us. Then he pulled out that revolver of his and flashed as he went by."[3]

"Oh, Cinda," said Will. "He never pointed it at us. And we ain't hurt. Hell, even the wagon was fine. Let's not let that spoil a beautiful day like this."

John Terrell put down his fork, an uneaten piece of cake still on it. He stood and, without saying a word, walked out of the house and onto the porch.

After the meal, the pall caused by Cinda's revelation seemed to pass. Finally, some of the day's joy returned as the womenfolk cleaned up, and the men found a shady spot outside to smoke and swap stories. But John stayed his distance. As far as anyone could later remember, he didn't say another word until it was time to leave.

It was mid-afternoon when John Terrell and his family returned home.[4] Farm chores did not stop because of birthdays, and there was much work to be done before sundown. Everyone changed from Sunday clothes into work clothes, John wearing a strapped undershirt and overalls.

By five o'clock, Catherine had finished her work in the house. She grabbed four pails and headed across the train tracks where the cows awaited milking. John worked around the barn, getting ready to feed the livestock. Lucy stood near the well while Mabel and Georgia played in the barnyard.

Perhaps a quarter mile away, John saw the dust thrown up from two buggies heading south toward them on the Camden-Bluffton road. John rested on his pitchfork, watching. One-year-old Mabel toddled over to John, grabbing his pants leg for balance.

The lead carriage with a young couple seated close together passed by John, perhaps sixty yards ahead of a second buggy. But as the second rig came closer, John recognized the unmistakable figure of Melvin Wolfe. Sitting next to him was his stepsister.[5]

John started to turn away but couldn't without causing Mabel to lose her balance and fall. Then he heard Mel's buggy slow.

"Hold up the little bastard!" Mel yelled, his voice sharp. "I want to see it." Then he laughed—a laugh that cut straight through John.[6]

Mel urged his horse to a quick trot. John could still hear him laughing over the horse clops and turning buggy wheels.

John laid down his pitchfork and started toward the house. Just after he crossed the road, near the wind pump, he fell. Lucy dashed to her father where he had fallen. He was ashen, with froth at the edges of his mouth. Lucy helped him to his feet and led him into the house, where he crumpled into a rocker.

She went outside to tend to the children, and when she returned, John was coming down the stairs, his shotgun in one hand and a box of ammunition in the other. Without saying a word, he walked past Lucy and out the door.

Not more than twenty minutes later, John saw dust being thrown up by the two carriages on their northbound return. John broke open his double-barrel shotgun and checked the breach. He slipped two new cartridges into the barrels, then closed the gun with a snap. He moved into the roadside ditch among a stand of foxtails, buckhorn, goldenrod, and thistle and knelt like he was hunting rabbit or pheasant. Waiting.

The first buggy went by at a moderate trot. The couple talked quietly enough that John could not understand what they were saying. But he knew it wasn't Wolfe.

A minute or so later, John heard the second buggy approaching. Melvin Wolfe was talking with his stepsister. John waited. And waited. And waited. As the horse drew even, John stood.

The buggy was no more than six feet away. John pulled the shotgun toward the firing position, but too soon the gun boomed. John's eager finger had hit the first firing trigger and the shot discharged into the road just behind the horse.[7]

John cursed, then pulled the gun steady. Mel was struggling to pull the reins and calm the horse. John calculated how much to lead his aim, then squeezed the second trigger. The shot cracked, and John saw Mel fall forward, grabbing for his right leg. Blood immediately soaked Melvin's pants.

John reached into his pocket for fresh shells, but by the time he had the cartridges in hand and the gun ready to reload, Mel's buggy was dashing wildly down the road, already out of range.

John knew he had only hit Mel in his thigh. It was a damaging blast, but John knew Melvin Wolfe was still alive. The task was not done.

John emptied the spent cartridges and reloaded, once again snapping shut the breach. He walked into the barn and hitched the waiting horse to his buggy, then climbed in. Holding the gun in one hand and the reins in the other, John sent the horse out of the barn and onto the road. Ahead of him, a trail of dust rose in the direction of Petroleum.

John was determined to finish the job he had started.

Ahead, Della Reed fought for control of the reins and urged the horse on as fast as possible. Mel lay next to her, color draining from his face. He clutched his leg, his pants soaked with blood.[8]

"Hold tight, Mel. I'll get you to Doc Saunders. He'll patch you up."

Mel gave an agonized groan but no other response.

Tears streamed down Della's face as she urged the horses on.

John saw the dust cloud ahead of him. He gave the beast full rein and urged it on. It was as near a gallop as a horse could go while hitched to a rig. It wasn't a fast horse, but it was only a bit over a mile to Petroleum. He would not lose much ground as he chased Wolfe.

Melvin leaned heavily against Della as she arrived at Petroleum. She slowed and turned from Bluffton-Camden Pike onto Air-Line Pike, the peculiarly named main east-west road in Petroleum. A block later, she turned north and brought the buggy to a stop in front of Doc Saunders's office.[9]

Della yelled out. "Help! Help! I need the doctor!"

Dr. Jesse Saunders's office was a small roughly crafted building, twelve feet wide and twenty-six feet long. It consisted of two rooms. The front room was the largest, about eighteen feet long, with shelves for medicine lining two walls. A five-plank door separated the reception area from the smaller room where Dr. Saunders performed his surgeries. It held his surgical tools, anesthesia supplies, and an operating chair that looked not much different than a dental chair or even the chair at the local barber shop without the padded leather seat. The chair back could be lowered into an operating table when needed.[10]

Dr. Saunders was inside his office chatting with J. M. Hopkins when they heard the cry for a doctor. They both walked outside, where two other men, Dick Risser and William Kirkwood, were approaching the wagon.[11]

In his early thirties, Dr. Saunders immediately saw that a young man was stricken. He walked to the far side of the buggy to get a better look. Melvin Wolfe was conscious, but barely. He moaned but did not say anything. Blood covered Mel's clothing, the seat, and the floor of the buggy. Blood was still pouring through a shredded pants leg from an obvious wound several inches above the knee of the right leg.

"He's been shot," Doc Saunders said reflexively. "He's going to bleed to death if we don't hurry. Help me carry him into the operating room. Grab him by his arms. Hop, you grab his uninjured leg. I'll take care of carrying the injured one. We'll make a saddle and carry him in."

Risser and Kirkwood lifted Mel under his arms. When they got his body mostly out of the buggy, Hopkins grabbed the uninjured leg, and Saunders cradled the injured man under his buttocks. It was awkward, but they only had to carry him a few feet through the front office into the operating room.

A trail of blood marked their path.[12]

Della didn't follow the men. She had seen the trail of dust behind her and suspected John Terrell was pursuing them. Whether from fear for her safety, queasiness from all the blood, or just shock, she left Melvin and walked back to Bluffton-Camden Pike, then down the street to Oliver's Restaurant, where she took a seat among the supper crowd.

Dr. Saunders led the men through his office and into the surgical room. They sat Melvin down in the operating chair, then Dr. Saunders lowered the chair to make an operating table.

"Water," Mel said, his voice hoarse and barely above a whisper.

The men looked up at Dr. Saunders. "Go ahead," Dr. Saunders said. "It can't hurt him."

The well was just outside the office. Risser and Hopkins started for the front door to retrieve a drink for Mel. As they got to the door, they heard a commotion.[13]

John raced into Petroleum at full speed, reins in one hand and his shotgun held over his head in the other. He saw Melvin Wolfe's empty buggy pulled near Dr. Saunders's office. John maneuvered his horse and wagon behind Melvin's and pulled his rig to a stop, a dust cloud following in his wake.

John didn't bother tying the horse to a post. He got down from the buggy, gun in hand, and followed a trail of blood leading from Melvin's carriage to the door of Dr. Saunders's office.[14]

As John approached the steps, Dick Risser and J. M. Hopkins stepped out, looking to retrieve water for Melvin Wolfe. They stood side by side, blocking the entrance. John stood at the base of the steps, his face white, his hair on end, his eyes bulging. He pulled his shotgun up, pointing between the two men.

"God damn the man that comes between me and Wolfe."[15]

Risser and Hopkins glanced at each other, then back at John. Hopkins shook his head, stepped off the porch, and headed toward Witmer's Store. Risser stood still on the top step.

"Dick, don't you try and stop me. I will kill you if you do."[16]

Risser paused for a moment, then stepped aside. John brushed past him and into Dr. Saunders's office, his shotgun leading the way.

· · ·

Inside the surgery room, both Dr. Saunders and William Kirkwood heard the exchange on the steps. "Latch the door," Saunders said. Kirkwood did what he was told, shutting the wood plank door, then throwing the deadbolt latch.

The two men looked at each other, then down at Melvin on the operating table.

"We gotta go," Dr. Saunders said to Kirkwood.

Kirkwood and Saunders went out the back door of the surgery room. Kirkwood headed toward the livery stable. Saunders took off running in the opposite direction toward his house.

Melvin Wolfe lay on the table, his leg shattered and weakened by blood loss. Alone.[17]

John attempted to open the door to the surgery room, but it would not open. He stepped back and, using the barrel of his gun as a battering ram, repeatedly pounded on the wood planks. Finally, a panel broke with a loud crack.

Inside the surgery, Mel, even in his weakened state, knew that John Terrell was coming for him.

There was a second loud crack as John used his shotgun barrel to break through a second board. With the butt end of the gun, John cleared away the two broken planks.[18]

Mel struggled, trying to force himself to his feet, but his right thigh bone was in pieces. It could not support him, and blood loss left him helpless.

Behind Mel, John slid his shotgun through the broken door. He raised his gun as Mel lifted his back off the operating table, not quite in a sitting position.

John pulled the first trigger, and the room exploded with the reverberation of the shotgun. The first shot hit Mel in the back, just below his left shoulder blade, sending steel shot ripping through his chest, heart, and lungs.

Mel fell back, collapsing onto the table.

John wasn't finished. He put the shotgun inches from Mel's left ear and pulled the second trigger. Mel's head jerked as the shot exploded. Blood and brains flowed onto the table.

Melvin Wolfe was dead.[19]

10

"He Killed My Boy"

John left Dr. Saunders's office. He walked along the side of the building and peered in a window, assuring himself that Melvin was dead. As he turned around, he said to no one in particular, "He won't ruin any more girls."[1]

John returned to his wagon and headed south at a brisk trot, arriving back at his farm a few minutes later. He drove into the barn lot, got out of the buggy, and headed toward the house. Three neighbors who heard the gunshots were standing near the front gate. Lucy came out as her father walked past his neighbors and through the gate.

Lucy could tell something was wrong. Her father's face was pale, his hair standing up. John said something as he walked by his daughter, but she was uncertain what it was. Inside the house, John went upstairs, changed into a fresh shirt, and retrieved his bowler hat.

As he came downstairs, Lucy was waiting. "Pa, come and sit down with me a bit."

John ignored his daughter and headed to his wagon. He spoke briefly to one of the neighbors, asking him to look after his family. Then John climbed into his rig and, without saying another word, headed back north to Petroleum.

About ten minutes after the shooting in Petroleum, Dr. Saunders approached his office. The acrid smell of the shotgun blasts still hung in the air. William Kirkwood and Dick Risser met Saunders on the office steps.

"Well, I guess we best go inside and see," Dr. Saunders said.

Saunders walked into his operating room, followed by Risser and Kirkwood.

"Holy Jesus," Dick Risser said when he glimpsed Melvin Wolfe.

Mel's body lay sprawled across the operating table, a hole just above his left ear. Blood and brains were still oozing out and onto the table.[2]

Dr. Saunders felt for a pulse, then checked his watch. It was a formality. William Kirkwood volunteered to get his father, Harry Kirkwood, the local justice of the peace and former sheriff. Someone in authority had to notify Jacob Wolfe that his son was dead.

Dr. John Dickason, a forty-two-year-old physician and friend of John Terrell, arrived back in Petroleum shortly before seven o'clock. He had been in Nottingham tending to a sick family. As his horse led Dr. Dickason's rig along, he noticed a larger-than-usual congregation of men and women on the streets.[3]

As he pulled the buggy to a stop near his house, William Kirkwood ran by and shouted the news. "John Terrell just shot Melvin Wolfe. Killed him dead."

Dickason had known John Terrell for nearly twenty years. He grew up not more than half a mile from the Terrell farm and considered them neighbors. When Dickason returned from medical training four years earlier and set up practice in Petroleum, he started treating John for his headaches and nervous stomach, as well as treating other members of the Terrell family.[4]

After hearing the news, Dickason saw John in his buggy stopped near Witmer's Store, where thirty-seven-year-old Byron Witmer owned one of the few telephones in Petroleum.

"Byron," John said in a raspy voice. "I wish you would call the sheriff."

Witmer responded, "I already did, John."[5]

Only a block away from where John was getting out of his buggy was the Oliver house. In its doorway stood Cinda Terrell Books, John's middle daughter. She was visiting Emma Oliver when the commotion drew them outside. Someone passing by shouted that John had shot and killed Melvin Wolfe. Cinda's face was drained of all color, and she looked as if she would collapse.

Standing next to Cinda, Emma Oliver yelled out toward John, "Look what you've done to your daughter!"[6]

John said nothing. He reached into his wagon and grabbed his shotgun. Loosely holding the gun with its barrel pointed down, he walked toward where John Dickason and his wife Ida stood near their house.[7]

"Where you going, John?" Dr. Dickason asked.

John looked around. "I . . . I don't rightly know. I guess you need to take me to the sheriff."

Dr. Dickason nodded. "Let me look after your daughter, then I'll take you. You can wait in my house until I'm ready to go."

They ambled to the Dickason house, where Dr. Dickason guided John into the parlor.

Ida Dickason greeted John, then held out her hand. "I will take the gun," she said in a firm voice.

John held it out. Ida took it and disappeared into the kitchen, where she put it out of sight.

Dr. Dickason picked up his medical bag and left to tend to Cinda. Ida Dickason stayed in the kitchen, leaving John alone. She looked in on him every few minutes and saw him pacing and mumbling. She could not make out what he was saying other than occasionally she heard him say "Lucy."[8]

Twenty minutes after he left, Dr. Dickason returned. He put his arm on John's shoulder. "Cinda will be fine. I'll take you to Bluffton to the sheriff now." It was after 7:30 when Dr. Dickason directed his horse out of his barn and headed north on Bluffton-Camden Pike.

About the same time Dr. Dickason was pulling out in his carriage to take John to the sheriff, Harry Kirkwood, township justice of the peace, rode up to Jacob Wolfe's house to notify Jacob that his twenty-two-year-old son was dead.

Dr. Dickason urged his horse along at a steady gait. They had been on the road for perhaps twenty minutes when John Terrell spoke, his voice measured. "I have killed him."[9]

Dickason turned and faced John. "Who?"

"My son-in-law, Melvin Wolfe."

"Are you sure you killed him?"

"Well, I shot him." He did not say another word.

A few minutes later, Dickason saw the dust rising on the pike from two approaching wagons. As they drew near, Dickason recognized Sheriff James R. Johnston in the lead rig and the coroner, James Alfred "Fred" McBride, in the carriage that followed. Dickason pulled his horse to a stop. When the sheriff drew alongside, he stopped his buggy. So did the coroner. The sheriff got down and walked to where John was seated.

"Well, John, from what I hear, you shot Mel Wolfe. That right?"

John lifted his hat and ran his hand through his gray hair. But he said nothing.

"I'm gonna have to take you to the jail, John, 'til we get this all sorted out. So climb on down out of there."

John nodded and got out of Dickason's buggy. Without saying a word, he walked the few steps to the sheriff's carriage and climbed up to take his seat.[10]

. . .

The Wells County coroner was James Alfred McBride, thirty-three, a Bluffton undertaker whom everyone called Fred.[11] He arrived at Petroleum just before 8 P.M. and immediately went to Dr. Saunders's office.

Through the shattered door to Dr. Saunders's surgical room, McBride saw the body of Melvin Wolfe. The blasts into Melvin's head and leg were apparent. Blood pooled under his head and around his leg and was beginning to dry.

"You fellas get along outside," McBride said to those standing around. "Dr. Saunders and me have work to do."

A few minutes after McBride arrived, so did Jacob Wolfe.

Jacob walked into Dr. Saunders's office, his breathing as heavy as his footsteps, his voice harsh as dried corn husks. "Where's my boy? I come to take him home."

"Hello, Jacob," McBride said, his voice quiet. "Your boy's in the next room. It's not a pleasant sight. He hasn't been cleaned up. You don't have to look at him that way."

"I wanna see him," Jacob said.[12]

Jacob followed Harry Kirkwood and Dr. Saunders through the shattered door that had been pushed open. Jacob walked to the operating table and stood over Melvin's lifeless body. Tears formed in the old man's eyes, then he broke into great heaving sobs. "He killed my boy," was all he said. Then he left the room.

At about the same time Jacob Wolfe was seeing his dead son, Sheriff Johnston turned the key to lock John Terrell in a cell on the second floor of the Wells County Jail.

"Make yourself comfortable, John," the sheriff said. "You want something to eat? My wife can cook up something for you."

John didn't respond. He just turned and looked out the barred east-facing window in his cell. Night had fallen. Dim candlelight dotted a few of the homes visible from the narrow window. By the end of the month, the Bluffton Electric Light Company would be formed with plans to bring electric lighting to the city.[13] But for now, wood fires and candles provided the only lights John could see from his cell window.

"Suit yourself. I got a feeling you're gonna be here for quite a spell."

Harry Kirkwood and Dr. Saunders undressed the body. They found steel balls in Melvin's back, just under his left shoulder blade, and on the operating table just below the wound to Melvin's head. Dr. Saunders, Fred McBride, and Harry Kirkwood slowly examined the corpse.[14] It was nearing midnight when they finished.

Outside, a small group of men gathered around Jacob Wolfe, consoling him on the loss of his son. "We ought to string John Terrell up!" someone in the crowd shouted.[15]

"I'll hear none of that," Harry Kirkwood said. As a former sheriff, he knew how to make his voice carry the authority needed to break up a crowd. "We got to get this boy home to his family."

The men went silent.

A stretcher was retrieved from McBride's wagon. It was after midnight when Mel's body had been cleaned, wrapped in sheets, put on the stretcher, and loaded onto Harry Kirkwood's wagon. Kirkwood led the procession to the Wolfe house.

It was one o'clock in the morning when the informal cortege arrived at the Wolfe house.[16] Melvin's body was carried inside and placed on the family's library table.

Kirkwood followed with Melvin's clothes neatly folded and tied with twine. "Here's the boy's clothes," Harry said as he laid the clothes on the table. As Jacob watched, two steel shotgun balls dropped from the clothes and bounced on the floor with a harsh bang.[17]

Part II

Castle of Iron Bars

I know not whether Laws be right,
Or whether Laws be wrong;
All that we know who be in jail
Is that the wall is strong.

OSCAR WILDE

My occupation now, I suppose, is jail inmate.

THEODORE KACZYNSKI

11

Headlines across the Nation

The news of John Terrell's operating room murder of his son-in-law Melvin Wolfe was perfect for the sensational journalism style of the times, often referred to as yellow journalism. It was a style born from the newspaper wars of the 1890s, particularly the no-holds-barred newspaper competition in New York City between William Randolph Hearst's *New York Journal* and Joseph Pulitzer's *New York World*.[1]

At the heart of yellow journalism was reporting of sensational crimes involving sex, betrayal, scandal, and lurid details. As one commentator observed, it was the "florid bloom of crime and underwear."[2] Stories were filled with graphic details "unimpeded by minor problems created by fact," while "any concept of objectivity took a back seat."[3]

Readers of Hearst's *New York Journal* wanted "to look at page one and say, 'Gee Whiz,' to turn to page two and exclaim, 'Holy Moses,' and then at page three, shout, 'God Almighty.'"[4] No doubt, the story of John Terrell elicited the latter response.

With elements of illicit love, an abandoned mother and child, a father's revenge, and death by shotgun in a doctor's operating room, the story of John Terrell murdering his son-in-law touched on nearly every element that newspapers looked for in the screaming headlines of the day.

By the day following murder, the Associated Press Wire Service carried the story across the nation, where it made attention-grabbing headlines in hundreds of newspapers,[5] including on the front page of the *New York Times*,[6] as well as stories in the *Boston Globe*,[7] *New Orleans Times-Democrat*,[8] Illinois's *Champaign Daily News*,[9] Texas's *Austin American-Statesman*,[10] Pittsburgh *Press*,[11] *Minneapolis Tribune*,[12] *Nashville American*,[13] *Nebraska State Journal*,[14] Montana's *Butte Miner*,[15] Iowa's *Davenport Democrat*,[16] *Bangor Daily News*,[17] and North Dakota's *Sioux City Journal*.[18]

Bold headlines grabbed attention, gave newsboys fodder for hawking papers, and drove newsstand sales.

BLEW OFF HEAD OF SON-IN-LAW
Wells County Man Murders
Daughter's Husband in Tragical Style
—*Fort Wayne Evening Sentinel*

HORRIBLE WAY OF REVENGE
Farmer Kills His Son-in-Law
While Latter Is on Operating Table
—*Evening Item* (Richmond, IN)

FATHER AVENGES
CHILD'S WRONGS
—*Daily News-Democrat* (Huntington, IN)

Father-in-Law Fires Both Barrels of a
Shotgun into Victim's Head
—A Bloody Crime
—*Princeton (IN) Daily-Clarion*

Indiana Farmer Wounds Son-in-Law,
Follows Him to Doctor's Operating Table
Blows His Brains Out While Victim Is Under Opiate
—*St. Paul Globe*

Got Him!
—*Boston Globe*

The Associated Press report contained numerous errors. It claimed Melvin and Lucy were married for four years and that Melvin deserted Lucy "with child in her arms." In fact, they lived together for only six months, were married less than two years at the time of the shooting, and their child was not yet born when they separated. Headlines across the country announced that John shot Melvin while Dr. Saunders, knife in hand, was amputating Melvin's leg. By his own admission, Dr. Saunders ran out the back door of his office before he started operating on Melvin.

But despite the errors, the entire nation read the Associated Press account.[19]

In an era of journalism where facts were often just the starting point for a good story, an enterprising rewrite man at the *New York Sun* found the story, as dramatic as it was, needed embellishing. So the nameless writer added his own imaginings. As a result, the account sounded like something from a dime-store novel and was closer to a novelist's vivid imagination than a reporter's objectivity.

Surrounded by ads for cures for sexual weakness,[20] nervous disability,[21] and contagious blood poisoning,[22] the rewritten story ran in the *New York Sun* and *Buffalo Examiner*.

SLAIN WHILE SURGEON WAS USING KNIFE.
Man Blows Out Son-in-Law's Brains as He Lies on Operating Table Undergoing Amputation of Leg—Murder of Extraordinary Character

(SPECIAL TO THE *BUFFALO ENQUIRER* FROM THE *NEW YORK SUN*)
BLUFFTON, Ind. July 13.—In a manner perhaps never heard of anywhere in the world before, John Terrell murdered his son-in-law, Melvin Wolfe, yesterday afternoon. First, he had wounded the man with a barrel load from his shotgun that struck Wolfe in the leg, and then, while the wounded man lay on an operating table in a doctor's office, with the surgeon at work amputating his limb, the old man fought his way through a crowd into the room, and, lifting his shotgun, blew out the brains of his victim.

Against the wishes of John Terrell, who is a wealthy farmer living near Petroleum, his pretty daughter married Melvin Wolfe four years ago. The old man threatened to disinherit the girl. His doubts as to Wolfe's fitness as a husband to his daughter were born out about a year and a half after the marriage when the husband deserted his wife, leaving her with a little child.

Old John Terrell's heart softened toward his daughter when she came to this extremity, and he took her back to his home. He was determined, however, that Wolfe should not escape his just responsibilities, and time and again, he had the young man hauled to court to answer proceedings for non-support.

Bitterly the feud has grown between the two so that at the sight of each other, the men had broken out into insults almost invariably. Within the last week or so, Wolfe took to driving past the fine old Terrell house, standing up in the carriage as he passed and shouting objurgations at the old farmer and his daughter and shaking his fist at them.

With face as white as his hair, but his eyes fiery with passion, the old man leaped out of the carriage and made his way through the crowd up the steps and to the doorway. The men standing by, seeing him in a fiery passion and armed, sought to stop him, but one long arm shot out furiously, while with the other he swung the gun, and those who did not give him way were sent reeling to all sides.

Some men in the crowd thought to follow him into the doctor's office and there overpower him, but the old fellow suddenly wheeled, and the barrel of his gun gaped at them.

"Don't follow," he said. They did not.

Suddenly the surgeon and his assistants heard the door slam open, striking against the wall as it swung. They turned to confront the mad old man. Wolfe, with a sob of pain, half lifted his head. Horror and fear leaped into his eyes at the sight of his father-in-law.

"I'm after him, and I am going to kill him," the old man said deliberately. Then he fired the contents of both barrels into his son-in-law's brain.[23]

12

No Sorrow for the Deed

On Monday, as the nation was learning of the events in Petroleum, John Terrell was recovering from his first night in confinement. He was no longer tearful, but instead he summoned his lawyers to his cell. Levi Mock, a literal and figurative giant of the Indiana bar arrived with his son, George Mock.[1] They were followed a few minutes later by Arthur L. Sharpe, a lawyer with Sturgis & Stine and a close friend of John.[2] Sharpe also served as the Bluffton postmaster.[3]

"How you feeling?" Sharpe asked.

John stood and walked to the barred window and looked out. He said nothing, but tears were streaming down his face when he turned back toward the lawyers.

Levi knew about murder cases. He had tried six, and none of his clients went to the gallows. Of those who were convicted, none served a complete sentence. Only George King, who killed a man in a drunken bar fight, received a life sentence, but he was paroled eight years after his conviction. Ike Ruth killed a man in a rage, hitting him with a wagon wheel. Mock convinced the jury to give him a two-year sentence. Levi represented two women who killed their lovers, preventing them from even being indicted.[4] Most people in the county knew Levi Mock was the lawyer they wanted on their side if they found themselves in serious legal trouble.

"You can't be saying anything about the shooting," Levi said. The other two lawyers nodded in agreement.[5] Levi then explained the upcoming arraignment for murder to which John would plead not guilty.

John looked up and spoke for the first time. "Then do I get to go home?"

Levi shook his head. "Sorry, John. You'll have to stay in jail until the Grand Jury can hear the case. That won't be until the September term. So until then, just try to make yourself comfortable. And keep your mouth shut about the shooting."

Not long after 10 A.M., the entire Terrell family arrived at the jail. In Lucy's arms, she carried one-year-old Mabel.[6] As they stepped into the cell, Lucy broke into tears, followed by her mother and sisters. John uncharacteristically reached out to hug each of them, himself dissolving into tears.

They spent most of the day together but said little.

On Tuesday, extensive articles appeared in the *Indianapolis News* and the *Muncie Morning Star*.[7] Photos of John and Melvin ran on page 1 of both newspapers. In addition, the *Muncie Morning Star* carried a photograph of Lucy holding Mabel.

Shortly before ten o'clock on Tuesday morning, Wells County coroner Fred McBride pulled up to Jacob Wolfe's house to conduct the coroner's inquest. It had to be completed before Melvin's body could be released for his funeral at Disciples Church, a small church located just over a mile from the Wolfe house in the small crossroads town of Domestic.[8]

Fred knew that the inquest was only a legal formality. It would be Prosecutor John Burns who would determine if charges were filed. But the law required an inquest, and Fred would carry out his legal obligation.

McBride stood before the open coffin where Melvin Wolfe lay, dressed in a navy suit, high collar, and navy-and-gold-striped tie, and called the coroner's inquest into session. "I'm not here to say who is guilty or not guilty. I'm here to find out what caused Mr. Wolfe's death."

McBride called Dr. Saunders and Nottingham justice of the peace Harry Kirkwood as witnesses. Both testified about finding Melvin Wolfe dead with shotgun wounds in his leg, back, and head. After twenty minutes, McBride had heard enough.

A dozen miles from the Wolfe house, as the inquest was winding down, Sheriff Johnston led John Terrell, followed by his lawyers, on a short walk to the office of the justice of the peace. Several men shouted their greetings to John. He kept his head down and said nothing.[9]

Inside the office, John and his lawyers sat in straight-back chairs in front of a battered maple desk where forty-three-year-old Martin Walbert held informal court proceedings. Sheriff Johnston took a seat in a back corner of the room where a handful of news reporters gathered, pad and pencils in hand.

Shortly after John Terrell arrived, Walbert and Prosecutor John Burns walked in through a door that led to Walbert's law office. Burns was a short man with sharp features, receding black hair, and small eyes behind rimless spectacles. He had the beginnings of a middle-aged paunch that bulged under his vest. He did not smile and exchanged only perfunctory greetings with John's lawyers.

"Well, it seems we have quite a case here," Walbert said, sitting in a high-backed swivel chair behind his desk. "The prosecutor has advised me that Mr. John Terrell is being held on a charge of first-degree murder."

Levi Mock stood. "Yes, your honor. Mr. Terrell recognizes the charges, waives a preliminary hearing, and pleads not guilty."

"I will accept that plea at this time. Do you plan to assert a defense of insanity?"

"We are still gathering information," Levi responded. "We will decide on our defenses at a later date, including whether we might assert an insanity defense. But that decision is a-ways off yet."

Walbert nodded. "This matter will have to be presented to the Grand Jury. The next Grand Jury term starts in September, is that right, Mr. Burns?"

Burned stood. "Yes, sir. I'll call the Grand Jury the first week in September."

Again, Walbert nodded. "Very well. Because this is a murder case, Mr. Terrell will have to remain in jail."

"Yes, sir," Levi said. "Mr. Terrell fully understands that."

"Anything else?"

Levi and Prosecutor Burns responded quickly, "No, sir."

With that, the arraignment ended.

When John walked out of the arraignment, he saw Lucy standing in front of W. A. Gutelins's drugstore, holding Mabel in her arms. John walked to her without asking permission, took the baby in his arms, and kissed her. With his other arm, he reached for Lucy, hugging her.

"I got some things to buy," he said to Sheriff Johnston. Then, carrying the baby in his arms, John walked into the drugstore. He was warmly greeted by the owner, the clerk, and two customers, although another customer scurried out the door as John walked in. He purchased paper and envelopes for letters and a box of cigars. As he walked out, a reporter was waiting on the sidewalk.

"Tell us what happened, John."

John shook his head. "I won't talk about that," he said. John then pulled a cigar out of the recently purchased box and handed it to the reporter. "I'll give you this if you can tell me how the newspapers are reporting this. Are they for me or against me?"

The reporter took the cigar and ran it under his nose, inhaling the tobacco scent. "It seems mixed," the reporter said. "I'll tell you what. I'll bring as many newspapers as I can to the jail, and if you ever want to talk, you make sure I'm the reporter you talk to."

"I ain't talking about the shooting," John said. "But I'd thank you much for bringing some newspapers by."

At one o'clock, as the July heat rose to near ninety degrees, six pallbearers loaded the body of Melvin Wolfe into a horse-drawn hearse. Fred McBride, in his mourning coat, sat next to the driver. Jacob Wolfe sat in a carriage immediately behind the hearse, his wife and stepdaughter alongside.

The cortege pulled out on the mile-and-a-half journey to Disciples Church in the small crossroads town of Domestic. The procession of buggies, carriages, and wagons stretched half a mile. A reporter counted more than three hundred horse-drawn rigs.[10]

The grief and heat were overbearing in the small country church. Mourners crowded together, trying to make room for all who wanted inside. Less than half of those in the procession could find seats or even standing room along the sides and back of the church. The rest tried to find space around windows and doors where they could hear the service.

Reverend Balduc from Oxford, Ohio, a Wolfe family friend, presided at the funeral. He was not a preacher of love and forgiveness but an Old Testament preacher of wrath and vengeance upon those who broke God's commandments. Using the story of Joab and David as the foundation of his message, he spared none of his energy in condemning atheist and murderer John Terrell.

After nearly an hour of forceful preaching, Reverend Balduc offered soothing words of condolence to the victim's family. "Melvin might have had his faults, but he was a faithful young man who regularly went to church and believed in Jesus. So this is the Lord's promise to you, Jacob, and your family. Upon your house, there shall be peace forever from the Lord."

Reverend Balduc paused and again wiped his face. He concluded with a prayer that was not so much for comfort as for justice. "Let the stern justice of the law settle all questions, and the good name of our state and the peace of our home be thereby secured for us and future generations. Amen."

Jacob and the rest of his family walked to the shade of the nearest tree and shook hands with the line of mourners. Mourners lined up to shake hands and express their condolences. A few said that John Terrell would hang, but most limited their comments to ones of sorrow and comfort.

Melvin's body was removed from the church and loaded into the hearse and transported a mile east to Alberson Cemetery, where he was laid to rest next to his mother's grave.

About the time a gravedigger was shoveling dirt onto Melvin Wolfe's coffin, Charles DelaCour arrived at the Wells County Jail to visit John Terrell.

13

Jailhouse, Opera House, and Charles DelaCour

Nothing in Charles DelaCour's physical stature hinted at the presence he carried with him when he entered a room. He was short, not more than five feet, seven inches tall, with a slender build betrayed only by a vaguely discernible middle-aged paunch beneath his brown pin-striped suit and vest. He walked with his head up, his prominent chin pointing the way forward. At age thirty-seven, he combed his dark hair to cover as much as he could of a bald spot expanding from the back of his head. Yet there was something—an energy about his person, the way he held himself, his engaging smile and ready laugh—that immediately drew people to him.

Charles walked into John's jail cell carrying a small cloth valise. He extended his hand and a smile spread wide across his face. "John, how are you doing, my friend?"

John smiled and firmly grabbed Charles's hand. "Better now that you're here, Charles. Have a seat," John said, pointing to the only chair in the cell.

Charles sat, placing the valise on the floor between his feet. "I'm sorry this mess with your son-in-law had to come to this, but he deserved it. I'm sure your lawyers will get you off."

"They're working on it."

"I've been trying to help best I can. I talked to some reporters to tell your side of the story." Charles opened the valise and pulled out several newspapers. He read a few excerpts from the stories, all pointing out that Melvin Wolfe had mistreated Lucy.[1] "He was goaded into fury by his son-in-law's prolonged annoyance and mistreatment of his daughter" was Charles's favorite quotation.[2] Charles also pointed to a story in the *Indianapolis News* about John's family, titled "Member of Good Family."[3]

"Can you leave the newspapers for me?"

"Sure, John. By the way, did you hear the news about Doc Saunders? He's marrying Harry Kirkwood's daughter, Rose. They got their marriage license this morning."[4]

"Well, I hope he treats her better than Melvin treated Lucy."

Charles handed the newspapers to John, and the two men sat quietly for several minutes while John read. Charles broke the silence. "I need to talk to you about the opera house."

For the past seven months, the construction of a new grand opera house in Bluffton had been the most talked about subject in the city, if not the entire county. The men behind the project were John, Charles, and postmaster/lawyer Arthur L. Sharpe. Charles had the driving creative vision, and John provided most of the money.[5]

Despite graduating from the Michigan University School of Law,[6] Charles made his living as a partner in DelaCour and Fields Theatrical Producers and as a part-time actor.[7] DelaCour and Fields produced and promoted plays and variety shows that traveled the circuit of theaters and opera houses throughout the Midwest. On occasion, they produced performances in New York City. But the constant travel wore on Charles and his young family. He looked for an opportunity to settle down. Bluffton presented that opportunity.

The old opera house in Bluffton burned down a decade earlier. Despite some recent proposals, it had not been replaced.[8] Charles thought building and managing a theater in Bluffton would give him a home base. All he needed was to find an investor—someone with money. And in the fall of 1902, he was introduced to John Terrell.

John was interested and enthusiastic. He offered his business property across from the Wells County Jail as the site. William Kapp currently rented the building where he cut and sold marble for buildings and tombstones, but John did not see that as an impediment.

John convinced his friend, Arthur Sharpe, that it was a good investment. By early spring, with initial funds from Terrell and Sharpe, Charles hired George O. Garnsey, a noted Chicago architect known for theaters, to design a grand opera house to be built on a lot owned by John Terrell. A few days before the shooting, Garnsey traveled to Bluffton to inspect the site and present the drawings and specifications to Charles.[9]

The three-story opera house was planned as the most opulent building in northeastern Indiana, perhaps in the entire state. It would be constructed with a front of pressed brick and Bedford stone over a frame of steel girders. The interior would be accented with Tennessee marble, hardwoods, brass railing, and a mosaic floor. Fifteen hundred electric lights were planned even though the formation of the Bluffton Electric Light Company to bring electricity to the city would not be announced until the end of July. The theater, including its balcony, would seat thirteen hundred. The cost was estimated at an astounding $30,000.[10]

Charles leaned forward on the rickety jailhouse chair, ensuring he had John's attention. "There's a lot of concern about the opera house," Charles said. "Business folks and bankers keep stopping me and want to know how this shooting impacts the opera house. Most of them seem to think that it won't be built. Then there's the Elks. They want to lease the top two floors for their new lodge. They need to know right away if you're not going forward with the project." After a short pause, Charles added, "I need to know."

John rubbed his hand across his bare head and gave a dismissive huff. "Nothing's changed. You tell everyone I'm going ahead. Hell, the lot is right outside my cell window. I can oversee it from here."[11]

Charles gave an audible sigh, then a small laugh. "By God, you are a card, John. You are a card. I'll let everybody know it's full steam ahead."

The two men sat for several moments before Charles spoke again. "Just one more thing, John. You've been a good man, and I appreciate your belief in the opera house project. I'd like to help you out with this mess. I don't know if I told you, but I'm a lawyer. I talked with Arthur Sharpe, and he said he'd be happy to have me help, as long as it's okay with you."

John nodded his head. "It's okay with me as long as you don't charge me too much."

By the second week in jail, John Terrell's life had become a routine. He met with his family before noon and his lawyers in the late afternoon. Businessmen and bankers stopped by in the morning or sometimes after lunch to discuss business. But John was frustrated trying to keep up with his business in the confines of his cell. Finally, in the middle of the second week, he sent word that he needed to talk to Sheriff Johnston.[12]

Sheriff Johnston, who was a longtime friend of John, made his way to John's second-floor cell. "Understand you wanted to see me."

John nodded. "You've seen all these businessmen and bankers coming here to talk with me. Well, I just can't keep up this away." John swept his arm to show the conditions of the cell. "This ain't no way to do business."

Sheriff Johnston gave a sympathetic laugh. "I know, John, but I can't let you out."

"Ain't asking that. I need some stuff from home so I can do right by my business while I'm here. The papers and pens I bought last week down at Gutelins's drugstore done run out."

"You need more paper?"

"I need my contracts, my ledger books, and my correspondence. I even need some cash. And I need my desk and my safe to keep all that in. I can get the boys on my farm to bring all of that up here."

Sheriff Johnston looked around the cell, rubbing his chin and trying to picture how the cell would look. "That's an awful big heap of stuff. Sure you need all that?"

"I measured it. It'll fit. I can't keep my business going without it. I ain't been convicted yet. It ain't fair to take my business away from me before I ever had a trial."

Sheriff Johnston considered the situation. He had never had such a request, but then he had never had a prisoner like John Terrell, possibly the richest man in the county. He had some sympathy for what John had done and didn't want to see his business go to ruin. And there were other factors. What was bad for John's business was probably bad for a lot of businesses in the county. The last thing any politician like Sheriff Johnston wanted was to have the county's bankers and most influential businessmen howling at him.

"You can bring your safe and desk and chairs up here and put them in your cell," Johnston said. "But you have to pay for everything."

"Yes, sir," said John.

The next day, John's son, Jake, and three muscular workers from John's farm loaded the safe, rolltop desk, office chair, and two chairs into two sturdy wagons. Everything was transported to the jail and carried into John's second-floor cell.

"Got to admit," Sheriff Johnston said, looking at the cell. "It all fits."

"Just one more thing," John added. "I need my stenographer to come over each day and take down my correspondence."

With his business relocated to his cell, John kept busy. On September 1, incorporation documents for the Bluffton Opera House Company were filed in Indianapolis. John Terrell, Arthur Sharpe, and Charles DelaCour were listed as the incorporating members and board of directors. The capitalized stock was valued at $32,000.[13]

Two days later, George O. Garnsey, the Chicago architect of the new opera house, arrived in Bluffton by train, along with W. C. Wiley, president of Wiley Brothers Construction, a Chicago theater construction company. In front of a few businessmen and two reporters, they signed the construction contract to build the Terrell Grand Opera House.

The *Bluffton Banner* credited Charles DelaCour, "who has so persistently and faithfully carried to a successful termination" the theater project. Completion was scheduled in ninety days, about the time John Terrell's case was expected to go to trial.[14]

14

Shadow of the Gallows

During the first two weeks of September, the six men of the grand jury convened (women could not serve as jurors). Guided by Wells County prosecutor John Burns, they heard testimony from forty-three witnesses without cross-examination. The result was a foregone conclusion, but Burns wanted to make sure he was dotting all the i's and crossing all the t's. Unfortunately, for the State's case, no one caught the typographical errors in the indictment, the significance of which would not be known for another three years.

On Saturday afternoon, September 12, the grand jury returned its indictment of John W. Terrell for the murder of his son-in-law, Leo Melvin Wolfe. Wolfe's name was misspelled throughout the indictment.

Indictment #1204, September 12, 1903:
"Indictment for Murder by Shooting"
The State of Indiana vs. John W. Terrell.
Indictment for Murder by Shooting

The Grand Jurors for the County of Wells, State of Indiana, upon their oath, charge and present that John W Terrell, on the 12th day of July in the year 18903 [sic], at and in the County of Wells, in the State of Indiana, did then there, unlawfully, and feloniously, purposely and with premeditated malice kill and murder one Melvin Wolf [sic] by then and there unlawfully, feloniously, purposely and with premeditated malice shooting at and against and thereby mortally wounding the said Melvin Wolf [sic] with a certain deadly weapon called a shot gun then and there loaded with gun powder and leaden balls which said shot gun he the said John W. Terrell then and there had and held in his hands of which mortal wound the said Melvin Wolf [sic] then and there instantly died, contrary to the form of the Statute in such case made and provided and against the peace and dignity of the State of Indiana.

/s/ John Burns, Prosecuting Attorney[1]

John took the news of the indictment as he would the latest price of corn. It was part of his daily business. "Guess this means we can finally get a trial," he told Levi Mock when the lawyer delivered the news. But other than that, John had little to say about the indictment, even to his family.

On September 21, just a little over a week after the indictment, Sheriff Johnston led John from his cell to the courthouse. Waiting in the courtroom were John's lawyers: Levi Mock, his sons George and John, Arthur Sharpe, and Charles DelaCour. As he entered the courthouse, the newspaper described John as "looking hale and hearty and smoking a cigar, with evident satisfaction."[2]

The 10 A.M. hearing to take John's plea on the indictment was delayed by another matter. As the lawyers and a handful of John's friends waited for Judge Vaughn, John casually walked around the room, greeting people and swapping stories. A newspaper reporter present wrote, "He does not seem worried nor bothered with cares of any kind. In the courtroom, he shook hands with several attorneys and others assembled there and was courteous and pleasant as anyone present."

At 10:30, Judge Vaughn took his seat. Levi Mock waived a reading of the indictment, and John pleaded not guilty. No trial date was set, but Judge Vaughn indicated he wanted to get the case tried before the end of the year.

John's indictment and plea drew some attention, but interest in the case had waned until a full-page article in the *Indianapolis Sunday Sentinel* on September 23. The report provided a detailed account of John's life behind bars, complete with photos of John, Lucy, baby Mabel, Melvin, and the Wells County Jail, along with a page-length drawing of John Terrell leaning from his jail cell window, delivering orders to a worker on the Terrell Grand Opera House.[3]

In much of Wells County, and indeed throughout much of the state of Indiana, there was sympathy for John as a father who had acted to defend his wronged daughter. But the *Indianapolis Sentinel* story had many people rethinking their sentiments. In the days before television and radio, jail was an isolated existence. Only an occasional visit from family and friends broke the tedium.

But that was not how John Terrell was spending his time. Visitors came and went on a day-to-day basis. He ran his business from his cell much as he would if he was sitting in his office at home. It was not how most people expected a man in jail awaiting trial for murder would be living.

Although John's wealth was likely between $50,000 and $100,000,[4] the *Sunday Sentinel* story painted John as a millionaire who, despite being jailed for murder, could buy a lifestyle available to few, whether behind bars or walking free. The story characterized John as "the imprisoned millionaire—the self-confessed murderer who is financing his millions in the shadows of the gallows."[5]

John's daily schedule did not look much different from any other industrious wealthy businessman.[6] He met with bankers in the morning, family and friends over midday, and his lawyers in the afternoon. Nor did his cell differ much from a business office, except for the bars: "Terrell's cell has been made to appear office-like. In one corner stands his huge iron safe, containing all his valuable papers and numerous rolls of bills, approximating about $60,000. To the right of that is his rolltop desk and his luxurious office chair.... By the side of his desk sits his stenographer—a pretty, dainty little stenographer."[7]

John spent most of his afternoon hours attending to construction of the opera house. He met with architects and contractors when needed. But most of his time was spent standing by his jail cell window, overseeing the construction work across the street. A worker was assigned to stand below John's window to receive his instructions and relay them to the construction crew.

The *Sentinel* was unforgiving in its assessment of the privileges extended to John.

> To some it may seem strange that a practically condemned murderer would be allowed all these concessions, which are more than unusual to criminal history, but then the fact must not be forgotten: Terrell is a financier—he is a man of millions. Money, you know, will do almost anything. And no man who owns 350 acres of the richest oil-producing land in Indiana ought to be able to command almost anything money can buy.[8]

The article seemed to express admiration for John's single-mindedness toward his work, terming him "a Napoleon of the finance in a castle of bars."[9] Despite the legal Sword of Damocles hanging over him, he continued to work.

The chilly shadow of the gallows would naturally quench anything but a trembling dread as to what the dark and terrible future held. Not so much with Terrell. He is a man of too much strength of will and, it might as well be said, character. Feeling justified in doing what he did, as he himself expresses it, he gives no more thought, apparently, to his crime.[10]

But regardless of the *Sentinel*'s admiration, the newspaper article wondered about what demons might visit John when he was alone in the quiet of the night.

As to what the night holds—ah, one may easily conjecture. Business is a good antidote for a burden of the conscience in the day time, so long as those around one keep the interest alive, but when the night comes, when the huge outer door clangs to open again no more until the morrow, when the sounds of life from the happy and free outside world are stilled, then—then business becomes a mocking illusion that evades a grasp and a relentless Nemesis, in the throbbing pangs of a guilty conscience, paints pictures that drive men mad. "I feel justified" fails to quiet the voice: "Thou shalt not kill!"[11]

. . .

The *Sunday Sentinel*'s full-page feature on John used many of the features of yellow journalism of the day, exaggerating John's wealth and creating dramatic imagery that at times only touched upon the truth. It is apparent that the story did not help public sentiment for John as his trial drew closer. While John was a wealthy man by Wells County standards, he was far from the multimillionaire portrayed in the *Sentinel*. The article also magnified the opulence of the new opera house under construction, doubling its costs. And while Sheriff Johnston's longtime friendship with John undoubtedly resulted in some favoritism, there is no indication that John was buying special treatment.

After the *Sentinel* article, there is little question that many, even some of his supporters, viewed John differently. The sympathy many had for a father acting in defense of a wronged daughter began fading.

The public perception took another hit three weeks later. On the afternoon of Monday, October 19, Sheriff Johnston escorted John from the jail and across the street to the construction site of the new opera house for the laying of the cornerstone. Nearly three hundred people crowded around the Washington Street lot owned by John Terrell, where construction of the opera house was in progress. Many were there to see the cornerstone laid. Others simply wanted to get a glimpse of John Terrell.[12]

John was animated as he walked to the corner of Washington and Johnson Streets, shaking hands and greeting friends and local businessmen. Charles DelaCour stood next to the stone, directing the activities. Architect George O. Garnsey and general contractor W. C. Wiley stood alongside. DelaCour hosted the ceremony, talking about how the magnificent opera house would mark Bluffton as one of the most progressive cities in Indiana.

The stone was laid, and the principals shook hands and exchanged congratulations. When they were done, Sheriff Johnston escorted John back to his cell.

The story of the man accused of murder being released to lay a cornerstone made newspapers across Indiana. The *Indianapolis News* observed, "The site is immediately opposite the jail, and from his cell window Terrell can watch the rise to completion."[13]

The stories of the stone-laying struck yet another dissonant chord among many residents—that John's money was buying him favors in the legal system. It did not sit well with many of the humble, hardworking, God-fearing citizens who would sit on his jury.

15

The Cusp of Trial

In early October, a date had not yet been set for the trial of John Terrell, but everyone anticipated it would be before the first of the year. The lawyers were busy with trial preparation, interviewing and reinterviewing witnesses, lining up doctors as experts on the insanity defense, researching the law for evidence fights, drafting instructions, and preparing trial strategies.

Every lawyer on both sides, indeed nearly every person in the county, knew that few facts were in dispute. Everyone knew that John shot Melvin Wolfe. The question was whether the jury would excuse his actions on the legal basis of temporary insanity or irresistible impulse. Few juries can be convinced of the wisdom of releasing a murderer because of mental deficiency. But an irresistible impulse defense could be used as cover for the real defense argument—convincing the jury that Mel Wolfe deserved what he got. If John's lawyers could do that, there was the possibility of acquittal no matter how the judge instructed the jury about insanity.

But when Levi Mock walked into John's cell on October 10, it wasn't to discuss witnesses, legal issues, insanity, or trial strategy. Instead, it was to talk about money.

Levi did not take his customary seat next to the rolltop desk in John's cell. Instead, he stood towering over the accused. Rather than his usual satchel filled with legal papers, he carried only a single sheet of paper. Levi got right to the point. "You haven't paid our latest bill. I sent you a bill for $1,000 for our work, and you haven't paid it. It's past due."

"I ain't paying no $1,000, Levi." John's voice was firm. "That's way too much."

"We've known each other for too long for you to say that," Levi said.

"I'll pay you $500 for what you done, but not a penny more. That's fair. Anything more than that is just robbery."

"I can't take that, John. Five hundred dollars is not fair to my sons or me for all the time we've put in on this case."

John stood up, pointing upward at Levi as he spoke. "You think you got me over a barrel being in here? You been readin' them stories about me having millions, and you want a piece of that."

"That's not true. I just want to be fair. Fair to you, but also fair to my boys and me."

"Ol' Sharpe can try this case. He's as good a lawyer as you."

"Arthur is a good lawyer, but he's never tried a murder case."

John swiveled in his desk chair and spun the combination dial to open his safe. He pulled out his bank draft book. Without saying another word, John wrote a check for $500 and handed it to Levi. "I ain't a-paying you no more than that."

Levi took the check and walked out of the jail. It was the end of his law firm's long relationship with John Terrell. The next day, Levi walked into the Wells County Circuit Court and filed a lawsuit for the remaining unpaid legal fees against John Terrell and a motion to withdraw as John's lawyer.[1]

As soon as Levi left, John sent word that he wanted to see Arthur Sharpe. When the fifty-six-year-old Sharpe arrived, his ill health was evident. His skin was pale, and he had a persistent hacking cough.

John was direct about the reason for the meeting. "Levi quit on me. I need you to take over the case."

Surprise registered on Arthur's face. "Surely not. Levi wouldn't do that."

"He was trying to hold me up for a thousand dollars, with more to be paid later. I told him no, and he said he wasn't doing no more work for me. So, I guess this is your case now. You and Charles DelaCour."

Arthur rubbed his hand across his face and took a thoughtful moment before responding. "I wish you'd reconsider. Levi's the best lawyer around. But, in a case like this, two good lawyers are better than one. Even Prosecutor Burns has hired William Eichhorn to help him—and he's about as good a courtroom lawyer as there is in these parts."

"Well, I ain't paying Levi no more than the $500 I paid him. And you got DelaCour to help you."

"Charles is a smart guy. He can help some, but he's never tried a case."

"That's the way it's gonna be."

A few minutes later, Postmaster Arthur Sharpe walked out of the Wells County Jail as John Terrell's lead trial lawyer.

Rumors spread around the county that Levi Mock quit the Terrell case because he knew John was guilty and couldn't win the case. The rumors became so persistent that Levi called the editor of the *Bluffton Banner* on Friday, November 13, to give an interview about withdrawing from the case. "The decision was a business one, pure and simple," Levi told the newspaper. "I was loth [*sic*] to bring the action because I was afraid it might somehow damage Mr. Terrell's case. But after considering the situation and my own family, I felt I was required to withdraw from representing Mr. Terrell and file suit to protect my own interests. I do not have anything further to say on the case."[2]

John became the subject of even more rumors when a notice of the public sale of his farm equipment was published in the *Bluffton Banner.*

PUBLIC SALE TO BE HELD

THURSDAY, NOVEMBER 24, 1903, COMMENCING AT 9 A.M.

Public sale by auction of all farming equipment and tools located at the John W. Terrell farm, 1¼ miles south of Petroleum. Items for sale include plows, disks, harvester, combine, farm wagon, fencing equipment, harnesses, hand tools, and various other farming equipment.

TERMS: CASH. ALL SALES FINAL

SELLER'S NOTE: Sale to be on November 24. Thereafter, my family will move to Bluffton as we wish to have more congenial neighbors.

/s/ John W. Terrell[3]

Some speculated that the murder case had taken a toll on John's finances and that he was selling off property to meet his legal debts. Others guessed that he was selling his property to make his fortune more liquid so that he could transfer it in expectation of going to prison. No one knew for sure because John was not talking. But that didn't stop people from talking in restaurants and taverns and at church socials.

Gossip was fueled even more when the next day, the *Fort Wayne Daily News* contained a front-page article with a drawing of the new Terrell Grand Opera House. The newspaper reported that construction of the opera house was on time. Charles DelaCour announced that the opening show was expected shortly after January 1.[4]

But as exciting as the news was about the opera house, the center of interest and discussion was the upcoming trial of John Terrell.

· · ·

By mid-November, Judge Edwin C. Vaughn determined it was time to bring the John Terrell case to trial. At 1:30 P.M. on November 15, he brought the lawyers before the court to decide the trial date.[5]

"Let's get this case set for trial," Judge Vaughn said. "December term starts November 30. I suggest we set the trial to begin on that date. Any problem with that?"

"The State is agreeable to that date," Prosecutor John Burns said.

Arthur Sharpe rose. "Your honor, the defense is agreeable to that date as long as the court has sufficient days on its calendar. I think this may be quite a long trial."

Judge Vaughn looked over his glasses at Sharpe. "The Court is aware that the parties expect a lengthy trial. If we start on November 30, we can finish in time for the jurors and the lawyers to have a nice Christmas. Now how long will this take?

"The State can put its case on in two days," Burns said.

Sharpe shook his head. "It will take the defense considerably longer. I expect it will take a week for our side. Maybe more."

"Well, Mr. Sharpe, see if you can move things along a little faster. As much as people have talked and read about this case, I suspect we will have to call more jurors than usual. I'm going to start by ordering the clerk to draw fifty names. That should be enough to get twelve jurors."

Judge Vaughn removed his glasses and looked toward the ceiling, obviously thinking. After a moment, he looked directly at Arthur Sharpe. "I've heard some talk from other lawyers that you are going to file a motion for a change of judge. Is that so?"

Sharpe stood, his mouth hanging open for a second. "That's the first I've heard of it." Sharpe then glanced to where his client was seated. He started to ask his client, but something in John's expression told him it was a question best asked in private.

"Well, Dr. Sharpe, I would be glad to be relieved of the case as no judge cares to sit on a murder case. But we are less than two weeks out from the trial. It would be a great hardship on the court to secure a judge from a neighboring county to come to Bluffton on such short notice. So, if you are going to file such a motion, you need to file it promptly."

"Yes, your honor."

On November 24, only six days before John Terrell's trial began, Arthur Sharpe filed a sworn Motion for Change of Judge. However, Sharpe did not sign it. Instead, it was signed by John Terrell, claiming "bias and prejudice of said judge against him."[6]

Judge Vaughn immediately granted the motion, happy to be rid of the case. He named John M. Smith, a forty-nine-year-old judge in neighboring Jay County, as the special judge. Smith was completing the fifth year of his six-year term and would not seek a second term.[7]

With the new judge in place, the case of *State of Indiana vs. John W. Terrell* was ready for trial.

Part III

Trial

If a madman or a natural fool, or a lunatic in
the time of his lunacy do kill a man, this is
no felonious act, for they cannot be said to
have any understanding or will.

STATEMENT OF BRITISH LAW, 1581

A jury consists of twelve persons chosen
to decide who has the better lawyer.

ROBERT FROST

16

Twelve Men Tried and True

It was still dark with a late-November chill that penetrated the jail cell when John Terrell woke at his usual time of 6 A.M. for breakfast on the first day of his murder trial. After a breakfast of eggs, bacon, and fried mush, he cleaned up and changed into one of his two dark wool suits. He sat quietly at his desk, reading and waiting for his lawyers.

Shortly after 9 A.M., Sheriff Johnston came to his cell. "You ready, John? Your lawyers are waiting downstairs. So's some of your family."

John stood without talking and accompanied the sheriff. On the ground floor, perhaps the most extensive legal team ever to try a case in Wells County waited. Arthur Sharpe was acting as lead counsel. Joining him were law partners Charles Sturgis and Robert Stine, their young associate Robert Landfair, and self-promoter Charles DelaCour. Joining them at the courthouse would be Ralph Gregory. Two months short of his sixtieth birthday, the gray-bearded Gregory was revered in legal circles throughout eastern Indiana for his powerful oratory.

Several members of the Terrell family were also waiting to accompany John to the first day of trial. Lucy held Mabel, now eighteen months old. With her were John's son, Jake, now nearly twenty, and Sally, accompanied by her husband, John Schott.

"You ready, John?" Sharpe asked, putting a hand on John's shoulder.

John nodded. "Let's get it over with." John leaned over toward Lucy. "Let me carry the baby a bit," he said.

The procession headed out for the two-block walk to the courthouse, the lawyers leading the way. John followed, holding his granddaughter, then Lucy. Sheriff Johnston and a deputy walked a few paces behind.[1]

Built in 1889, the Wells County Courthouse still had the shine of a new building. The circuit courtroom was on the third floor. It was a large room full of dark walnut and the smell of furniture oil. Benches for spectators, which were already half filled, stood ten rows deep, separated by a broad center aisle. Each side of the aisle seated perhaps a dozen citizens dressed in their Sunday best, possibly two more if they were willing to squeeze together. The first row behind the defense table was reserved for the Terrell family; the one behind the prosecution was reserved for the Wolfe family. Several rows were marked off for the fifty prospective jurors, most of whom were already in place when John, his lawyers, and family entered.

A highly polished wooden rail with a single swinging gate separated the public from the participants. Twelve chairs were arranged in two rows of six on the judge's left, facing the witness chair to the judge's right. Two tables sat across from the judge's bench, one for the prosecution and one for the defense. Several chairs were set off to the side, reserved for the reporters and a courtroom artist who would be covering the trial.

As he walked to the defense table, John carried the baby in his arms. He sat in the chair indicated by one of the lawyers, still holding the baby, whom he started bouncing on his knee, sometimes quietly singing the ditty, "Went out to milk, didn't know how. Hung the bucket on the horn of a cow."

A few minutes after the defense team arrived, Prosecutor John Burns walked through the door carrying his well-worn leather valise. Behind him, tall and slender, walking with assurance to the point of arrogance, was William Eichhorn, a thirty-four-year-old lawyer who had already made his reputation for his dynamic, aggressive, and quick-minded courtroom performances. Behind them, carrying satchels filled with papers and law books, were young lawyer George Matlack and veteran J. K. Rinehart, followed by the Wolfe family.

Jacob Wolfe, his posture erect and stiff, his face stern and unsmiling, glared at Terrell as Prosecutor Burns pointed Wolfe to a seat at the defense table. John concentrated on his granddaughter bouncing on his lap and took no notice of Wolfe entering the courtroom.

Mary Wolfe and Della Reed took seats immediately behind the prosecution table. Mary sneered at the Terrell family. Della lowered her head as if this was the last place on Earth she wanted to be.

At 9:45 A.M. by the courtroom clock, Bailiff Adnah Hall moved to his place next to the judge's imposing bench. He slammed his gavel, and the sound carried like a rifle shot, causing some to jump in their seats. His voice boomed.

"Hear ye! Hear ye! Hear ye! The Wells County Circuit Court is now open, Special Judge John M. Smith presiding. All rise!"

Those in the courtroom rose in nearly a single motion. The door behind the bench opened, and Judge Smith, wearing a black robe and carrying the case file under his arm, strode to his high-backed black leather chair and took his seat.

Judge Smith looked like he could be related to the faces on the widely used Smith Brothers cough drops. His dark beard hung several inches off his chin but was well trimmed. Even though he was forty-nine, he appeared much younger than most judges. When Judge Vaughn called him about accepting an appointment as special judge in the John Terrell trial, he had been hesitant. But after consideration, he took it as his duty.

Lawyers regarded Judge Smith as fair but firm. He did not like passing judgment on others. When his term as Jay County circuit judge expired at the end of 1904, he would return to private law practice and never again seek election to the bench.[2]

Judge Smith began by hearing the several pretrial motions that no one expected to be granted—a motion to dismiss by the defense and a prosecution's motion to strike the defense plea of insanity. After brief arguments, Judge Smith summarily denied the motions. He then addressed the prospective jurors, setting out the expected daily schedule and his intolerance for anyone being late.

He then turned to the lawyers. "Is the State ready for trial?"

John Burns stood. "The State is ready."

"Is the defense ready?"

Arthur Sharpe stood. "We are, your honor."

"Very well. Let's get a jury selected."

Selecting a jury would not be easy. Each side was given twenty preemptory challenges for which no cause was needed, more than the usual dozen.[3] Judge Smith made clear that simply hearing about the case, or even forming an opinion about the case from news stories, was not enough to disqualify a juror. "However, if any man who has formed a strong opinion about guilt or innocence, that will be sufficient cause to excuse that man from the jury."

Judge Smith took a small sip from his water cup, then continued. "This is a capital case, and one of the penalties provided by statute upon conviction is a possible sentence of death by hanging. The law in this state is clear that every juror empaneled must be able to follow the law and, consequently, upon conviction, must be able to vote for a sentence of death when warranted. Should a prospective juror not be able to do so for reason of conscience or religious belief, that man shall not be able to sit on the jury and will immediately be excused."

A few minutes before 11 A.M., the jury selection process began.[4]

The first man questioned was J. B. Schott, a farmer from Nottingham Township, where the Terrell and Wolfe families lived and where the shooting occurred. Schott pronounced that he had strong opinions about the case and was excused. He was followed by Henry S. Cloud, another farmer, who answered that he had "strong opinions I cannot get rid of" and was excused. Next was William Baker, who served as prosecutor for the small town of Keystone and was immediately dismissed with little questioning. Alonzo Poison, a Keystone-area farmer, followed him and bluntly stated, "I have an opinion about the guilt of the defendant, and nothing's gonna change my mind." Next, the lawyers questioned C. M. Miller, who likewise was excused. The next juror, David H. Marris, was related to one of the lawyers and was promptly dismissed.

The court reached the noon recess, and all that had been accomplished was excusing six of the fifty men called to jury duty. It was now apparent that selecting a jury would be even more difficult than the judge and lawyers envisioned.

After a ninety-minute break for dinner, questioning of prospective jurors followed. Edwin Hawley, a Jefferson Township farmer, told the court, "My conscience will not allow me to impose the death penalty." He was followed by William Walker, James Ryder, Frank Mosier, William Shady, and J. S. Grimes, all of whom, except for Shady, said they could not sentence a man to be hanged. Shady told the court that his son was home with typhoid fever and needed his father's attention. All were excused.

As the afternoon wore on, it became evident that fifty men on the jury panel would not be enough. Accordingly, Judge Smith sent word to the jury commissioners to draw thirty more names.

At six o'clock, the court adjourned for the day. The entire venire of fifty men was nearly exhausted, and the court was not much closer to having a jury than when the day started. Judge Smith had excused half of the men questioned for their conscientious objection to sentencing a man to death. Many of the other men held strong opinions about the case that prevented them from serving. At the end of the day, the State had used only one of its twenty peremptory challenges; the defense, none.

After the prospective jurors had left, Judge Smith commented to Bailiff Hall, "It seems that the death penalty is exceedingly unpopular in Wells County."

"It is, indeed, your honor," Hall responded.[5]

The jury commissioners gathered in the courtroom and selected thirty more names. Sheriff Johnston and three deputies set out across the county to serve the summons on citizens just sitting down to supper. Some did not receive the summons until they were in bed.[6]

On Tuesday morning, John's wife Catherine joined the family on the bench behind the defense table. She had battled illnesses for the past several years, and the strain of John's time in jail added to that. Tired and exceedingly frail, she shuffled down the aisle to her seat.

Day two began sharply at 9 A.M. Questioning droned on with little more success at seating the jury than the first day. More were excused for opposition to the death penalty and strong opinions about the guilt or innocence of John Terrell. Two were dismissed for defective hearing, and two because their wives had typhoid fever.

Thirty minutes before the dinner break, the lawyers exhausted the original fifty potential jurors and began questioning the thirty who were summoned only the night before. By early afternoon, it was apparent the additional thirty would not be enough.[7]

As the afternoon session dragged on, John showed weariness for the first time since his arrest. For most of the two days, he sat with his granddaughter on his lap. He smoothed Mabel's fine blonde hair, at times idly twirling curls in his fingertips, sometimes softly cooing in her ear. At one point, Mabel wandered away from Lucy and over to the table where Prosecutor John Burns was sitting. There were smiles around the courtroom as Burns picked up the little girl, gave her a hug and a pat, then returned her to Lucy.[8] Lucy took the child back with a gracious "Thank you." At counsel table, John leaned forward, resting his head on his hands, not paying attention to the questions or the answers of those who would ultimately decide his fate.[9]

At 3 P.M., the court called a recess but ordered the lawyers back into chambers. "Gentlemen, I still don't think we have enough to fill the jury, so I'm going to have the jury commissioners draw thirty more names. We can do this by having the names drawn from the jury box, or I can have the sheriff go out there and just start picking out bystanders in the courtroom. And if that's not enough, he can have his men go walking the streets and telling people to report to the courthouse. I'd just as soon skip the formality, but it's up to you, gentlemen. Do you have any objections to doing that?"[10]

"I would object," Prosecutor Burns said. "The statutes require we use the jury box, and the State will object to picking jurors any other way."

"Okay. That decides for us," Judge Smith said. "I'll bring the jury commissioners in and draw thirty more to report tomorrow morning."

With a new batch of prospective jurors in their seats, the third trial day began at 9 A.M. with the continuation of jury selection. Finally, at 9:50, Prosecutor Burns rose. "We accept the current twelve as members of the jury."[11]

After a few minutes of discussion among the defense counsel, Arthur Sharpe stood. "The defense accepts the jury."

A collective sigh of relief went across the courtroom. After more than two full days of questioning ninety-seven prospective jurors, the trial was ready to begin.

The jury that would decide John Terrell's fate was in place. The oldest juror was sixty-six-year-old Fred Hiser. The youngest was thirty-three-year-old Theodore Redding. Only three of the dozen were younger than fifty, selected from property tax rolls. They had three things in common: they were all men, they were all farmers, and they all believed in the death penalty.

Judge Smith decided that the jurors would be housed in the courtroom until the case was completed. Eighty-one-year-old bailiff John Poffenberger was placed in charge of the jury. Perhaps the oldest man to occupy such a position in the country, Poffenberger proudly referred to the all-male jurors as "my boys." Poffenberger had already secured a supply of cots and bedding, which he had stored in the jury room.[12]

For the next three weeks, the jurors would call the Wells County Courthouse their home.

17

The State's Case Begins

After a short break, Judge Smith read his preliminary instructions to the jury, including reciting the indictment, John Terrell's plea of not guilty, and the special plea that the defendant was not guilty because he was of unsound mind at the time of the incident. When Judge Smith finished, he nodded toward the prosecution table.

Prosecutor John Burns walked to a spot in front of the jury and delivered his opening statement.[1] Burns's presentation was well rehearsed. He portrayed the victim, Melvin Wolfe, as a young, hardworking, God-fearing man from a good family who was a regular churchgoer. While he had a bit of a wild side common to many young men, he tried to do right by Lucy Wolfe. They got married, but like many couples, they had problems, and so they went their own ways. But after that, the real problems began. John Terrell repeatedly threatened Melvin, just as he had threatened others in his past.

Burns recited his version of the shooting along the road in front of the Terrell house, followed by the shooting of an injured Melvin Wolfe in Dr. Saunders's office. In the gallery, just behind the prosecution table, there was a sob from Mary Wolfe. Jacob Wolfe sat stoically, but tears streamed down his weathered face.

Burns concluded with his practiced eloquence. "The State will prove beyond any reasonable doubt that John Terrell killed Melvin Wolfe in cold blood and with calculated premeditation. If the State so proves, it will be your duty to find him guilty of murder in the first degree."

The defense exercised its option to hold its opening statement until the defense was ready to present its case. With that, the prosecution began its case.

Jacob Wolfe was called as the trial's first witness.[2] Jacob was somber as he began his testimony. Melvin was the youngest of Jacob's two children. Melvin's mother died from consumption on his seventh birthday. On the day of the shooting, Melvin "lacked two months and fifteen days of being twenty-three years old."

On July 12, Jacob was at home on the farm when Melvin, his stepsister Della Reed, and two others went on a buggy ride. It was around five o'clock when he saw the buggy head north from the Wolfe farm.

"Tell the jury, did you ever see your son after that alive?"

The words caught in his throat. "No, sir," he finally was able to answer. "I did not."

Jacob testified that he saw Melvin's body later that day at Dr. Saunders's office. There was blood on the table and a wound behind Melvin's left ear. His body was brought home and laid on a stretcher in the house. It was there that Jacob found leaden balls on the floor beneath where his son's body was placed.

"Do you have those balls now?"

"Yes, sir. They been in my possession ever since I found them."

Jacob reached into his suit jacket and pulled out a small paper bag. He handed it to Burns. On the prosecutor's motion, Judge Smith admitted the lead balls into evidence. With that, Prosecutor Burns concluded his exam.

Arthur Sharpe rose from his seat. "No questions, your honor."

Coroner James A. "Fred" McBride was the next witness.[3] On the day of the shooting in Petroleum, McBride was called to Dr. Saunders's office at around 8 P.M. When he arrived, he found the body of Melvin Wolfe lying on the operating table.

Melvin had a wound on his leg, starting about six inches above the knee. McBride examined the wound and determined that both leg bones were shattered and the main artery in the leg was severed, resulting in significant blood loss.

There was also a hole in Melvin's shoulder, located behind the heart near the shoulder blade. The wound was about an inch and a half in circumference with ragged edges, and the clothing over the shoulder wound appeared burned or torn. Additionally, there was another wound, this one behind the ear, about an inch and a half in size, that caused severe damage to the skull and jaw bones.

Again, John's defense counsel did not cross-examine the witness.

Rosa Downing was the first witness to the shooting to be called.[4] A petite young woman, she appeared every bit the music teacher she was, dressed in a periwinkle cotton dress with a white sash and a small straw hat with a floral band. Her voice was soft and her eyes downcast as she testified.

She described being at the Wolfes' house on late Sunday afternoon, July 12, where she met with Clarence Turner, Della Reed, and Melvin Wolfe. Around five o'clock Rosa got in a buggy with Clarence Turner and Della got in Melvin's buggy. They traveled north about half a mile, then west to Petroleum. From there, they went south to Nottingham, passing the Terrell farm. Someplace south of Nottingham, they turned around and began retracing the route they had followed.

"When you came back to a place a mile and a half south of Petroleum, was there any shooting?"

Rosa looked straight across the room at the jury for the first time. "Yes, there was. About opposite Mr. Terrell's house. He was concealed there, and he jumped out in the road."

Judge Smith checked the courtroom clock. "It's noon. This is a good place to stop for dinner. We will resume at 1:30."

When John Terrell returned from the dinner break, a buzz went through the courtroom. Accompanying him was an elderly couple, seventy-four-year-old William Terrell and his sixty-seven-year-old wife Mary—John's father and stepmother.[5] They had arrived the previous night from their home in eastern Delaware County, more than fifty miles away.

The arduous trip had worn on the elderly couple. They both walked with faltering steps, taking their seats on the reserved bench behind the defense table. As they took their seats, John took his father's hat and placed it on the hat rack inside the area reserved for trial participants. He brought his father a glass of water before returning to his seat. As the testimony resumed, John focused more on his father's comfort than on the testimony.

After lunch, Prosecutor Burns resumed his questioning of Rosa Downing, picking up with her dramatic account of the roadside shooting.

Rosa stated that the buggy in which she and Clarence were riding was in front of Melvin's buggy. They had just passed where Terrell was in hiding when she saw him jump onto the road. Until that moment, she had not seen him. Rosa recounted, "We had just gone past, I think, just a little. Mr. Terrell was nearly even with our rig because when he jumped out, it frightened our horse."

"After he jumped out, did you see him do anything?"

Rosa nodded. Her voice was raised and breathless, and her face glowed red as if replaying the event in her mind. "I saw him shoot into the rig, the one Della and Mr. Wolfe was in."

After the shooting, Melvin's buggy raced around the one carrying Rosa and Clarence. They followed at a distance into Petroleum, where they saw men assisting Melvin outside Dr. Saunders's office.

"Did you see the defendant, Mr. Terrell, while you were in Petroleum?"

"Yes, sir. It was not many minutes until he came. I saw him when he drove up there in the buggy, and I saw him enter the front door into Doctor Saunders's office."

"Did Terrell have anything in his hands?"

"I can't remember about it," Rosa said, dropping her head. "I just don't remember."

Rosa did remember that the next day she saw Melvin Wolfe's body at his home.

Burns nodded, then walked back to his seat. "Pass the witness."

Ralph Gregory rose to cross-examine his first witness. He pulled at his gray beard as he took his place in front of the defense table. He also took care not to block the jury's view of the witness. His shoulders were slightly stooped with age, but his rich voice commanded the courtroom.

Gregory began questioning Rosa about her observations and actions during a buggy ride. She confirmed that she and Clarence Turner were engaged in conversation throughout the ride. When asked if she looked back to see how far behind Melvin and his stepsister were, she admitted that she didn't. Only when she heard the shot did she rise in the wagon and look back.

After Melvin's buggy ran past the one she was riding in, she and Clarence chased after them toward Petroleum. To the best she could recall, they were a quarter of a mile behind Melvin's buggy and, despite going as fast as their horse would carry them, didn't gain any distance.

Rosa's memory faltered when it came to what happened upon her arrival in Petroleum. Gregory used his experience to drill in on Rosa's lack of memory to the point that some in the gallery began to titter.

"When you got to Petroleum, what became of the horse and buggy you were riding in?"

"I don't know."

"When you first saw Mr. Terrell in Petroleum, where was he?"

"He was in his buggy."

"Did he get out of the buggy?"

"Yes, sir."

"What did he do with his horse?"

"I don't know what the man done with his horse."

"Did you see him hitch his horse?"

"No, sir."

"Did he jump out and leave his horse standing in the street?"

"No, sir. I don't know that at all."

"When he got out of the buggy, did he have anything in his hand?"

"I didn't notice anything."

"Tell the jury how he got from his buggy to Doctor Saunders's office if you can."

"I can't remember just how he did get there."

Rosa stated that she entered a residence in Petroleum, but she didn't remember whose house it was or what was said during her short visit. After a short time, she went to Oliver's Restaurant, where she met Della Reed. Despite sitting across from the woman who was in the buggy with Melvin when he was shot, Rosa said she did not know if she and Della talked. Under intense questioning by Gregory, she finally admitted that they did talk, but Gregory was never able to elicit the substance of their conversation.

Gregory, satisfied that he had destroyed Rosa's credibility as a witness, nodded toward the judge, signaling the end of his questioning.

The following two witnesses called by the prosecution were Ida Clark[6] and Orville Burgess.[7] The young couple also took a buggy ride on that fateful Sunday afternoon. They were south of the Terrell farm, heading north toward Petroleum, when two buggies passed them, the first buggy carrying Clarence Turner and Rosa Downing and, a few minutes later, a second carrying Melvin Wolfe and Della Reed. They did not speak to either as they passed.

Ida Clark's recollection of events was incomplete and, at times, contradictory. About a quarter mile south of the Terrell farm, she heard a gunshot. Looking up, she saw John Terrell crossing the road, but then changed her testimony to say she saw Mr. Terrell at the side of the road "with something in his hand." She later clarified that she saw him with a gun in his hand and saw him raise it. "I saw smoke from the gun and then saw him walk across the road." Ida did not know where Mr. Terrell was aiming his gun when he fired it.

Ida and Orville continued toward Petroleum. They were not far down the road when Ida pulled her buggy to the side of the road, and John Terrell passed in his rig.

Twenty-two-year-old farmer Orville Burgess, Ida's companion in the buggy, followed her to the witness stand. Dressed in a dark wool suit, he sat stiffly in the witness chair. As a farmer, he used rods to testify as to distance, each rod equaling sixteen and a half feet. He testified that he and Ida were "about 40 rods south of Mr. Terrell's farm" when they were passed by the two carriages with Clarence Turner and Rosa Downing in the lead, followed by Melvin Wolfe and Della Reed.

"Did anything attract your attention near the Terrell residence?"

"Well, I was looking down the road ahead like, and I saw Mr. Terrell rise up from the side of the road—the west side. He was in a side ditch with some bushes and weeds. He came up from behind a burdock bush."

Terrell rose up from the weeds with a shotgun in "kind of a shooting position." Before Terrell straightened, Burgess heard the first shot. "He was not standing straight." After the first shot, Terrell straightened and moved to the edge of the road. He raised the gun to his shoulder, aimed, and fired the second shot when he was only about ten feet from Wolfe's buggy.

"Did you see Mr. Terrell after firing the second shot?"

"Yes."

"What, if anything, did he do then?"

"Loading his gun."

"What happened next?"

"He ran across the road and set the gun in his buggy."

Burgess testified that when he and Ida stopped at Luther Fenton's house, they saw John Terrell race past. He and Ida then continued on to Petroleum.

Prosecutor Burns nodded and stepped closer to the witness. He lowered his voice, so the jury had to strain to hear the question. "Did you see Melvin Wolfe again after you got to Petroleum?"

"I did."

"Where?"

"He was laid on the dissecting table at Doctor Saunders's office. He was dead."

Burns let the words hang in the air for nearly a minute. He then led Burgess through describing the wounds on Melvin's body.

"Did you observe any wounds on Mr. Wolfe's corpse?"

"There was a shot in the right leg a few inches above the knee. There was another one between the shoulders, and one at the side of the ear in his head."

Burns turned and slowly walked back to his seat at the prosecution table. "I pass the witness for cross-examination."

Unlike Rosa Downing and Ida Clark, Orville Burgess has been certain and detailed in his recollection of events. There was little ground for Arthur Sharpe to attack Burgess in his cross-examination. After several futile efforts to sow doubt into his testimony, Sharpe became more aggressive in his questioning. Judge Smith sustained a series of objections from the prosecution. It was becoming evident that Judge Smith would not do the defense any favors in his rulings.

Sharpe accomplished little by his cross-examination. Rather than jeopardize his own credibility with the jury, the lawyer asked another handful of ineffective questions, then sat down.

18

Della's Story

The courtroom was now filled with every seat taken. A buzz crossed the courtroom as Prosecutor Burns called Melvin's nineteen-year-old stepsister Della Reed to testify.[1] She wore a full black skirt with a ruffled white blouse under a fitted black jacket. Raven feathers accented her small black hat. As she walked to the witness chair, she glared at John Terrell, her jaw fixed and teeth clenched. Terrell looked straight ahead, not taking notice of her.

After swearing in, Prosecutor Burns wasted no time trying to paint Melvin and Della as Godly young people, which he planned to contrast with the atheist John Terrell.

"Turning your attention to the day of the shooting. Where were you that Sunday morning?"

"I was at Sabbath School in Petroleum."

"Where was your stepbrother that morning?"

"He was in church at New Salem. I saw him when he was coming home."

Della said that around eleven o'clock, Rosa Downing and Clarence Turner visited. In the afternoon, they left on a buggy ride, with Rosa and Clarence in the lead buggy and Della and Melvin following behind. When they reached Petroleum, they headed south on Bluffton-Camden Pike, passing the John Terrell farm. As they passed, Della said she did not see anyone in the Terrell family. All the doors and windows on the house appeared closed. Neither she nor Melvin spoke or interacted with any members of the Terrell family.

After riding on for a while, they turned and headed back the way they came.

As they approached the Terrell house, Della saw John Terrell in a ditch along the side of the road. "He wasn't standing quite straight. Sorta getting up from where he was crouching."

"How far away from your buggy was he?"

"Not very far. Probably six or eight feet as near as I can tell."

"What side was Melvin sitting in the buggy?"

"He was on the side closest to Mr. Terrell."

"Did he have anything in his hands?"

"A gun."

The courtroom was completely silent as Della recounted the events. Burns paused, letting the impact of Della's words sink in with the jury.

"After you saw the defendant, what happened next?"

Della turned in her chair and gave an icy stare directly at John. "I saw him raise the gun and aim it at the buggy. He shot toward the buggy."

"How many times?"

"Twice. One shot hit Melvin in the leg."

As a result of the gunshots, the horse started running. It ran about half a mile before slowing down near Fenton's. Della took control of the buggy and continued driving Melvin to Dr. Saunders's office in Petroleum. Along the way, she noticed the wound on Melvin's leg. "I saw the wound where the load had went, there on top of his leg. I saw blood. It was on his clothing, and on my dress, and on in the buggy. It run clear across the buggy."

"Did Melvin say anything as you rode along toward Petroleum?"

For the first time, tears formed in Della's eyes and began streaming down her cheeks. She wiped her eyes with the handkerchief she held in her hands. When she started to speak, her voice broke. "He said his leg was broken. He . . . He said, 'I'm gonna be a cripple for life.' And he kept groaning something awful and saying how bad it hurt. Then he started saying that everything was turning green."

By the time they arrived at Dr. Saunders's office, Melvin was turning gray. Dr. Saunders, William Kirkwood, and two other men helped carry Melvin into the doctor's office. After Melvin was carried away, Della went to Samuel Green's house nearby, then after a few minutes walked to Oliver's Restaurant just down the street.

"Did you see the defendant, John W. Terrell, any time after you got to Petroleum?"

The rage returned to Della's face, and she looked straight at John as she answered, "Yes, sir. I saw him head up the steps to Saunders's office. There were two men were on the steps, and I heard him yell at them to step aside."

"Did he have anything in his hands?"

"He had a gun."

"What happened next?"

"I heard the reports of a gun."

"How many reports?"

"Two."

Not that it was necessary, but at Burns's request, Della stood in the witness box and extended a finger, identifying John Terrell as the shooter.

Burns walked back to the prosecution table, looking at his notes, allowing the jury to absorb the impact of Della's testimony. Nearly a moment of silence passed before he spoke again.

"Your witness."

Arthur Sharpe questioned Della Reed about her encounter with Mr. Terrell as she and Melvin rode past the Terrell farm the first time. Della insisted that there had not been any encounter and that she did not see anyone at the Terrell place. It was about thirty minutes later when they passed by the Terrell house on the return trip.

It was then that Sharpe drove his stake into Della's credibility.

"When you came back, Mr. Terrell was in the ditch alongside the east side of the road."

"Yes."

"How did he know you had passed his house and were coming back?"

Della's jaw dropped open, and she stammered. That gave Prosecutor Burns time to jump to his feet. "Objection, your honor. That calls for speculation."

Judge Smith, doing no favors for the defense, sustained the objection. Still, Sharpe was confident that just asking the question made his point. How could Della have known that John Terrell was waiting along the side of the road had he not had a previous encounter with Melvin Wolfe? Despite the judge's ruling, Sharpe kept hammering at Della's version of events.

"Had you talked with Mr. Terrell, telling him you were going to come back that way?"

"No, sir."

"Had you passed him on the road after you passed by his home?"

"No, sir."

Sharpe turned to the jury, his face in mock confusion, then turned back toward the witness. "Do you know how he happened to be out there in the ditch with a gun?"

Burns objected, but this time Judge Smith overruled the objection.

Della stared icily at Sharpe for a long moment. "No, sir," she finally answered.

Sharpe then questioned Della about her relationship with Mr. Terrell, but the prosecution objected several times, stating it was beyond the scope of cross-examination. The objections were sustained. Despite this, Sharpe continued to inquire about any feelings or troubles between Della and Mr. Terrell. The judge finally yielded and permitted the question.

"What feelings have you toward Mr. Terrell? Do you understand that?"

"No, I don't."

Judge Smith held up his hand to stop Sharpe's next question, then turned toward Della, who sat with her jaw firm and eyes glaring at the defense attorney. "Miss Reed, the question is this: Do you entertain any feeling and ill-will or hatred against Mr. Terrell, the defendant?"

Della took a deep breath as if calculating the impact of her answer. "I don't know as I do."

Sharpe suppressed a smile of satisfaction. No one doubted that she hated John Terrell. They could see it on her face, hear it in her words. But now the jury knew she would lie when she thought it was needed.

Sharpe held up his hands. "No more questions of this witness."

Judge Smith looked at the clock. It was just past 5:30. "Gentlemen, we will continue tomorrow morning. Court adjourned." With that, the first day of testimony concluded.

As the lawyers packed up and spectators began slowly making their way out, Bailiff Adnah Hall enlisted the help of Bailiff John Poffenberger and several onlookers and began to move a dozen cots into the courtroom. That night was the first in confinement for the jury. They would not be allowed to separate or go home until the case was decided. Few suspected it would be nearly three weeks until they again slept in their own beds.

When the cots were in place, Hall gathered the jurors together. "Well, boys, where do you want to go for supper?"

One of the older jurors spoke up, his voice filled with irritation. "Home."

The next morning, Della returned to the witness chair for redirect examination. As soon as she was seated, Prosecutor Burns had Della identify the coat, shirt, and trousers that Melvin was wearing at the time of the shooting. Her eyes glistened as she held the clothes and pointed out the holes from the shotgun blasts and the places that were stained with dried blood.

"And can you tell the court and jury if they are in the same condition they were prior to the shooting?"

Tears flowed down Della's cheeks. "There were no holes in them before the shooting."

Della also identified Melvin's suspenders, cuffs, and collar that he was wearing that day, all soaked in blood. Over the defense's objection, the judge allowed the prosecutor to pass the clothes to the jury. Each man inspected the clothes, knowing that Melvin had died while wearing them.

19

Three Times Dead

The prosecution changed focus to the events in Petroleum, calling J. M. "Hop" Hopkins,[1] Clarence "Dick" Risser,[2] and William Kirkwood[3] in succession. The three men helped carry Melvin into Dr. Saunders's office. They were also present when John Terrell arrived minutes later with his shotgun in hand.

Hopkins was visiting Dr. Saunders in his office when the buggy carrying Melvin Wolfe and Della Reed pulled up. He heard Della yelling for help, and he and Dr. Saunders went out. Hopkins observed that Melvin was shot in the leg just above the knee, and blood covered the buggy.

Hopkins testified that William Kirkwood and Dick Risser were nearby and walked over to help. Melvin was "perfectly helpless, almost unconscious." The four men carried Melvin into the back room at Dr. Saunders's office and placed him on the operating chair, where Melvin asked for a drink of water.

Hopkins and Risser went to retrieve a drink for the injured man. They stepped into the front doorway. "That's where I saw Mr. Terrell," Risser said.

"What did he say? Use his language."

"He said, 'Hop, get out of there, or I will kill you. I am going to get him.'"

"What did you do then?"

Hopkins shrugged his shoulders a bit. "I got out of the way. I went over to Dr. Saunders's barn."

As he left toward the barn, Hopkins heard the sound of boards breaking inside Dr. Saunders's office, then heard two shots fired. A half hour later, Hopkins returned to the doctor's office. He found the wooden door to the operating room broken. Inside the operating room, he found Melvin on the operating table. "He was dead."

On cross-examination, Sharpe focused on John's appearance. "His face was white. His eyes were sticking way out away from his face, and his hair was standing straight up."

"Was his motion full of energy or passive."

"He was wild."

Dick Risser, a twenty-three-year-old oil worker, followed Hopkins to the witness seat. He was in Petroleum when he saw the buggy carrying Melvin Wolfe pull up near Dr. Saunders's office and heard Della Reed call for help. He walked over and saw Melvin Wolfe in the carriage. His leg was broken just above the knee, and blood was on his pants and in the buggy. "He was helpless."

Risser helped carry Wolfe into Dr. Saunders's back office and placed him on the operating table. He heard Melvin ask for water. As he walked to the front of the office to help retrieve a glass of water, Risser saw John Terrell approach. As he stood in the front door, John Terrell said, "Dick Risser, don't you stop me. I will kill you if you do."

"Did he have anything in his hands at that time?"

"He had a shotgun."

Risser stepped aside but stayed close enough that he saw John walk to the entrance door to the surgery room. "I seen him bust in two panels of the door." Risser left immediately, heading uptown. As he did, he heard two reports of a shotgun.

A half hour later, he returned to Dr. Saunders's office and saw Melvin on the operating table. Melvin had two new wounds, one on the left side of his head and the other in his shoulder blade.

"Was he dead or alive?"

"He was dead."

Sharpe could do little on cross-examination and limited his questions.

William Kirkwood, the son of former sheriff Harry Kirkwood, took the stand next. He repeated much the same story as Hopkins and Risser, except that when Melvin asked for water, Kirkwood stayed in the operating room with Dr. Saunders.

Kirkwood saw John Terrell entering the doctor's outer office. He immediately shut and latched the partition door between the main office and the operating room.

"After the partition door was shut and locked, what did you and Dr. Saunders do?"

"There was a rear door to the operating room. We went out it."

"When you left, was Melvin conscious or unconscious?"

"Conscious."

There was some buzz throughout the courtroom at the prospect of leaving a critical injured man alone, but a stern look from Judge Smith silenced the room.

Kirkwood jumped a fence and headed north toward a nearby barn. Dr. Saunders headed south.

"Once outside, did you hear any noise?"

"I heard a sound of something like splitting of boards. Then I heard the report of a gun."

"How many times?"

"Twice."

Kirkwood later returned to the doctor's operating room. "There was blood on the floor and operating table, and Melvin's brains oozed out on the operating table."

On cross, Sharpe asked why Kirkwood and Dr. Saunders had fled the operating room, leaving Melvin to face a shotgun-wielding John Terrell.

Kirkwood stared blankly across the room. Then, with a defensive tone in his voice, he finally answered. "Because I wanted to get out of the way."

What Sharpe was hoping to accomplish is beyond comprehension, but he continued. "Now, what was it that induced you to go away?"

"There was a shotgun carried by Mr. Terrell and pointed in the direction where we were standing. That caused us to go away."

"Did Mr. Terrell say anything?"

"He says, 'God damn the man that comes between me and Wolfe. I will kill them just as quick as I will kill Wolfe.'"

"Were you scared on account of the presence of Mr. Terrell?"

"Yes, I was. Here was a man standing with a shotgun and saying, 'Damn the man that comes between me and Wolfe.' That was enough to scare me."

Sharpe realized he was doing nothing but damaging the defense case, and he stopped his cross-examination.

Prosecutor Burns turned to what happened in Petroleum the night before the shooting. In 1903 Wells County and most of Indiana, running water was not common outside of the county seat, telephones were rare, and electricity generally was not available. In today's world of the internet, streaming services, and smart phones, turn-of-the-century Indiana is likely viewed as a land filled with uneducated rubes, a dull time when people went to bed with the chickens and rose with the sun, and towns rolled up their sidewalks at sundown.

But the testimony about what happened on the Saturday night before the shooting of Melvin Wolfe requires some readjustment in many popular views of rural life in turn-of-the-century rural Indiana. Rather than a sleepy village, Petroleum on a Saturday night was a bustling town into the late hours. At 10 P.M. and later, the grocery, barber shop, and restaurant were full of people socializing.

Oscar Oliver, the owner of Oliver's Restaurant, saw John Terrell between 10 and 11 P.M. at the barber shop in Petroleum. They had a brief conversation in which John mentioned that his son Jake had some trouble earlier that week with Clifford Shakley.[4]

Two teenage boys who were hanging out in town, Merle Stine[5] and Frank Kelly,[6] saw John Terrell's buggy hitched to a rail in town on the Saturday night before the shooting. They saw a shotgun lying on the carriage floor. On a dare, Merle climbed into the rig, picked up the gun, and then put it back where he found it.

Burns then called Harry Kirkwood.[7] The fifty-eight-year-old former sheriff and now justice of the peace in Nottingham Township was known by nearly everyone in the county. As he took the stand, he carried an air of somber authority and respect.

Kirkwood arrived at Dr. Saunders's office about 7 P.M. Melvin Wolfe lay on the operating table, already dead. Kirkwood helped Dr. Saunders remove Melvin's clothing and wrapped it in a single bundle, which he later took to Mr. Wolfe's house along with the corpse.

Kirkwood noticed a substantial pool of blood on the operating chair, which had dripped onto the floor. As he examined Melvin's body, Kirkwood observed brain matter oozing out of the head. Another wound was discovered under the left shoulder, approximately the size of a silver dollar. When asked about the wound's depth, Kirkwood said, "You could put your finger in it and could not reach the bottom."

Again, Sharpe's cross-examination seemed to only allow the witness to restate his testimony on direct exam and perhaps satisfy some morbid curiosity. "Did you put your finger in that wound as far as you could?"

"I did."

"You couldn't probe to the bottom of it?"

"No, sir."

. . .

The prosecutor recalled Jacob Wolfe.[8] He had been sitting at the prosecution table for the entire trial. Except for the tears that rolled down his face during Burns's opening statement and his testimony, he remained stoic, his eyes rarely straying from the witness and never glancing toward John Terrell. Jacob struggled to rise from his seat. He walked slowly across the courtroom and sat in the witness chair.

One by one, Prosecutor Burns handed each article of torn, blood-stained clothing that Melvin was wearing. Jacob identified each. After Burns completed the identification, Burns turned to the judge, the bloodstained clothing hanging over his arms. "We now offer to exhibit the clothing to the jury."

Sharpe rose and offered an extended objection as to the relevancy and materiality of the exhibits, as well as numerous technical evidentiary objections.

"Overruled," Judge Smith said without hesitation.[9]

Bailiff Hall took the garments from Burns and walked to the jury box. Judge Smith turned his chair to face the jury. "Gentlemen of the Jury, you are to hand them to each other without comment."

For the next several minutes, the calloused hands of the twelve farmer-jurors, some missing fingers, handled the clothes Melvin Wolfe was wearing when he was shot to death. They explored the holes that the shotgun balls had torn and rubbed their fingers across the blood-soaked cloth, touching Melvin Wolfe's dried blood. Several jurors somberly shook their heads as they passed the clothes to the next man in line.

Dr. Jesse E. Saunders was the next witness.[10] Only thirty-three years old, he had practiced medicine in Petroleum, near where he grew up, for the past seven years. Saunders was in his office when he saw the buggy with Melvin Wolfe and Della Reed pull to a stop. He went out to the carriage with J. M. Hopkins where he found Melvin looking "like he was very weak. He was very white."

Saunders joined William Kirkwood, Risser, and Hopkins in carrying Melvin into his office and placing him on the operating table. Melvin's leg was so badly injured that it "seemed almost off. He had no use of it. And there was a tremendous loss of blood."

Before Dr. Saunders was able to begin treating the injured man, there was a commotion outside. Kirkwood slammed and latched the door, and both Dr. Saunders and Kirkwood went out the back door. Shortly after, Dr. Saunders heard two gunshots.

A few minutes after the gunshots, Dr. Saunders walked back into his operating room. No one was there but Melvin Wolfe. "He was still laying on his back. His right leg hung off the chair, and his left arm was hanging loosely."

Melvin's head was still in roughly the same position as when Dr. Saunders left, except "there was a hole in the side of his head."

About three hours later, after Fred McBride and Harry Kirkwood arrived, Dr. Saunders performed an examination of the body. Dr. Saunders found three areas of major wounds: the head, the scapula, and the left leg. He testified in detail about his finding in examining each wound.

"The whole side of the head and face was shot out just below the back of the left ear," he testified. "The left jaw was broken, and brains ran out over the chair and floor."

Several jurors flinched at the description.

Dr. Saunders found a wound under the left shoulder, just below the shoulder blade. "It was immediately behind the heart, about four inches deep, I should judge. Possibly more. The wound punctured the lung and heart."

The description of the injuries to Melvin's leg were equally gruesome. "There was about four or five inches of the femur shot out. Shot up, so there was none of it there. The femoral artery was severed. The flesh was lacerated quite bad. I could put my hand in."

Burns then turned to Melvin Wolfe's cause of death. Dr. Saunders spoke without hesitation. The injury to the leg, to the back, and to the head, each standing on its own, was sufficient to cause Melvin's death.

Burns nodded, then turned and gave a signal to the prosecution table. Two of the lawyers stood, reached behind them, and lifted a shattered door panel. There was a small gasp around the courtroom. Dr. Saunders identified it as the door that separated his office from the surgical room. He also identified scrape marks on the two shattered panels as being consistent with the door being battered with the barrel of a shotgun. The door was admitted into evidence and exhibited to the jury. With that, Burns sat down. "Your witness."

Sharpe knew there was little he could accomplish on cross-examination, but he needed to make some effort. Dr. Saunders admitted that he did not know who was in the front office when he left through the rear door.

"Why was it you went out?"

Dr. Saunders looked down. His voice was barely loud enough for the jury to hear. "I got afraid."

"Of what?"

"I don't know. There was somebody hollered, 'Let's get out!' And someone yelled, 'John Terrell is coming.'" Dr. Saunders testified that he had treated John and wasn't afraid of him. But under further questioning, Dr. Saunders explained that he heard a rumor that Wolfe had been shot by John Terrell. "I didn't care to be in front of a gun."

Only a few minutes after exiting his office, Dr. Saunders saw John. He described John's appearance as pale with fixed, staring eyes and straight-up hair, and he was holding a shotgun as he walked.

Sharpe ended his cross-exam without challenging Dr. Saunders's examination of Melvin's body or his determination of the cause of death.

Prosecutor Burns called Sheriff James Johnston as the next witness.[11] He was dressed sharply in a black suit and matching tie, which he considered his go-to-court suit. Johnston was stout, with a round face and trimmed moustache, and bore more than a passing resemblance to then president Theodore Roosevelt.[12] He carried the demeanor of a man familiar with testifying.

Sheriff Johnston testified that he was notified of the shooting by a telephone call from Byron Witmer, who owned the grocery in Petroleum. He headed south out of Bluffton along the Camden-Bluffton gravel road. Along the way, he met John Terrell, being driven by Dr. Dickason. John Terrell's shotgun was in the buggy, and Sheriff Johnston took possession of it. Both barrels were loaded.

The shotgun was admitted into evidence and passed among the jury. Each of the twelve farmers owned shotguns and knew how to use them. Except for those who served in the Civil War, it was a new experience—holding a weapon that took another man's life.

Prosecutor Burns stood. "Your honor, the State rests."

In just a little over a full day of testimony, the State had called seventeen witnesses and presented its case that John Terrell had committed first-degree murder and should be hanged. It was now time for John's lawyers to present a defense that would save him from the gallows or spending the rest of his life in prison.

20

In Defense of John Terrell

After the prosecution rested its case on Thursday afternoon, Arthur Sharpe began his opening statement for the defense precisely at 3:30.[1] He thanked the jury for their attention and briefly discussed the crux of the State's evidence. Sharpe then set about to make John Terrell a sympathetic character who was more victim and defender of his family than the perpetrator of a heinous crime.

Sharpe described John as a respected man from a minister's family (omitting that John was an atheist) who lived a peaceful and prosperous life on his farm in Wells County. He told the jury that John's life took a turn when oil was discovered on his land, attracting troublemakers known for exploiting naive country girls. Terrell's two older daughters married oil workers who abused, then abandoned them.

The pivotal moment in John's life was when his favorite daughter, Lucy, was seduced and mistreated by Melvin Wolfe. Wolfe subjected Lucy to infidelity and forced her to leave their home, causing immense anguish.

Sharpe explained that John's behavior became increasingly unusual due to a family history of insanity, exacerbated by head injuries and stress. Wolfe's taunting and threats, including derogatory rumors about Lucy, pushed Terrell to the brink of temporary insanity. "We will show that John Terrell was standing near his barn and that Melvin Wolfe shook his fist at him. We will also show that Melvin Wolfe shouted an insult about his grandchild. This was the last straw. After that, John Terrell was a crazy man."

There it was. For the first time in the case, the jury heard the defense. John Terrell committed the murder of Melvin Wolfe in a state of temporary insanity.

The insanity defense was far from a new or novel idea at the time of the John Terrell case. Indeed, insanity as an excuse for criminal culpability dates as far back as the ancient civilizations of Greece and Rome.[2] As early as the sixth century BC, Hebrew scriptures pronounced that children and the insane should not be held criminally at fault.[3] English common law followed suit. In the 1500s, leading English jurist Lorde Coke pronounced that a "man or a natural foole" would not be guilty if his mind was "like a child or beast."[4]

The landmark development in the insanity defense arose out of the 1843 trial of Daniel M'Naghten, who attempted to assassinate British prime minister Robert Peel. He failed, killing Peel's secretary, Edward Drummond, instead. When the jury found M'Naghten not guilty due to insanity, there was public outrage. In response, the judges responded to an inquiry by the House of Lords that became the principal test for criminal insanity: the accused, at the time of the act, must have been acting under such defect of reason he did not know the nature and quality of the act or that the act was wrong.[5]

What became known as the M'Naghten test was quickly adopted by American jurisprudence. Nearly two centuries later, the M'Naghten test remains the law in federal courts and in seventeen states.[6]

The first pronouncement of what became known as the Irresistible Impulse Test came two years before M'Naghten in the 1840 English case of *Regina v. Oxford.*[7] It was also the first case to allow expert medical testimony on the issue of insanity.[8]

The Irresistible Impulse Test centers on whether a person, even if he or she knew the act was wrong, was unable in that moment to resist an impulse to commit it.[9] The test focused on the moment of the act and therefore was often an integral part of the more generalized term *temporary insanity.* Importantly for John Terrell's case, Indiana was one of the earliest states to adopt the concept of irresistible impulse. In the 1869 case of *Bradley v. State,* the Indiana Supreme Court held that the defendant must not only be able to comprehend the nature and consequences of his act, but his willpower must not be so impaired at the moment of the act that he cannot resist an impulse to commit the crime.[10] By 1900, irresistible impulse was firmly established as part of Indiana law.[11]

Any lawyer relying on an insanity defense knows the steep road before them. The lawyer will try to convince a jury that the defendant, even though the person committed the act, should not be held accountable for his or her actions because in that instant in time, the defendant was temporarily insane.

As Sharpe concluded his opening statement by thanking the jury for their attention, he knew he faced a monumental legal challenge.

Judge Smith checked the clock. "We'll pick up with the defense testimony tomorrow morning." With that, he banged the gavel and adjourned the second day of testimony.

Bailiff John Poffenberger, in his eighties, was a frail man, balding with a flowing white beard. He was in charge of the jury for the second night. First, he took them to dinner and then for a walk along the Wabash River and back. They finished the evening by going to an entertainment venue called the People's Store where, according to the *Bluffton Banner*, they saw "Major Winner, the midget."[12]

Afterward, they returned to the courthouse, sleeping yet another night in the courtroom.

On Friday morning, Arthur Sharpe began laying the foundation for the insanity defense. First, he called Ida Clark back to stand.[13] Ida and Orville Burgess had testified in the State's case about being in a buggy when John Terrell raced by only moments after hearing a gunshot.

Ida described John's appearance as he raced by. "He looked very wild and agitated. He was bare-headed. His hair was flying in the air. And his eyes were starey—you know, staring off, not focused on anything."

As John went by, he stood with one hand holding the reins on the horses and the other holding a gun. He was talking, but Ida could not understand anything he was saying.

Ida testified that she had known John Terrell since she was a little girl. She often saw him at Witmer's Store when she worked there. She also saw him at other places around Petroleum and Nottingham Township when she was about town.

Sharpe then asked for the first time what would become the most frequent and perhaps most important question throughout the trial.

"From the action of Mr. Terrell on that day and what you observed of him that day and before, did you consider Mr. Terrell of sound or unsound mind on that day?"

Prosecutor Burns was on his feet. "Objection."

Before Burns could say more, Judge Smith overruled the objection. He leaned toward the witness and, in a fatherly voice, said, "What was your opinion about it, if you know, or if you have any?"

"My opinion was it was a very strange action for a man with the judgment Mr. Terrell had. That is all the opinion I had. I never seen him angry before."

. . .

Sharpe called J. M. Hopkins back to the witness chair.[14] Sharpe probed about John Terrell's appearance when Hopkins saw John outside Dr. Saunders's office. "His actions were that of a wild man," Hopkins said, waving his arms to emphasize his testimony. "He had that double-barreled shotgun and was looking right in my face."

Hopkins described John's appearance as "terribly excited. Very wild. His face was white. His hair stood straight up. His eyes were, I would say, starey."

When asked if he thought John Terrell was of unsound mind, Hopkins answered, "I think he had lost control of himself."

Attorney William Eichhorn, who would handle much of the insanity evidence for the prosecution, did the cross-examination. Hopkins admitted that prior to the day of the shooting, he had never seen John angry. However, on that day, standing outside Dr. Saunders's office, John said he was going to "get" Melvin Wolfe. He did so with a determined, emphatic look.

Eichhorn used his experience in the courtroom to ask a series of questions to draw into doubt Hopkins's opinion of John Terrell's madness. "Did you think he was insane because he called you by your nickname, Hop?"

"No, sir."

"Did you think he was an insane man because he recognized you?"

"No, sir."

"Did you consider him insane because he told you to get out of his way so he could get at Wolfe?"

"Not because he said it."

"When you stepped aside, did he make any more threats to you?"

"No, sir."

Eichhorn wisely knew when to move on to his final point. He had Hopkins confirm that he saw John Terrell walk out of Dr. Saunders's office only moments after Hopkins heard two shots. John was still carrying his shotgun.

"What did he do with the gun?"

"Broke it open and took out two shells and reloaded it."

Dr. John Dickason was the next witness.[15] He testified that he learned of the shooting from William Kirkwood as he arrived back in Petroleum from seeing a patient. He saw John at about seven o'clock. He took John to the Dickason house and told him to stay there while Dr. Dickason went to call on his daughter. Dickason told John that when he returned, he would take John to Bluffton to the sheriff.

Dickason described John as having "a wild stare look." His face was flushed and white, and his speech was random and disconnected.

Dickason had known John for eighteen years and, for the past four years, had served as the Terrell family physician. He treated John for nervousness and nervous headaches. His complaints were always at the base of his brain at the back of his head. Dr. Dickason treated him with gelsemium[16] and veratrium,[17] which Dr. Dickason mixed himself.

After treating John's daughter, Dickason returned home, finding John in the same spot where he had left him, as if he had not moved. Dickason helped John into the doctor's carriage, and they rode north toward Bluffton. About halfway to town, they met Sheriff Johnston coming south and moved John into the sheriff's buggy to be transported to the county jail.

Sharpe finished his direct exam by asking Dickason, as a doctor and a longtime friend, his opinion as to the state of John's mind on the Sunday evening of the shooting when Dickason saw John.

Dickason did not hesitate. "At that time, unsound."

On cross-examination, Eichhorn wasted no time challenging Dr. Dickason's observations on John Terrell's state of mind. Dickason talked with John in Petroleum the night before the shooting and found him of sound mind. Two or three days after the shooting, Dickason met with John in his jail cell.

"At that time, was he of sound mind?"

"He seemed rational."

Eichhorn questioned Dr. Dickason about the ailments and headaches that John suffered. It was the jury's first dose of what would become a nearly endless barrage of scientific and pseudoscientific testimony. The questions displayed the limits of medical understanding in turn-of-the-century rural Indiana. Dr. Dickason testified about John's "misery at the base of the brain." The testimony delved into headaches connected to an enlargement of the spinal cord and references to the pneumogastric nerve, the sympathetic nerve, and the medulla oblongata. None of the testimony was within the comprehension of the twelve farmers of limited education who sat on the jury.

Eichhorn finished his cross-examination by asking Dickason about any conversation he had with John while on the way to meet the sheriff. Dickason twice denied that he and John talked about the shooting. But Eichhorn, experienced in the courtroom beyond his relatively young years, did not accept Dickason's answers.

With a disbelieving scowl, Eichhorn said, "Now, doctor, didn't he say to you on the way to town, 'I have killed him,' and you said, 'Who?' and he said he had killed his son-in-law, killed Melvin Wolfe. Wasn't that said between you on the way to town?"

Dr. Dickason paused, then he gave a slight nod. With a soft voice, he answered, "I think, sir, he did."

"Then did you not say to him, 'Are you sure?' and did he not answer to that and say, 'Well, I shot him.'"

Again, Dickason was trapped by the truth. After a long pause, he finally answered. "Yes, something to that effect anyway."

"Then, did you not say to him, 'When did you do it?' and did he not say, 'Just before I came to town.'"

Dickason hung his head. "Something like that, yes."

Ida Dickason followed her husband to the witness chair.[18] She testified that John Terrell was still carrying his shotgun when Dr. Dickason brought him into the front parlor of their house, which made her a "little alarmed." At her insistence, John handed the gun to her. She took it into the kitchen and leaned it against the wall. Dr. Dickason tended to John Terrell's daughter, Cinda Books, for about twenty minutes. During that time, John stayed in the front parlor, pacing back and forth and mumbling. The only word she could make out in his ramblings was "Lucy."

From her observations following the shooting, Ida joined the growing list of witnesses who testified that John Terrell was of unsound mind.

The next witness was Emma Oliver,[19] who, along with her husband, Oscar Oliver, owned and operated the restaurant in Petroleum. Even though the world was still two weeks from the first powered flight of the Wright Brothers at Kitty Hawk, she and her husband lived on the peculiarly named Air-Line Pike.[20]

Emma only knew John to see him on the street. Around six o'clock on the day of the shooting, she saw him ride by, standing in his buggy with a shotgun in one hand and the reins to the horse in the other. After word of the shooting spread, John Terrell's daughter, Cinda Books, found her way to the Oliver house. Emma could tell that Cinda was upset.

About half an hour after first seeing John, Emma saw him again in his buggy as he was going by her house. She yelled at him to look at his daughter, but John ignored her. "He was yelling very loud, and he said something about he will not ruin a third girl or break up any more families. Something to that effect."

Emma described John as having a fierce look. "His eyes seemed as though they were bulged right out of his head." But when pressed, she could provide few other details. "I was too excited to know what was said or done."

Sharpe concluded Emma's direct exam by asking her opinion of John Terrell's sanity when she saw him that Sunday. She joined the growing list who opined that he was of unsound mind.

Although only thirty-seven, William Henry Eichhorn was known in northeast Indiana legal circles as a compelling courtroom advocate.[21] He was about to demonstrate to the jury why he had that reputation.

Eichhorn established that Emma had known John Terrell only since she moved from Ohio a matter of days before the shooting. When pressed by Eichhorn, Emma admitted that she could not remember whether Cinda Books, John's daughter, had come to Emma's house before or after news of the shooting had spread, nor could she remember whether she went to the store before or after the shooting.

"The fact is you do not remember much about it," Eichhorn said.

Eichhorn turned his attack to the limited basis for Emma's conclusion that John was of unsound mind.

"You never saw him angry before?"

"No, sir."

"You never saw him when he was excited?"

"No, sir."

"You do not know how he usually appeared when he was angry?"

"No, sir."

Eichhorn nodded, then turned and walked several paces toward the jury before turning back to the witness for his final question. "Your statement that at that time, the defendant was of unsound mind was only based solely on what you told the jury you had seen that day, wasn't it?"

"Yes, sir."

As he sat down, his examination concluded, Eichhorn was content that he had established that Emma Oliver didn't have a basis to decide whether John Terrell was insane or simply enraged.

In a major murder case, defense lawyers spend countless hours debating and mapping out their strategy, deciding what witnesses to call and what questions to ask. Sometimes the most important decisions are what questions not to ask, for once a door is opened by one side, a judge will not close it for questioning by the opposing side.

One of the key moments in John Terrell's trial was not recognized as such by those watching. David Kelly, a young farm laborer, was an unassuming witness. He did not draw any particular attention in the courtroom. When the transcript was prepared, his direct examination took just four lines more than a single page.[22] But in looking back, the defense may have been better served had it never called Kelly as a witness. The handful of questions Sharpe asked Kelly opened the door to some of the most damaging testimony against

John Terrell about his past. Ultimately, it would also lead to testimony about John's strong antireligious opinions in front of twelve God-fearing jurors in the heart of the Bible Belt.

Kelly testified on direct examination that he had grown up on a farm less than a mile from John Terrell and had known John for nearly eighteen years. He was well acquainted with all of his neighbors.

"Up to the twelfth day of July last, are you acquainted with his general reputation for peace and quietude in the neighborhood?"

"Yes, I was."

"Was that reputation good or bad?"

"As far as I know, it was good."

And with that question, Arthur Sharpe opened the door to exploring John Terrell's reputation.

Prosecutor Burns bounded from his seat and strode to a spot only a few feet from the witness chair. His voice boomed as he began his cross-examination.

"By saying as far as you know, do you mean from your own experience with him?"

"Yes, sir."

"Had you heard about the defendant having trouble with Mel Moore?"

"Yes, sir."

"About John Terrell striking him with a board?"

"I heard he did."

"Knocking him down?"

"Yes, sir."

"You heard of his having been arrested and fined for that, did you not?"

"Yes, sir."

"You heard of his having trouble with John Shull and quarreling with him, did you not?"

"Yes, sir."

"You have heard of him having trouble and quarreling with other people, have you not?"

"Only one other that I remember of is John Newhouse."

"You had heard all these things talked about in that neighborhood, had you not?"

"Yes, sir."

"What do you understand by reputation for peace and quietude?"

"The way I understand that—a man, whatever he agrees to do with his neighbors, he does."

"You did not have reference to his being quarrelsome and having fights?"

"I never heard of him having many of them. Those three is all I know of."

"You heard it generally talked that he was quarrelsome and high-tempered?"

"No, sir."

"Did you now hear it generally talked about that he was high-tempered?"

"No, sir."

"Were you not asked before the grand jury, and did you not answer in reference to his being a high-tempered man, that you heard he was a high-tempered man?"

"I don't remember of answering that question that way."

Burns moved away from the witness chair as if he had finished, but he turned back to the witness just before sitting.

"You are renting from Mr. Terrell, are you not?"

"Yes. I rent his livery barn at Petroleum."

"You became his tenant since he was in jail?"

"Yes, sir."

Burns nodded and looked toward the jury as he sat down. Sharpe tried to repair the damage on redirect, eliciting that the incident with Melvin Moore was "quite a little bit ago," and the fight with Newsom was about sixteen years ago. But the reputation issue was now open, and the jury would hear far more about it before deciding John Terrell's fate.

21

Hold up the Bastard

Sharpe recalled Dr. Saunders to the witness box.[1] From the doctor's long relationship with John, Sharpe clearly expected Saunders to be a friendly witness. He had known John for six or seven years, treating his family for grippe and similar maladies, including John's complaints of headaches, which Dr. Saunders attributed to John being "nervous more than anything else."

There is an old lawyer adage that an attorney should never ask a question when he doesn't know the answer he will get. When Sharpe turned his questions to John's state of mind, he may have thought he knew the answer from John's friend, but it became apparent that he had miscalculated.

Dr. Saunders saw John only a few minutes after the shooting. Saunders testified that John's face was white and his eyes "looked starey," a term for staring unfocused into the distance. As he had with earlier witnesses, this led Sharpe to the key question on which the insanity defense rested.

"From what you saw of him on that day, and from your acquaintance with Mr. Terrell, and from your knowledge as a physician who had treated him, tell the jury whether, in your opinion, on Sunday, July 12, was he a person of sound or unsound mind."

"At the time of the shooting?"

"Yes."

Dr. Saunders looked across the room and fixed his focus on the jury. "He seemed to be determined."

Sharpe persisted. "The question is whether he was of sound or unsound mind."

Dr. Saunders shook his head, his reluctance pulpable. "That is a hard question to answer, Mr. Sharpe. I don't feel justified in answering that. There might be two answers to it."

Either oblivious to what the witness was signaling, or so certain that the doctor would ultimately answer in favor of his friend, Sharpe continued bulling forward. "You have all the facts?"

"Yes, sir."

"Now, your opinion based on those facts is what I want. What is your opinion?"

Judge Smith held up his hand to stop the interrogation. He leaned toward the witness. "If you have an opinion."

Dr. Saunders took a deep breath and exhaled slowly. "I can't answer that question."

Sharpe gave a small sigh, a final concession that he would not get the answer he sought. He moved on but with no more success. Sharpe asked the doctor about John's reputation for peace and quietude in the neighborhood around Petroleum and Nottingham Township.

"Well, I never heard very much either way."

Sharpe's exam had foundered badly. He ignored the rule of even a novice lawyer and had charged forward. The result was a significant strike against John Terrell's defense.

There is no quarter given among lawyers in a courtroom. Attorney Eichhorn knew how to jump on a weakness in direct examination. He wasted no time doing so with Dr. Saunders.

Eichhorn first attacked John's reputation, for which John's own attorney had opened the door. While Saunders had not heard much about John's reputation in the community, Eichhorn elicited that Saunders had heard of John's "taking a board and knocking down Melvin Moore" and that John had continued with his attack until he was restrained. Saunders also had heard of a quarrel John had with a man named Cummings.

"Did you hear it said that Mr. Terrell was a high-tempered man?"

"Yes, I have heard that."

Eichhorn knew how to close his cross-examination with his strongest point. Using leading questions permitted on cross-examination to his fullest advantage, Eichhorn got Dr. Saunders to testify that a few minutes after the shooting, he saw John Terrell looking in the window of Saunders's surgical room.

"He looked in your office window there?"

"I think he did, yes."

"You heard him speak there, too, did you not?"

Trying to prevent what he knew was coming, Sharpe objected on the basis that Eichhorn was going beyond the scope of direct examination. Judge Smith overruled the objection.

Dr. Saunders looked at John, then across at the jury. His voice was firm and clear. "He said he wanted to see if the son of a bitch was dead."

Everyone in the courtroom knew that Dr. Saunders's testimony had been devastating to John's defense. It was not a good way to begin the major part of the defense case.

Like an Egyptian pyramid, John's insanity defense was built on a three-sided foundation: John's past head injuries, the Terrell family history of mental illness and idiocy, and opinions that John was of unsound mind by eyewitnesses and a parade of medical experts. Arthur Sharpe began trying to establish John's history of head injuries by calling William Eberly, a farmer near the crossroads town of Balbec in neighboring Jay County and a three-term justice of the peace.[2]

Eberly had known John Terrell since he first came to Wells County more than twenty years earlier. On a late afternoon in May 1894, he came across John lying on the road near an old railroad grade crossing. His wagon, loaded with bags of corn, was nearby.

"He told me he got a very hard fall off the wagon. He fell on his shoulders, and he struck his head against the pike." Eberly helped John on to his horse, and he went home, leaving the wagon where it sat.

Eberly was followed to the stand by Dr. Charles Caylor,[3] who treated John for his head injury in 1894. He recalled a scalp wound on the back of the head and John's complaint of a headache. However, John's pupils responded to light and were the same size.

Asked about the possible effects of the head injury, Dr. Caylor testified, "It might produce a fracture with compression, contusion of the brain, rupture of minute blood vessels, unconscious condition—quite a number of symptoms. It might produce a headache that would come on in intervals afterwards so long as the man might live."

On cross-examination, Eichhorn attacked the seriousness of the head injury. Dr. Caylor admitted that there was no fracture, no pressure on the skull, the pupils reacted normally, and the wound did not require stitches.

Perhaps aggravated by his poor performance during his examination of Dr. Saunders, Sharpe did not give up so easily on Dr. Caylor. On redirect, Sharpe got his witness to testify that he had read books about head injuries that had lain dormant for years before resulting in patients being driven to "suicidal mania" or "driving a patient crazy," or even "homicidal mania."

On Eichhorn's recross, Dr. Caylor admitted that any homicidal mania would be indiscriminate. "He would probably kill the first person he came in contact with, friend or foe."

Eichhorn nodded and sat down, his examination complete.

The defense called four men from the Randolph-Delaware County area. John grew up and lived in western Randolph County along the Delaware County line until after he was married. The four men were called to testify about John's reputation and the Terrell family's history of insanity.

The first of the four men was Peter Helm, a distant cousin of John Terrell who lived in Randolph County near where John lived before moving to Wells County. Sharpe began asking about the mental state of a grandson of a cousin of John's mother. It was the second step in Sharpe's plan to establish John's insanity by showing his family history of insanity and idiocy. Eichhorn was immediately up from his seat.

"Objection! This relative is far too distant to be relevant to the issues of this case."

Judge Smith leaned forward. "What relation is this son to the defendant?"

Sharpe responded, "The grandmother was a first cousin to John Terrell's mother."

Judge Smith shook his head. "There has been no testimony that the insanity claimed in the defendant was or could have been a hereditary. For that reason, it does not appear that the insanity now inquired about could have been in any way transmitted, or the taint appearing, that it could have transmitted to the defendant."

It was another blow to the defense. Sharpe withdrew the question, but it would not be the end of the issue.

Three more men from the same area took the stand.[4] They were all asked about John's reputation where he grew up for peace and quietude, and all answered it was "good." However, on cross-examination, the men admitted they had not heard anyone talk about John's reputation. The testimony seemed to do no harm, but the fact that reputation testimony was now freely being admitted would eventually hit hard at John's defense

After several witnesses who seemed to accomplish little for the defense, things changed with calling Lemuel Bouse to the witness stand.[5] His testimony changed the focus back to the conduct of Melvin Wolfe. While there was no legal defense of justification, the defense lawyers knew that the insanity defense would not succeed unless the jury understood that Melvin Wolfe had brought his fate upon himself and that given the same circumstances, any of the twelve men in the jury box would have done the same thing as John.

A thirty-nine-year-old resident of Nottingham, Bouse had known John for eighteen years and sometimes did business with him. On June 1, six weeks before the shooting, Bouse was talking with John in the barn lot at the Terrell home. John's wife, Catherine, and his daughter, Lucy, were standing nearby. John's two grandchildren were playing near him. As John reached down to pick up Lucy's daughter, Mabel, a buggy with Melvin Wolfe went past.

Bouse testified that Wolfe yelled, "Hold up the bastard until I can see it!" Wolfe then drove north at a rapid pace. As Wolfe rode away, Bouse turned to John and said, "Isn't that awful." John said nothing but held his head down and walked away.

Prosecutor Burns cross-examined Bouse, probing for every detail of the encounter with Melvin. Bouse remained calm, answering each question matter-of-factly. After nearly half an hour of questions, Burns concluded his exam, failing to poke any holes in Bouse's testimony.

Sharpe made his second effort to delve into the Terrell family history of insanity by calling sixty-three-year-old Louisa Terrell,[6] who was married to John's second cousin. Louisa lived in neighboring Huntington County for the past fifteen years, but before that she lived near the Terrell family in the small town of Windsor in Randolph County. Louisa was well acquainted with John, his father, William Wesley Terrell, and his grandfather, George Wesley Terrell, known as Wesley.

Louisa testified that Wesley's youngest son, George (William's much younger brother), was killed in a battle near the end of the Civil War. When Sharpe asked about the effect this had on Wesley, Burns objected on the basis that it was "immaterial and irrelevant." Consistent with his prior ruling, Judge Smith sustained the objection.

Despite the court's ruling, Sharpe persisted. "After Wesley Terrell received the news of the death of his son, you may tell the jury how he acted, what he said, what he did."

Again, Burns was on his feet, objecting because it inquired into collateral matter. "There has been no evidence offered that the insanity inquired about now, or the mental affliction, was transmissible to the defendant."

Judge Smith folded his hands in front of him. He sat in silence for a long minute before turning to Sharpe. "I think you will have to show it is transmissible."

"We propose to offer evidence of that kind," Sharpe responded, without specifying what the evidence would be. It was an earlier version of the practice still found in a modern courtroom of a lawyer promising that if questionable evidence is allowed, the lawyer will later "link it up."

Judge Smith nodded. "In view of your statement that you will show that, the court will overrule the objection."

Sharpe had succeeded. It was a major victory in his strategy to show the Terrell family history of mental health problems. Sharpe turned to the witness. "You may answer the question. How did Wesley Terrell act after his son's death?"

Louisa explained that she frequently saw Wesley, John's grandfather, after his son's death in the Civil War. "He seemed very despondent, very much down, melancholy. He hadn't much to say to anyone." The fact that George had died so far from home, and could not be brought home for burial "seemed to bear great weight on his mind."[7] Louisa heard Wesley "talk about the end of time." He imagined signs and believed the end of the world was coming. And he claimed to see "chariots sailing in the heavens."

After George's death, Wesley became fearful, particularly at night. He kept his window blinds drawn and doors barred at night, and he always kept a light burning.

"How long did this melancholy continue after his son's death?"

"I think always. I don't think it ever entirely left him."

Prosecutor Burns undertook the cross-examination, raising questions about whether Wesley's visions of the end times were anything new after his son's death. Under prompting by Burns, Louisa testified that Wesley was a "fire and brimstone, old-fashioned, old school preacher" who believed in a literal construction of the Bible.

Louisa said that when news arrived that George was killed in the war, the impact on Wesley was immediate and profound. "He lamented that his son was killed so far away from home and that he could not give him a Christian burial."

Louisa's husband, D. S. Terrell,[8] followed her to the witness chair. His testimony was much the same as his wife's. His memory of the specifics about George Terrell's death had faded, but he had no doubt that Wesley was of unsound mind after the death of his son.

Prosecutor Burns moved to strike the testimony regarding whether Wesley Terrell was of unsound mind, but consistent with his prior ruling, Judge Smith overruled the motion. Burns moved into his cross-examination. He focused on showing that Wesley's belief in the end of the world predated his son's death.

D. S. Terrell testified that Wesley was a minister, preaching his entire life until about a year before his death. He would preach that the world would come to an end as was prophesied in the Book of Revelation and that people should be ready for it.

"Now, about his talking about chariots and angels, he took the Bible for his foundation."

"That is right."

D. S. Terrell admitted that he "never could see a great deal of difference" in Wesley's preaching after his son's death. Then Burns took a chance and led the witness into delivering a devastating blow to the defense argument about the insanity of John's grandfather.

"The fact that he took the Bible for his foundation, and said that according to the Bible, the world would come to an end, or that according to the Bible, there was angels and chariots in the sky, the fact that he backed those assertions up with the Bible, was not evidence of his unsoundness of mind, was it, Mr. Terrell, in your opinion?"

"Why, I don't think that would be. No, I don't."

With that devastating blow to the defense, the court recessed for the day. Judge Smith had business to attend to the next morning, so court would not reconvene until Saturday afternoon. When the court reconvened, it would be the best show in town.

22

The Heavens Will Pass Away

A Saturday in rural Indiana was when people would head into nearby towns or perhaps the county seat to shop at markets and pharmacies and hardware stores, and with Christmas approaching, to window-shop for gifts. They would do their banking, buy treats at the bakery, and socialize with friends doing the same.

But Saturday, December 5, 1903, in Wells County was different. John Terrell was on trial for the murder of his son-in-law. It dominated newspapers across the state and was the talk of taverns, restaurants, and church socials from Fort Wayne to Indianapolis. And for many, Saturday was a day when they could see the drama for themselves.

Wagons and buggies crowded the roadways, bringing people to Bluffton. Railroad cars and interurbans from Hartford City, Muncie, and Fort Wayne were packed with the curious who wanted to look at John Terrell and his wronged daughter, hear the salacious testimony for themselves, and be entertained by some of the area's best lawyers.

Court was scheduled to convene at 1:30, but by noon, the largest crowd to date gathered in the courthouse. By 1 P.M., every seat in the courtroom was taken, and the areas alongside and behind the benches were lined with those standing. Outside the courtroom, men and women filled the corridors and the stairs from the third-floor courtroom to the ground floor.

With all the spaces filled, Judge Smith ordered fifty-seven-year-old bailiff Adnah Hall, a slight man with a sharp features and sallow complexion, to close the courtroom doors and not let anyone except the lawyers and witnesses enter. He also directed Bailiff Hall to disperse the crowd in the hallways and stairways before any ladies in the crush fainted or were hurt. The bailiff stepped outside the courtroom and shouted his order to clear the halls and stairs. Unfortunately, his high-pitched voice lacked the command to get a response from the crowd dominated by rough-hewn men who made their living in fields and with livestock. As it became evident that those who remained outside the closed courtroom doors had little chance of witnessing the proceedings, the throng slowly dispersed, but most went no farther than the courthouse lawn.[1]

At precisely 1:30, Judge Smith gaveled the proceedings to order. The defense began by calling William Terrell, John's seventy-five-year-old father.[2]

William was a big man,[3] standing over six feet tall and carrying more than two hundred pounds. He lived near Windsor, a small town in western Randolph County, where he was a prominent farmer and, like his father, a well-known Methodist preacher. A life of hard work as a farmer and a weekend preacher had taken its toll. So, too, had the fifty-mile trip from Windsor to Bluffton. William struggled to rise from his seat and walked with arthritic stiffness as he made his way to the witness chair. His hearing was failing, so he carried an ear trumpet in one hand. Even so, when addressing him, the lawyers and judge had to nearly shout so the old man could understand what was being said.[4]

Defense lawyers had decided that Ralph Gregory, bearded and the eldest of John Terrell's lawyers, would examine the aged Terrell. Gregory was from Muncie and had met William before. John's lawyers all agreed that he might be more comfortable answering questions from someone closer to his age.

"What relation are you to John W. Terrell, the defendant in this case?"

"I am said to be his father."

Gregory hesitated, trying to take in William's peculiarly phrased answer. In all of his trials, never had an innocuous question been answered in such an atypical way. But Gregory continued.

William explained that John's mother, Rebecca Thornburg, died in 1854 before John was yet two years old. After Rebecca's death, John was sent to live with William's childless uncle and aunt, Drummond and Sarah Terrell. Eighteen months later, William married his first wife's cousin, Mary Ann Thornburg.[5] However, William did not reclaim his children from his first marriage. John remained with Drummond and Sarah. As William explained, "He raised John W. Terrell, my son."[6]

A murmur around the courtroom caused Judge Smith to hit his gavel. The room went silent.

William identified his father as George Wesley Terrell, whose neighbors called him Wesley. William also had one brother, George, who was much younger. George died in "about the last engagement in the Civil War on the skirmish line." There was sadness in the old man's voice, sorrow at the loss of a much-younger brother to the savages of war.

William described his father's conduct after the death of his youngest son. "He became afflicted a great deal. He was looking to George for a strong arm to lean on in old age, and that was taken away from him. He lamented losing George until the close of life."

There was a silence across the courtroom. Several of the older men in the courtroom had fought in the Civil War. They had seen men die. In sparsely populated Wells County, 234 Wells County men died in the war.[7] Nearly everyone in the room much over 40 knew or was related to at least one of them, often more.

William recalled his father's prophesying about the end of the world, referring to biblical accounts of the destruction of the world by fire. When pressed about specific things his father said, William's memory failed. "I can't remember anything, only the scripture he would quote. 'The heavens would pass away as a scroll, and the elements would melt with fervent heat.'"

William testified that after George's death, his father "was wonderfully fearful of a night," bolting doors and windows, which he had never done before. "He was despondent and often talked of giving up, and he did give up all earthly hope."

Gregory moved on to the key question, asking William if following the death of his son George, Wesley was a person of unsound mind.

William sat, his face furrowed as he thought over the question. "I will give my opinion in this," the old man said. "Wherever there is a letdown in a man that is not sound, let him interpret the matter. I don't want to say anything that is not true or anything that is not right."

Judge Smith raised his hand toward the witness. His voice was full of compassion for the elderly witness. "You may just give your own opinion. That is what the question asked for."

The old man nodded. "Unsound mind."

Gregory moved his questioning on to William's daughter Josephine, now thirty, married with three children and living in Cincinnati. When asked if Josephine was still living, William responded, "Yes, she was a few days ago." The answer drew a few chuckles from the packed courtroom, but later it seemed prophetic. In less than two years, she would be dead, the victim of a sudden coronary occlusion.

Gregory's intent was to add yet another example of mental illness in the Terrell family that could be linked to John. Led by Gregory's questioning, William told about Josephine's episodes when she was nine years old. She acted strangely, wandering through the house at night, calling for family members to see things that were not there. "She'd say, Look yonder. There is a dog or a horse, or some other animal. We all looked, but we couldn't see nothing." Her episodes lasted "perhaps six months, maybe a year. She didn't seem right."

Gregory again asked the key question: Was she of sound mind? Eichhorn objected, arguing that the temporary aberration of William's daughter had no relationship to the murder trial in front of the court. Judge Smith, perhaps in deference to the old man, allowed William to answer.

"She was of unsound mind," William said.

Eichhorn cross-examined the elderly man, at first with a gentle touch, not wishing to be seen by the jury as abusing him. William recounted how his father would preach for an hour or more, all without ever writing anything down. But Wesley gave up his regular preaching several years before George's death.

William recalled that after George's death, whenever Wesley spoke of George, it was always with a great sense of sorrow. "He was heartbroken. When the news reached of George's death, a change come over him that he never recovered from."

The gentleness Eichhorn used to address the elder Terrell faded as he focused on William's opinion that his father became of unsound mind. "Did you mean to tell the jury that your father was insane, as you understand that term?"

"Well, I would like to put your question so I can answer it. I want to tell the truth. That is what I live for, to tell the truth. I don't want to tell anything that is not so."

"My question is, was your father insane, as you understand that term."

"If I understand the word insanity, a man don't know nothing."

"Tell the jury. Was your father insane?"

"I mean to tell the jury he was of unsound mind. That is what I told them. Insanity means to know nothing."

"I'm not asking you what it means. Did you mean to tell the jury that your father was insane?"

"No, sir. I didn't tell them that. If you will allow me to qualify?"

But Eichhorn didn't. He moved on to William's daughter Josephine. William testified that his daughter was afflicted only for that single period of perhaps a year. "She never had any spells since that I know of."

On redirect examination, Sharpe tried to take advantage of what seemed overreaching at the expense of the elderly man. Gently, and with an eye toward the jury, he asked William to explain his understanding of insanity compared to unsoundness of mind. Judge Smith overruled Eichhorn's objection, and William answered.

"Unsoundness of mind—I can illustrate that by taking a bundle of sticks and break one. It is that strength gone, that much gone from the mind. That is what I understand of unsoundness of mind. Like a broken stick, part of the sticks are whole, and part of them are broken. Consequently, I couldn't class it with insanity. Insanity means insane, to know nothing if I understand the English language."

With that, the old man finished his testimony. He stepped down, looked at his son, whom he didn't raise, then slowly hobbled to his seat behind the defense table.

William's wife and John's stepmother, Mary, was the next witness.[8] She testified at length about her daughter Josephine's troubles when she was nine years old, repeating much of William's testimony. "She had no mind. She screamed and was frightened. We had to chloroform her to keep her quiet."

The elderly Terrell couple, approaching the end of their lives, had been forced to disclose some of the most personal experiences, their deepest secrets—a father ravaged by the heartbreak over the death of his son and a child tormented for a year by unexplainable terrors. Yet what had it accomplished? To this point, there was nothing to connect those sad stories to whatever went on in John Terrell's head on July 12, 1903. Maybe it was penance for a father, a preacher, a self-proclaimed man of God, who never retrieved his own son, leaving him to be raised by another man.

The remainder of the afternoon was filled with witnesses who testified about facts already covered. Four neighbors testified that they all believed John had a good reputation for peace and quietude and for being a law-abiding citizen.[9] However, they admitted they had heard he had trouble with Melvin Moore and a man named Newhouse, but that it was quite some time ago. George Harshman added that he also heard of John having problems with Fred Hostettler and a man named Shull.

Bert Stookey was the day's final witness.[10] Several days before the shooting, Stookey asked John to bring his shotgun to Petroleum on Saturday night, July 11, for a belling.[11] It was an important point that explained why the gun was in

John's buggy the night before the shooting. It mitigated against the prosecution's claim that the shooting was planned in advance.

With that, the first grueling week of John Terrell's trial ended. The lawyers and bailiffs showed signs of fatigue. Already the trial was the longest in memory in Wells County. Judge Smith had pushed the case forward, starting each day at 8:30 and pushing through until 5:30, with no breaks other than ninety minutes for lunch. The lawyers and judge anticipated that at the current pace, the trial would conclude by the end of the following week.[12]

Curious citizens had packed the gallery, taking every seat and lining the walls until Judge Smith ordered that no more people be admitted than the courtroom had seats. From that point forward, bailiffs Adnah Hall and John Poffenberger were tasked with counting those who walked in, then, when seats were full, to admit another person only when one of those in the room left. Some stood in line all day, hoping for an opportunity to see the great trial in person.[13]

As John Terrell returned to jail, the burden and stress of the trial showed noticeably on his face. The lines on his face were more pronounced, the half-moons beneath his eyes darker. He had maintained his impassive demeanor throughout the week, not responding to the ups and downs of the testimony, but as the week wore on, he sank deeper into his chair, dejectedly gnawing at his moustache and rubbing his chin. Those who knew him best could see the hints of his unease and fatigue as the days went by.[14]

The jurors seemed to be handling their confinement with grace. Over Sunday, the jury remained in the courtroom except when they left for walks under the watchful eyes of the bailiffs. On Sunday night, they slept in the courtroom, hoping the trial would quickly be over. But, unfortunately, the expectation of the lawyers and judge, and the hopes of the jury, would all be in vain.

John spent Sunday in his cell, visiting much of the day with his family. With the start of the trial, visits from friends were fewer, and none from his business associates. He remained quiet, not speaking much and not saying anything about the trial. Even when Lucy raged about Della Reed's testimony, calling her a lying whore, John did not respond. His only reaction came when his three granddaughters were brought by during the afternoon. He played with them, bouncing them on his knee and singing familiar children's ditties. It was the only time John laughed.

23

Lunatics and Idiots

Judge Smith opened the second week of trial by announcing a critical ruling he had reached after a weekend of research. Evidence concerning insanity among John Terrell's relatives, some as distant as second and third cousins, would be admitted. "All the cases I have found and studied have been open on this point," he stated. "Without specific guidance on the issue, I will leave it to the jury. They can hear the evidence, and if it has any weight in their opinion, they have the privilege of doing with it as they see fit."[1]

It was a major victory for the defense and a blow to the State, or so it seemed at the time. The defense would send a parade of witnesses who knew of mental deficiencies in John's family, including distant cousins. The prosecution it seemed, would now have to convince the jury that cases of mental illness and deficiencies in the Terrell family were not connected to the acts John committed on July 12.

But like prayers, sometimes lawyer motions are best when they are not granted. Before a lawyer can persuade, he must first get and keep the attention of the twelve souls sitting in the jury box. And over the next several hours, as testimony about Terrell relatives droned on, the defense came perilously close to losing the attention of the jury. And for a jury that was confined to the courtroom and could not sleep in their own beds until trial was over, perhaps a lawyer's worst sin was to waste the time of the jurors. It seemed something that Terrell's team of high-priced lawyers had forgotten.

Dr. Nelson T. Chenowith, a sixty-six-year-old physician from Windsor in Randolph County, was the first witness called to begin the second week of the trial.[2] He testified about observing and treating Josephine Terrell, John's half sister, when she was about nine years old, including using chloroform to combat her fits and rages.

The insanity defense parade continued with seventy-seven-year-old William Cecil,[3] who was married to a cousin of John's mother. His wife went insane about sixteen years earlier. He detailed her bouts of mental illness, concluding, "Finally, I had her took away to Mount Clemens. You might call it a crazy house."

Cecil also knew Betsy Chandler, a cousin of John's mother, who had two children who "just weren't right," not speaking and barely managing to feed themselves. Cecil also knew Cyrus Thornburg, his insane wife's brother who died from fits at age thirty-five.

William Fitzpatrick was next to the witness chair.[4] He echoed prior testimony about Wesley's behavior after his son's death, concluding he was "of unsound mind, I suppose." He also knew Betsy Chandler and her older son. "He didn't act like he had any sense to me. He couldn't talk to anybody so that anybody could understand him. He was an idiot."

Fitzpatrick added yet another to the growing list of mentally defective Terrells. Edith Dudley, a third cousin of John's mother, had a son, now thirty years old who talks, "but his talk is not very well connected."

On cross-examination, Fitzpatrick delivered a blow to the assertion that Wesley Terrell became unsound after the Civil War death of his son, George. Fitzpatrick rented a farm from Wesley. With some admiration, he stated that until the day he died, the old preacher could count money, take care of it himself, and pay his taxes.

Charles Dudley,[5] Jeremiah Smith,[6] and Cinda Halstead[7] continued the line of Randolph County witnesses. Each reiterated the testimony about Betsy Chandler's sons and Edith Dudley's son, classifying them all as idiots and providing various details about their behavior. However, they offered contradictory testimony on exactly how many children there were and what their names were.

Jeremiah Smith offered perhaps the only new testimony. His mother, Martha Terrell, was John's aunt. On cross-examination, he was asked, "There is no insanity in your family?" Jeremiah answered, "Not in my family. Of course, my mother was adjudged insane."

William Terrell was recalled.[8] He testified as to specific instances of peculiar behavior among John's second and third cousins, but the old man's memory failed about names and precise relationships, leaving his testimony largely worthless.

The jurors' attention waned as witness after witness told prolonged stories about a confusing family tree, of Thornburgs and Terrells, of aunts, uncles, cousins, spouses, and children of cousins. Their ailments ranged from an inability to converse "connectedly" to idiocy and being confined to asylums.

In a time when note-taking by jurors was prohibited, Terrell's lawyers seemed oblivious to the jury's difficulty in tracking the Terrell family and their maladies or how this airing of family defects bore any connection to the shooting of Melvin Wolfe. Not once did anyone link the conditions in the far-flung world of Terrells and Thornburgs directly to John or the events of July 12.

It seemed a collective sigh of relief swept through the jury and those in the gallery when the defense finally returned to calling witnesses with knowledge of the shooting. The *Bluffton Evening News* summed up the testimony on its front page as "very tedious to all concerned. That there were about a dozen distant relatives of Terrell who were lunatics and idiots has been very conclusively shown but what bearing that will have is doubtful."[9]

Ross Thompson,[10] a butcher in nearby Pennville, was in Petroleum the evening of the shooting. He observed John shortly after a shooting, describing him as "kind of wild." He saw Terrell, still in the buggy, gesturing and talking to himself. In Thompson's opinion, the defendant was of unsound mind.

On cross-examination, Eichhorn hinted that Terrell's business partner and now lawyer Charles DelaCour had been tampering with the witness. He stopped just short of making the accusation. However, Eichhorn did get Thompson to admit that John seemed angry when he saw him shortly after the shooting, and angry was not insane.

Sharpe recalled John's neighbor, George Harshman, as a witness.[11] He saw John when he returned home after the shooting. He described John as looking red and excited, with his eyes "popped out like." Harshman's opinion was that John was of unsound mind.

But Harshman also added an additional element. On a spring Sunday afternoon about a year before the shooting, Harshman observed Melvin Wolfe bring Lucy home.

"He pushed her out of the buggy, and picked her clothes up, and throwed them out against the gate."

"What did he do then?"

"He wheeled his horse and took north about as fast as his critter could pace."

"What did Lucy do?"

PETROLEUM TRAGEDY SHOCKS THE COMMUNITY-- HEARING AND FUNERAL TO-DAY

JOHN TERREL AND MELVIN WOLFE,

The Principal and the Victim of the Wells County Family Feud.

Left: Headline from *Fort Wayne Journal Gazette*, July 14, 1903, with drawn images of John W. Terrell and Melvin Wolfe (Courtesy of Newspapers.com)

Below: Courtroom drawing depicting main parties and lawyers. *From left*: John Terrell, Lucy Terrell, defense lawyers Ralph Gregory (bearded) and Arthur Sharpe (bald with glasses), Prosecutor John Burns (standing), Assistant Prosecutor William Eichhorn next to Noah Jacob Wolfe (white beard), and Mary Wolfe (hat). From *Bluffton Evening News*, December 3, 1903. (Courtesy of Wells County Public Library)

COURT SCENE IN THE FAMOUS TERRELL-WOLFE MURDER TRIAL.

GEO·BREHM BLUFFTON

Terrell and Daughter.   Ralph Gregory.   Dr. A. L. Sharpe.   Prosecutor John Burns.   W. H. Eichhorn.   Jacob Wolf.   Mrs. Jacob Wolf.

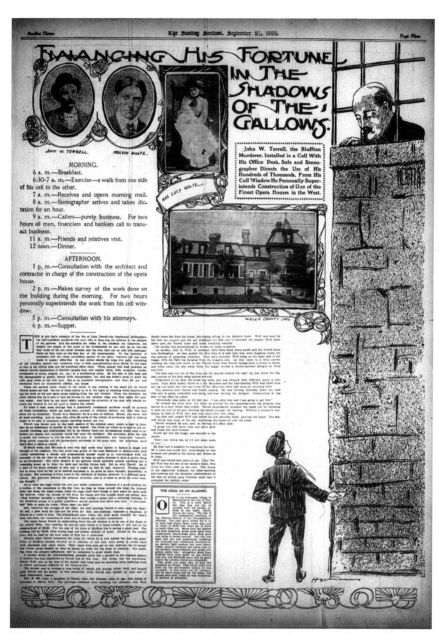

Headline and illustration from *Indianapolis Sunday Sentinel*, September 22, 1903
(Courtesy of Indiana State Library)

Wells County Circuit Courtroom, where John Terrell's trial was held for three weeks in December 1903, as it appeared in 2022 (Photo by the author)

Wells County Circuit Courthouse, where John Terrell's trial was held for three weeks in December 1903, as it appeared in 2022 (Photo by the author)

Above: The jury that convicted John Terrell in *Bluffton Evening News,* December 21, 1903 (Courtesy of Wells County Public Library)

Right: Drawing by Geo Bremm of John Terrell and Lucy Terrell Wolfe, who holds baby Mabel, in the courtroom at the start of the trial. From *Fort Wayne News,* December 2, 1903. (Courtesy of Wells County Public Library)

John Terrell's farmhouse as it appeared in 2023 (Photo by the author)

Wells County legal community circa 1903 with key characters identified: (1) Sheriff James T. Johnston, (2) Levi Mock, (3) 80-year-old bailiff John Poffenberger Sr., (4) clerk H. D. Studebaker, (5) Judge Edwin C. Vaughn, (6) Bailiff Adnah Hall, (7) Assistant Prosecutor J. K. Rinehart, (8) Magistrate M. W. Walbert, (9) defense attorney John Mock, (10) defense attorney C. E. Sturgis, (11) defense attorney George Mock, and (12) Assistant Prosecutor William H. Eichhorn. (Courtesy of Wells County Circuit Court, Hon. Kenton W. Kiracofe)

Drawing of John W. Terrell in *Fort Wayne Sentinel*,
December 21, 1903 (Courtesy of Newspapers.com)

SLAIN WHILE SURGEON WAS USING KNIFE.

Man Blows Out Son-in-law's Brains as He Lies on Operating Table Undergoing Amputation of Leg—Murder of Extraordinary Character.

[SPECIAL TO THE BUFFALO ENQUIRER FROM THE NEW YORK SUN.]

BLUFFTON, Ind., July 13.—In a manner perhaps never heard of anywhere in the world before, John Terrell murdered his son-in-law, Melvin Wolfe, yesterday afternoon. First he had wounded the man with a barrel swered grimly: "You'll do that once too often."

And yesterday Wolfe essayed to repeat the performance of driving past and shouting insults. This time Terrell awaited his coming with a loaded shotgun. As Wolfe appeared in his carriage, arose and began to call at

Headline in *Buffalo (NY) Enquirer*, July 13, 1903 (Courtesy of Newspapers.com)

Terrell, Who Murdered Son-in-Law, Expresses No Sorrow for the Deed

MELVIN WOLFE,
The Murdered Man.

MRS. MELVIN WOLFE AND BABY

JOHN W. TERRELL,
The Murderer.

Headline and photos of John, Lucy, and Melvin in *Muncie Morning Star*, July 14, 2008 (Courtesy of Newspapers.com)

Some, Who Think He Had Provocation for the Crime, Feel Sympathy for Him; No Fear of Mob Violence

He Orders Work to Proceed on the Opera House at Bluffton; a Sad Family Gathering at the Jail

[STAR'S SPECIAL SERVICE.]

BLUFFTON, Ind., July 13.—John W. Terrell, who murdered his son-in-law, Melvin Wolfe, Sunday evening by shooting him with a shot gun as the young man lay on the operating table at Petroleum, this county, passed a quiet day here in the county jail. He received very few visitors and asked Sheriff Johnson not to admit anybody unless he was consulted as to whether he wished to see them.

He refused to make any statements to the press in regard to the affair. He will not discuss the shooting with anybody, thus acting under instructions from his attorneys. He has not expressed sorrow for the deed, but said it was a bad thing.

Asked as to Public Sentiment.

The first question Terrell asked the reported, who saw him today, was what the public thought of it and what

the public sentiment was toward himself.

This forenoon Terrell was visited in the jail by his wife and four children, a son and three daughters. One of the latter is Mrs. Lucy Wolfe, the daughter whom Melvin Wolfe had wronged, married and deserted, and for which act Terrell took his life. She carried her baby. It was a sorrowful meeting of the family and all broke down and wept bitterly.

The father's tears mingling with those of his wife and children.

Counsel is Engaged.

The firm of lawyers already engaged by Mr. Terrell consists of Levi Mock and his two sons, Mayor John Mock and George Mock. They say that they have not yet outlined their defense and do not know whether there will be a plea of insanity. They will waive a preliminary hearing.

The coroner drove to the home of Melvin Wolfe's parents, J. N. Wolfe and wife, three miles east of Petroleum, today to hold the inquest. He had ordered the young man's body removed to his home last night.

The coroner has not yet rendered his verdict.

Drove By Three Times.

Later developments indicate that the murder of Wolfe was cold-blooded and premeditated, though in a measure provoked. He drove past Terrell's home three times Sunday afternoon in company with his step-sister, Delia King, Clarence Turner and Rosa Downing.

After shooting at Wolfe twice and wounding him as he passed, Terrell climbed into his buggy, which he had in waiting, and followed him as fast as he could drive to Petroleum. He stood up in his buggy in his bare head

and shouted, "I'll kill him." "I'll kill him."

Calmness Prevails.

Since Terrell was brought to jail there has been no disturbance worth mentioning and no motion of any kind toward mob violence. The murder has been about the chief topic of discussion today, but no threats have been made toward Terrell. Some express sympathy for him on account of his terrible provocation. He cannot be tried before September.

Terrell, from his cell in the jail, gave instructions to Charles Delacour this evening to go ahead with the construction of a $45,000 opera house here, for which they had the plans drawn. Terrell will furnish most of the money for the house. The opera house will occupy a lot located directly across the street from the jail, and Terrell can watch the work from his cell. Work had not yet been commenced.

THE EVENING NEWS.

TWELFTH YEAR NO 72

BLUFFTON, INDIANA SUNDAY DECEMBER 20 1903.

TEN CENTS A WEEK.

IMPRISONMENT FOR LIFE

Jury, Finds Terrell Guilty.
on First Ballot.

Four Ballots taken on the punishment. One man only vot for light sentence and eleven for Life imprisonment.

Headline from *Bluffton Evening News*, December 20, 1903 (Courtesy of Wells County Public Library)

"She stood still there. Put her hands up over her face. I think she was crying."

In a single moment, Harshman's answers brought the jury's focus back to the core of the case: a young woman, an abusive husband, and an enraged father.

On cross-examination, Harshman disclosed that John called out to him just before he headed to Petroleum with his shotgun in hand. "He said he wanted me to look after his little children." An hour later, Harshman saw John return and go in the house.

"Did he say anything to anyone?"

"Runs in my mind he said, I believe he said, 'Lucy, your husband is dead.'"

Harshman, Frank Fisher, and his wife gathered in the front yard of the Ter-rell house. John came out a short time later wearing a coat. As he headed back to his buggy, he called Harshman and Fisher over. "Look after my family a little." He then got in his rig and headed down the pike toward Petroleum.

As Harshman walked away from the witness chair, Arthur Sharpe stood and announced the next witness—Lucy Wolfe.

24

Lucy's Story

A buzz spread across the courtroom as twenty-two-year-old Lucy Terrell Wolfe stood, handed her eighteen-month-old daughter to her mother, and walked to the witness chair.[1] She wore a conservative dark brown wool suit with a double-breasted jacket cinched at the waist. The dress flared slightly to give her an hourglass shape that was in fashion. Her white shirt showed the slightest ruffles above the top jacket, and she wore no wedding ring or jewelry.

Judge Smith banged his gavel once for silence, and Lucy took the oath. At the defense table, John had spent most of the trial looking on with casual disinterest, seldom looking toward the witnesses. But now he edged forward, his eyes intently focused on his youngest daughter.

At the prosecution table, Prosecutor John Burns also leaned forward. He knew Lucy would be a critical witness and intended to rattle her and obstruct her sympathetic story as much as possible.

Lucy took her seat in the witness chair.[2] The gallery did not make a sound as her testimony began. It was 2:30 P.M. and Lucy would remain on the witness stand without a break until 4:45 P.M.[3]

Under gentle questioning from Arthur Sharpe, she told her story. She spoke in a quiet, confident voice, a contrast to the anger underlying Della Reed's testimony.

"When did you first meet Melvin Wolfe?"

Burns was quickly on his feet. "Objection. Immaterial."

"Sustained."

"When did you begin to keep company with him?"

"Objection. Immaterial."

"Sustained."

The opening salvos from the prosecution and Judge Smith sustaining the objections signaled to Sharpe that this would not be an easy examination. It was going to be difficult to get any of the story of Lucy's relationship with Melvin into evidence.

Lucy seemed momentarily confused, but she held her composure. She told of marrying Melvin Wolfe on November 20, 1901, when she was pregnant, then moving in with the Wolfe family. She identified Melvin as the father of her child.

Sharpe asked if Lucy talked with her father about Melvin promising to marry her.

Burns stood. "The State objects for the reason that the same could not be relevant to any issue in this case."

This got to the heart of the prosecution's effort to keep out Lucy's story. They wanted to restrict the case to what happened on July 12—a shooting along a roadside, the chase into Petroleum, and the shooting in the doctor's office. Deflowering a man's daughter was not a legal justification for murder. Were it otherwise, far fewer young men would be roaming free in Wells County. Nor was the abuse Lucy suffered while married to Melvin an excuse. Burns wanted to keep the case to just the facts of July 12.

Judge Smith had anticipated the issue and clearly had given it extended thought. He did not take argument from counsel but instead delivered a carefully thought-out explanation for his ruling. "The defendant's acts may be shown, but to go into a collateral matter, that is, to an inquiry as to justification, could not justify the defendant's actions. Therefore, we are not putting the evidence in on any justification, but only to show the condition of the defendant's mind. The court's ruling is that the collateral issue between Mrs. Wolfe and her husband is not on trial. What Mrs. Wolfe said to her father about her husband's treatment is competent, and the court will so hold. But whether what Mrs. Wolfe told her father is true or false is not competent."

When Judge Smith paused, Sharpe spoke. "The defense proposes to show that these facts were all communicated to the defendant."

Judge Smith nodded. "You may show any facts that this witness communicated to her father. That is not the question the court is ruling on. The question the court is ruling on is a conversation between Mr. Wolfe and this woman. That is being excluded."

So there it was—a split-the-baby, Solomon-like decision on the most important evidentiary issue of the case. Lucy would not be able to testify straightforwardly about what happened between her and Melvin. That was not an issue material to the murder trial. But since John's state of mind was an issue, she would be able to testify as to what she told her father. The ruling also meant that the State would not be able to call witnesses to counter Lucy's version of events because the only issue was what Lucy told her father, not whether what she told him was true. It was a technical evidentiary ruling that perhaps encouraged fabrication. Direct evidence that could not come in the front door could be brought in indirectly through the back as long as it was prefaced by saying it was told to John.

Sharpe acquiesced and tried a new approach—one to which the judge had clearly been leading him. "What did you tell your father about you and Melvin?"

"I told him that I was pregnant with a child. I told him Melvin was the father and that he refused to marry me." Lucy told of accompanying her father to Bluffton, where they met with Melvin's father, Jacob Wolfe.

Heading off a potential objection, Sharpe asked, "Were you present at that meeting?"

"I was." Lucy went on to describe how Jacob said he had paid Melvin's way out of one situation, and he would not do it again, and Melvin had to marry Lucy.

Lucy explained that initially she told her father that she was treated well by Mel and his family. However, when she saw her father again after a week, she informed him that she was being mistreated. She shared with her father a conversation she had with Mel on the porch of his house. Mel expressed his disdain for her and his preference for another girl named Chloa Blair, with whom he already had a child. She also quoted Mel's comment to her about their baby: "That kid don't belong to me. It belongs to your old gray-headed daddy."

A unified gasp went up from every corner of the courtroom. Judge Smith banged the gavel several times to silence the room. At the defense table, John dropped his head and closed his eyes for a long moment.

"What did you tell your father about your coming to town to have an abortion or an operation performed at your husband's request?"

Just the question evoked involuntary gasps.

Lucy looked straight ahead, her voice remaining steady. "I told my father that Mel offered me the money and wanted me to come to town to get an operation performed and then go home. And he said he would give me the money to pay my mother if she would take care of me."

Hat-clad ladies who were scattered across the courtroom shook their heads. Whispers of "Oh my," "That poor girl," and "Sweet Jesus" filtered up to the lawyers and jurors. Judge Smith banged his gavel for order.

Sharpe moved his questioning on to what Lucy told her father about Mel's relationship with his stepsister, Della Reed. Lucy calmly recounted how Mel would keep her confined while he went out at night with Della. She then told of the night she found them together in Della's bed.

John sat at the defense table, visibly distraught by his daughter's testimony. In the silence of the courtroom, his sobs could be heard.

Lucy testified about telling her father how she was ill and no one in the house would help her with her chores. Mel and his stepmother, Mary Wolfe, joined in the rants that Lucy had to move back home.

Lucy then recounted telling her father of her attempted suicide with laudanum. "I told him I took laudanum and took it with the intent to kill myself because Mel told me he wouldn't take care of me."

Sharpe asked Lucy to recount what she told her father about the night Melvin attempted to force himself on her. Remaining remarkably calm, Lucy said, "I told him Mel got up in bed and put his arms around my neck and pulled my head down. He tried to put my face down to his private part and put it in my mouth."

There was an audible gasp across the courtroom. At the defense table, John lowered his head into his hands and sobbed. Lucy continued, her voice steady. "I told him I wouldn't do it, and he hammered me on the back."

The courtroom fell into stunned silence. Nothing was said. No one whispered. The only sound was John sobbing with his head buried in his hands. Sharpe let the silence linger. In the witness chair, Lucy looked straight ahead. Not a single tear fell from her eyes. Finally, after a long silence, Sharpe resumed.

Lucy told about her final day in the Wolfe house and Mel taking her home, throwing her and her belongings out of his wagon. Two months later, Mabel Marie Wolfe was born. Sharpe asked if the child was in the courtroom. Burns objected, even though the jury had seen the child throughout the trial. Sharpe didn't wait for a ruling. He just shook his head and moved on to another question.

Lucy testified that after Mabel was born, she and her father would often see Melvin ride by. There were times when he would sing out loud the song "Bye, Oh, Baby." Not long after Mabel began walking, Melvin rode by and yelled to Lucy and her father, "Hold up the little bastard so I can see it." Several other times, he made dirty signs at Lucy, waggling his fingers with his thumb held to his nose. Lucy also told about an incident in Oliver's Restaurant in Petroleum where Melvin shoved her.

Sharpe then turned his attention to the day of the shootings. From the house, Lucy saw Wolfe in a buggy with his stepsister, headed south. Melvin shook his fist at John, then yelled out, "'How is the bastard' or something like that about the baby." Lucy, who was in the dining room, ran to the front porch. From there, she saw her father fall by the wind pump. She went to assist him in getting up. She got some water and bathed his face. "There was froth at his mouth."

Lucy took her father into the house and sat him in a chair, then left to find her mother, who was milking cows on another part of the farm more than half a mile away. By the time Lucy returned to the house, her father was gone. Lucy testified that her father returned home about seven o'clock.

Sharpe concluded his questioning of Lucy the same as he had with most witnesses by asking Lucy whether when she saw her father that evening, he was of sound mind.

"I think he was unsound."

With that, Sharpe ended his direct examination. The entire courtroom was quiet. John raised his head. His face was wet from tears.

Burns strode to a place only a few feet from Lucy. His demeanor and voice were stern. Burns went over Lucy's story about getting pregnant, telling her father, and the meeting between John and Mel's father. Lucy repeated the same testimony she gave on direct examination, adding that she was two months pregnant when she told Mel, then her parents about the pregnancy. When she told her parents, John cried.

After their marriage, Melvin would sometimes drive her home to visit her family, but he never went inside the Terrell house.

Burns pressed Lucy with questions about what her father said to her when she revealed Melvin and the Wolfe family's bad conduct toward her. Lucy responded that her father spoke little and never made any threats against Melvin in her presence. When Lucy told her father about Melvin's effort to get Lucy to have an abortion, "He told me not to do it."

Burns then turned to Lucy's testimony in September 1902 during her fraudulent marriage lawsuit against Melvin. The lawyer pressed on why many of the things she had just testified about were never mentioned in her previous testimony. Burns tried to use that testimony to challenge Lucy's credibility, but Lucy remained unshaken, simply recognizing that it was not in her earlier testimony but not offering any explanation.

Burns questioned Lucy extensively about the events of July 12. However, the examination did little but allow Lucy to repeat her account of that day. She did not provide new information or contradict her earlier testimony.

Burns and Sharpe squabbled through some meaningless questions on redirect and recross, but by 4:45, they had exhausted all their questions. Lucy stepped down from the witness chair. She had testified without a break for two hours and fifteen minutes.

Lucy glanced toward her father, whose eyes were still red. He gave her a slight nod, which she returned. Then, her head up and shoulders back, she walked confidently out of the courtroom, maintaining her composure. She walked until she was out of sight and sound of the courtroom, then stopped. Only then did she hang her head and break down in a flood of uncontrollable sobs.[4]

25

Atheist and Believers

After Lucy's testimony, Sharpe called Lucy's two sisters: Sarah Terrell Schott,[1] known by family and friends as Sally, and Lucinda Terrell Books,[2] known as Cinda. Sharpe got through the direct exam of Sally before the court concluded testimony for the day. On the following day, questioning took up with Burns's cross-examination.

During direct examination, Sharpe tried to elicit testimony from both women about being abandoned by their first husbands, the oil field–working Vandergriff brothers. In both cases, Judge Smith sustained prosecution objections and struck the testimony that was given. However, as every lawyer knew, it was impossible to "unring" the bell. The jury heard enough that they knew that John's two older daughters were abused and abandoned by their first husbands, whether it was considered evidence or not.

Under Sharpe's questioning, Sally testified about her father's head injury in 1894. He came home with a one-inch gash in the back of his head, which she said kept him in bed for a week or more. "He complained of his head ever since" and during those headaches often talked to himself. "It was a kind of ramble, and you could not understand what he would say."

Sharpe concluded his questioning by focusing on the day of the shooting. Sally described everyone in her family gathering for a surprise birthday dinner for her husband, John Schott. Sally overheard her sister Cinda talking about her encounter that morning with Melvin, which left their buggy "pretty near upset."

. . .

Eichhorn's cross-examination explored inconsistencies in Sally's testimony about the frequency and severity of her father's headaches and her lack of knowledge about any medications her father was taking.

Cinda, John's twenty-four-year-old middle daughter, described how her father walked the floor and cried during times of stress for his daughters. She detailed his behavior on May 11, 1902, when Melvin Wolfe brought Lucy home and threw her out of his buggy, and her father "went in the pantry and shut the door," where he remained for nearly half an hour. After he went to bed that night, "he got up once or twice and walked the floor, worried about Lucy."

Although Eichhorn's objections prevented Cinda from testifying about the abuse she suffered at the hands of her first husband, Ben Vandergriff, Eichhorn spent much of his cross-examination questioning Cinda about that same failed marriage. Eichhorn insinuated through his questions that John was aggressively hostile to Cinda's first husband, which Cinda denied.

On redirect, Sharpe probed into a line of questioning he omitted in his direct exam. After all, Cinda saw her father in Petroleum just after the shooting. She described him as "hair standing straight" and eyes "bulged out." His face was pale and purple. "He looked awful. Frightful." Cinda opined that her father was of unsound mind.

Cinda testified that the following day, when she saw her father in jail, he was still pale and his eyes were glassy. "His talk was not connected." Cinda's opinion was that her father, hours after the shooting, was still of unsound mind.

Eichhorn pounced on his cross-examination, attacking Cinda's observations and conclusions that her father was of unsound mind. Cinda stumbled with her words, at times contradicting earlier testimony. In just a few minutes, Eichhorn had reduced the impact of Cinda's testimony from a near-eyewitness to a young woman saying what she needed to save her father.

Even though he was the son of a Methodist minister and grandson of a fundamentalist John Wesley–inspired preacher, John Terrell was an unapologetic atheist. He spoke ill of organized religion and considered preachers men who were taking advantage of those who were gullible. In the early 1900s, that placed John in a small minority—and an even smaller minority who spoke out about their views.

The early 1900s were not a tolerant or accepting time for atheists. The Haymarket Riot in Chicago by eight "godless anarchists" left eleven people dead.[3] Even worse, on September 6, 1901, at the Pan American Exposition in Buffalo, Leon Czolgosz, an anarchist who rejected Catholic teachings, assassinated President William McKinley.[4] In the popular mind, atheism was un-American and linked to domestic terrorism.[5] Atheists' attacks on religion were presumed to lead to other dangerous ideas.[6] A lack of belief in God was linked to an absence of any of moral beliefs. The result "made atheists an easy minority to revile."[7]

Indeed, intolerance for atheists extended back to the nation's very roots. Political philosopher John Locke, who served as a guide for the nation's founding fathers, talked of the need for religious toleration. Yet Locke also stated, "Those are not at all to be tolerated who deny the being of God."[8]

When Alexis de Tocqueville traveled through the United States in the 1830s, he observed that an individual "who dared express his irreligion publicly and— even worse—to criticize religious beliefs, was almost immediately despised and shunned by other Americans."[9]

The village atheist was viewed as "dangerously unfit for equal citizenship."[10] So much so that until about 1840, most states prohibited atheists from holding office, serving as jurors, or even testifying.[11] By 1903, fourteen states still prohibited nonbelievers from testifying or serving on juries, although Indiana, by statute, was not among them.[12]

The next witness was Fred Goss,[13] a thirty-year-old oil field worker who had known and worked for John Terrell for seven years. Although called by the defense, it was his testimony on cross-examination that would squarely put John's atheism in evidence before the Bible Belt jury.

Goss testified that late at night, John often came to the powerhouse that served Terrell's oil wells. He would sit, talking for an hour or more with his head in his hands. Sometimes he would act nervous, shake his fist in the air, and "act crazy."

During the past March, Goss was visiting with John at the Terrell house. As they sat in the porch swing. Melvin Wolfe drove by with a team of horses and yelled out, "How do you like to take care of the bastard?"

On cross-exam, Eichhorn saw the opportunity to attack John's character in a way he knew would have a significant impact. Why John's lawyers did not object is inexplicable.

Goss admitted that on John's nocturnal visits to the power station, they would sometimes talk for as much as two hours.

"He talked religion?"

"Well, I don't remember anything in particular about his talking religion."

"He told you what his views were, did he not?"

"I think he expressed himself by reading some literature of some kind."

"What did he say about it?"

"I heard him remark that he thought Ingersoll was a very smart man. He had read a great deal about Ingersoll in different books and religious books and read about him."

Robert Green Ingersoll was a renowned orator, lawyer, and writer known as "The Great Agnostic" for his writings against religious beliefs and organized churches.[14] Ingersoll's writings were widely known, and it is very likely that most jury members, if not all of them, would know of Ingersoll and his opinions about religion. For the last thirty years of Robert Ingersoll's life, until his death in 1899, he regularly spoke to auditoriums and theaters filled with three thousand people a night, each paying one dollar for the privilege or to heckle his unbelief.[15] Newspapers across Indiana were regularly filled with editorials by local preachers attacking Ingersoll and his antireligion speeches, often openly praying in print for his conversion.[16]

In the heart of the Bible Belt, not believing in God or the Bible was nearly as bad as murder itself. Eichhorn had gotten before the jury that John Terrell was an adherent of Ingersoll's godless views. He ended his cross-examination on that point. But he knew there would be more to come. Before the case went to the jury, they would be told multiple times that the defendant was an atheist.

The stunning portrait of Melvin Wolfe's abusive conduct toward the Terrell family continued with the next witness, fifty-six-year-old farmer Emanuel Caves.[17] A lifelong resident of Nottingham Township, he had known John Terrell for about eighteen years. He also knew Melvin Wolfe. The month before the shooting, he was helping John Terrell shear sheep on the Terrell farm.

"I told John W. Terrell that, I says, Melvin Wolfe don't think very much of his wife, does he, the way he talks. And John says, 'I don't know.' And then I said to him what Mel had said to me."

Sharpe nodded encouragement. "State what you said to him at this time that Melvin Wolfe had stated to you."

Caves hesitated. He looked toward the judge, seeking a reprieve from the question, but Judge Smith nodded for him to answer. Caves took a deep breath, then answered. "I told him Melvin Wolfe told me, 'I made her suck my privates.'"

Not for the first time, there was an audible gasp in the courtroom. Women throughout the room ducked their heads. Some covered their faces as they turned shades of red. Others fanned themselves. Even men in the gallery showed their disgust. Judge Smith hit his gavel once for order.

"What did the defendant do after you told him this?"

"John didn't say nothing. He turned around and walked out of the shed. I don't know what he done after that."

On cross-examination, Eichhorn grilled Caves about a visit he had from John's attorney and business partner, Charles DelaCour. He tried to leave the impression that there was something nefarious in DelaCour's visit, and maybe DelaCour paid Caves for his testimony. But in the end, the jury would remember Caves's revelation about Melvin Wolfe and Lucy's brokenhearted father.

John's sons-in-law, John Schott and William Books, were called as witnesses.[18] They added little, only repeating the testimony about John Schott's birthday dinner and John closeting himself in the kitchen pantry. Both opined that when they saw John in jail the morning after the shooting, he was of unsound mind.

Jake, John's nineteen-year-old son, followed.[19] His testimony primarily recounted episodes regarding Melvin Wolfe's misconduct that were already in evidence.

He testified about his encounter on July 10 with Cliff Shakley and Melvin Wolfe in Petroleum. Wolfe was encouraging Shakley to fight Jake, and Jake saw Melvin carrying a revolver. He told his father about Mel carrying a firearm. He also told his father about the incident earlier that week with Minnie Kirkwood at Oliver's Restaurant when Melvin made fun of Minnie and Shakley slapped her.

Neighbors Cassius White,[20] Frank Kirkwood,[21] and Henry Stanley[22] testified about John having a good reputation. However, on cross-examination, all three admitted hearing about John's fight with Mel Moore several years earlier.

The defense changed directions, calling two physicians to the witness stand but for vastly different reasons. First was Bluffton physician Dr. Charles L. Landfair, forty-three,[23] whose younger brother was one of John's lawyers. He testified as to a conversation he had with John about Melvin Wolfe's visit to his office. In a time when patient confidentiality apparently was not quite so scrupulously maintained, Dr. Landfair testified he told John that Melvin Wolfe had asked him to perform an abortion or give him materials that would produce an abortion. Dr. Landfair refused to do either.

A buzz went across the courtroom. Words like "shame," "awful," and "Sweet Lord" could all be heard. Judge Smith responded with a bang of the gavel.

Landfair then testified that Melvin returned a second time seeking an abortion for his wife. When Landfair again refused, Melvin left. As he left, "Wolfe said he would get rid of the kid and the mother too. And if he failed to do that—the words he used—he said, he wouldn't live with anybody with a drop of Terrell's blood in them. That is what he said."

After a pause, Sharpe resumed questioning Dr. Landfair, this time about his examination of John the morning after the shooting. Dr. Landfair found that John had a temperature of 103 degrees, indicating "anxiety and agitation and exhilarated pulse." His pulse was "bounding, full and pounding." Dr. Landfair also noticed that John's pupils were dilated beyond normal and "he looked to be starey—staring out unfocused."

When asked for his diagnosis, Dr. Landfair answered, "Well, it would indicate that there was a super amount of hyperemic condition of the brain where the capillaries were engorged with blood where there was a dissension." Landfair determined that at the time he saw John in the jail the day after the shooting, "He was unsound. He wasn't right."

Cross-examination started with Dr. Landfair's visit to the jail. Eichhorn got Dr. Landfair to admit that he was with John only "but a few minutes." During the visit, Dr. Landfair said little to John, and John said even less in return. John said nothing about the events of the previous day nor how he was feeling.

Eichhorn then explored other causes for John's condition. He got Dr. Landfair to admit that the high temperature, the elevated pulse, and bulging eyes Landfair observed could have been caused by excitement, agitation, or anger. Anger could also produce the "congested condition of the blood vessels" that Landfair diagnosed.

Eichhorn then asked if Dr. Landfair had ever seen John Terrell when he thought he was insane except for the few minutes he saw him in the Wells County Jail.

Dr. Landfair hesitated, then answered quietly, "Well, I am not to be a judge of that."

Eichhorn had what he wanted and ended the examination.

The second doctor was H. H. Weir, who had practiced medicine in Bluffton for more than a dozen years before moving to Indianapolis in 1897 where he now practiced. Dr. Weir treated John Terrell in 1895 for pain in the back of the head, nervousness, and insomnia, diagnosing him with "basilar congestion of the brain." He believed the condition was caused by a fall Terrell had experienced from a high load of corn the previous year, and that the impact upon the blood vessels "would be to weaken them and the effect upon the head would be to make it permanent."

Under Eichhorn's cross-examination, Dr. Weir acknowledged that without further information, he could not determine if the fall caused a concussion but suggested that if the individual remained conscious and rational, there was likely no concussion. Sharpe and Eichhorn continued to banter with Dr.

Weir, but neither obtained the definitive statements they were seeking on whether John's fall in 1894 impacted his mental state nearly a decade later.

The afternoon testimony concluded with Catherine Terrell, John's fifty-seven-year-old wife.[24] Even in an era when women in their late fifties were expected to exhibit the wear of a life of hard work, she looked shockingly older than her years. Showing the effect of her decadelong fight with epilepsy and pernicious anemia, which often kept her bedridden, she walked to the witness stand with difficulty. The stress of sitting through nearly two weeks of her husband's murder trial had also taken its toll, evident from the deep lines on her face, the dark shadows under her eyes, and the weary-to-the-bone way she moved and spoke.

At the defense table, John watched his wife. He kept his gaze fixed and showed no emotion.

Catherine testified about her husband's history of fretting about his daughters and their troubles. When his daughters were abandoned by their first husbands, "he would walk the floor and set with his hands on his face." He would not sleep and ate little. When Lucy became pregnant with Melvin Wolfe's child, John would go out and walk at night, sometimes never going to sleep.

Catherine repeated the previous testimony about Melvin Wolfe's mistreatment of her daughter, and after their separation, Melvin's constant yelling of insults and taunts at the family as he passed in his wagon. On the day Melvin Wolfe brought Lucy home, John "just got up and walked the floor over the house, out and in and around, and would rub his head and face, and looked [as] though he had had a sick spell. He didn't sleep any. I don't think at all."

On cross-examination, the prosecution tried to establish that despite all of these issues, John continued to run his farms and businesses, making him one of the county's wealthiest men. But Catherine denied knowing anything about her husband's business affairs, not even knowing what properties he owned.

The court recessed for the day before the cross-examination was completed. The next morning when court began, Catherine was recalled to the stand. But as she approached the witness chair, she stumbled and nearly collapsed. The court's two bailiffs assisted her to the judge's chambers, where she lay on a couch while a doctor was summoned. The state eventually waived any further cross-examination, and Catherine remained on the judge's couch until near noon when she went home.[25]

After a thirty-minute delay caused by Catherine's collapse, Judge Smith called the court back in session. "Call your next witness, Mr. Sharpe."

Sharpe stood. His posture erect, his voice booming, he faced the jury. "The defense calls John W. Terrell."

26

John's Story

"It Got Night"

As he had been for the entire trial, John was dressed in a dark suit, white shirt with a collar, and a smartly tied black tie. John walked to the witness chair, his head up and chin jutting a bit forward. His look was stern, but he did not fix his gaze on anyone or anything in particular. He stood a head taller than Bailiff Adnah Hall. His skin, worn red and rough from a lifetime of working in fields, stood in contrast to the pasty complexion of the bailiff.

Sitting behind the prosecution table, as they had every day of the trial, were Jacob and Mary Wolfe. Jacob stared unblinking at John, his brow furrowed into a scowl. Mary huffed dramatically and turned her head away to show her disdain.

Sharpe began his questioning by trying to make John more sympathetic.[1] John recounted how his mother died when he was just a toddler. He was sent to be raised by his great-uncle and great-aunt, Drummond and Sarah Terrell. He described moving from Randolph County when he was twenty-seven to Wells County, where he had lived ever since with his family on his farm.

Sharpe tried to get into the details of the failed marriages of his two older daughters, who were abandoned by their oil field–working husbands. However, Judge Smith continually sustained the prosecutor's objections, holding that the treatment of John's daughters had nothing to do with Melvin Wolfe's murder. But despite the judge's rulings striking much of that testimony, the jury heard it.

John testified that Lucy and Melvin separated on May 11, 1902, when Melvin dropped Lucy at the Terrell home. Two months later, the baby was born. Lucy and the baby had lived in the Terrell home ever since.

Lucy told John about her mistreatment at the Wolfe house. "She wasn't allowed enough to eat. When she would come home, she would come home hungry." As Sharpe continued his questioning, John recounted how there would be times Mel wouldn't speak to her for a week, and when he did, he told her he didn't intend to keep living with her, and that she should move back home. He also recounted Lucy's version of how she found Melvin and his stepsister Della in bed one night.

John detailed his history of three head injuries from falls. "I have had a headache almost constant since."

Sharpe then turned his attention to John's encounters with Melvin Wolfe between the time Lucy moved home and the shooting. John recounted the times Melvin shouted insults as he passed, demanded that John "hold up the bastard," and directed other taunts at Lucy and John.

Even though evidence of the taunts previously had been admitted, the prosecution objected to each set of questions. Each objection was identical, with the message intended as much for the jury as it was for the judge. "The State objects for the reason that the question is immaterial. Whatever Wolfe said or did in passing the Terrell house would not be sufficient justification or provocation to justify the murder charge against the defendant."

The judge sustained each objection, precluding John from testifying about Melvin's conduct even though others had already testified to the same facts. Judge Smith allowed John to answer about Melvin's taunts only when Sharpe began questioning about the actual day of the shootings.

John testified that on the morning of July 12, he had a severe headache. At about eleven o'clock, he took his family to the house of his son-in-law John Schott for a surprise birthday dinner. They stayed until just after three o'clock.

They returned home mid-afternoon. After changing out of his Sunday clothes, John went to the barn lot to water the horse and feed his stock. It was then that Melvin Wolfe rode by in a buggy with Della Reed, headed south.

"What, if anything, did you see Melvin Wolfe do at that time?"

"He shook his fist at me."

"What did you hear him say?"

Prosecutor Burns stood. "The State objects for the reason that whatever might have been said, it would not be any justification or excuse for murder."

The objection was overruled, but Burns knew that the jury had heard his preemptive strike. Melvin's taunts weren't an excuse for murder.

"I heard him say, 'Hold up the bastard.'"

"Now, Mr. Terrell, after you heard that remark, what did you say?"

John shook his head. "I don't know. It got night. Dark."

Sharpe looked toward the jury and then back at John. "You say it got night, dark. Tell the jury what you mean by saying it got night."

Burns objected, this time his voice more demanding than before. "State objects for the reason that the same is incompetent, immaterial, and irrelevant."

Judge Smith sustained the objection, preventing John from testifying about what he meant by his testimony. "You have no right to couple with it the answer," the judge said, as if that explained his ruling.

Sharpe reformulated the question, but there was the same objection and the same ruling.

"Tell the jury what you know, if anything, about what you did after on that day?"

Again, John shook his head. "I don't know, only what I have learned from the papers and what people has talked."

Burns stood again. "State moves to strike out the last part of the answer. Everything after 'I don't know.'"

Judge Smith granted the motion and struck John's reference to what he had learned from newspapers and conversations.

Sharpe continued, asking what John remembered about having shot Melvin Wolfe as he passed in his buggy, about going to Dr. Saunders's office and shooting Melvin Wolfe in the operating room. Burns objected to each question, and Judge Smith sustained the objection.

Still, Sharpe continued. "Tell the jury whether or not, on the twelfth day of July, you intended to kill and murder Melvin Wolfe as charged in the indictment?"

Burns objected, but this time Judge Smith hesitated. Preventing a defendant from denying the charge in the indictment could be found on appeal to have interfered with the defendant's fundamental right to deny the accusations against him. On appeal, it could be grounds for reversal. Judge Smith overruled the objection and allowed John to answer.

John looked straight across at the jury. "I didn't."

"Tell the jury whether or not you intended to do Melvin Wolfe any personal harm."

"I didn't."

"Tell the jury whether you have any knowledge of having wounded, pursued, or hurt Melvin Wolfe on that day."

"I have no knowledge of it. Only as I learned in the papers."

"Tell the jury whether or not, on the twelfth day of July last, you entertained any malice or hatred towards the deceased Melvin Wolfe."

"I didn't. I felt sorry for him."

Burns had gotten his message across to the jury through his objections, but ultimately Sharpe got what he wanted into evidence. The question that remained was whether the jury would believe it. And if they believed it now, would they still believe it when Prosecutor Burns completed his cross-examination?

The court adjourned for a ninety-minute lunch break and resumed with the cross-examination of John Terrell. Burns began his cross-examination in a friendly manner, almost like John was his own client, repeating much of his earlier testimony about his background. John was a prosperous farmer, owning 365 acres of farm ground and business property, and was engaged in loaning money.

"Since July 12, what has been your business?"

John gave a short laugh. "Locked up down here." A smattering of laughter came from the packed courtroom.

Burns did not smile. "What business have you conducted, directed, and managed since being locked up?"

"I don't know that I have directed or conducted any business myself."

Burns gave an exaggerated look of surprise. "Now, since being locked up, you have had your iron safe and all your valuable documents and papers moved to the jail, have you not?"

"Yes, sir."

"And you have rented your lands, made contracts verbal and written since being locked up, have you not?"

"I don't remember I have made any written contracts."

"All verbal?"

"I think so."

"And you collected your rents from your properties?"

"Yes, sir."

"While you have been in jail, you have also ordered and directed the sale of grass and grain and other products from your farms?"

"Yes, I ordered the sale."

"You also ordered a public sale made of property, advertised it and employed auctioneers, did you not?"

"Yes, sir."

"You kept a bank account and kept track of your moneys?

"I wrote checks. I sent a boy with what I had for deposits. The bank kept track of what I had. I depended on them for that."

"And since July 12, you started an opera house company and have negotiated and directed it?"

"I am a stockholder in the opera house. I had but very little to do with the business part."

"The members of the opera house corporation are you and two of your lawyers, Dr. Sharpe and Charles DelaCour. You know that, do you not?"

"Yes, sir."

"And you are one of the officers of that corporation?"

"Yes. I am the vice president."

"What is it capitalized at?"

Sharpe was immediately on his feet. "Defendant objects. Mr. Terrell's finances are wholly irrelevant and immaterial."

Judge Smith nodded in agreement. "Objection sustained." But the objection had come far too late. The jury now knew, if they did not already, that since his arrest, John had been spending his time running his business from his jail cell, what for Wells County was a vast business empire. It certainly did not give the impression of a man disabled by severe headaches or an unsound mind.

Burns turned to the day of the shooting. John insisted that the last memory he had of July 12 was shortly after Melvin and Della Reed passed the farm in their buggy. The next thing he remembered was talking to his lawyer, Levi Mock, in the Wells County Jail. He denied any recollection of talking to Sheriff Johnston and telling him that he had a good night's sleep. He also denied remembering his conversation with William Kapp in which he told Kapp he would have to move out of John's business property to make way for the opera house.

Burns shifted his focus, asking if John remembered an incident about a month after Lucy returned home when, with a gun in his buggy, he met Al Vore on the road driving toward the Wolfe residence.

John didn't deny the incident. He answered softly, "I don't remember."

Burns questioned John about being in Petroleum the night before the shooting. He admitted having a shotgun with him, telling the courtroom that Bert Stookey had requested the gun for a belling. When he arrived, Stookey said he no longer needed it.

"Do you remember talking to Oscar Oliver at the jail?"

"I don't remember talking to Oscar Oliver since July 12."

Burns raised his voice and pointed at John. "I will ask you if you didn't, within a few days after the twelfth of July in the county jail, say to Oscar Oliver in a conversation that you didn't have any gun in Petroleum the Saturday night before the shooting?"

John straightened in the witness chair, his eyes unblinkingly fixed on the prosecutor. "I don't remember of it."

Burns walked to a place next to the corner of the jury box. It was time to paint John as an atheist and launch a direct attack on John's character in front of the God-fearing men of the jury.

"You know Fred Goss?"

"Yes, sir. He pumped oil on my farm for a year or two."

"While he pumped there, you would frequently go to the powerhouse and chat with him about the 'Great Agnostic' Bob Ingersoll, religion, and other subjects?"

Sharpe objected, but Judge Smith overruled the objection without any argument. Sharpe had not objected to the topic of John's religious beliefs—or lack of them—when it was first put in evidence. It was too late now.

"Yes, sir. We did."

"Turning to your headaches, when you would indulge in drinking some intoxicating liquors, would you then have severe headaches from that?"

"Not to my recollection that I thought it come from that."

"Mr. Terrell, going back to the time you lived in Randolph County, I will ask you if you are not the same John W. Terrell who was arrested on the 9th day of September in the year 1875 on a charge of bastardy preferred by Mary J. Clevenger, and tried in Middle Creek Township in Randolph County two days later, and were you not adjudged by the same court to be the father of the bastard child of Mary J. Clevenger?"

Sharpe was on his feet, his voice as dynamic as it had been at any point in the trial. "Defendant objects for the reason that the same is collateral. It was a civil matter, if at all, and is not put to the witness for the purpose of affecting his credibility or in any manner showing a disposition akin to the event now on trial."

Judge Smith nodded in agreement. "Sustained."

Again, Sharpe's objection was too late to prohibit the jury from the damning implication. The jury had heard what it could not unhear. John had been found to father an illegitimate child nearly thirty years earlier. The horse was out of the barn, and there was no way to put it back in.

But Prosecutor Burns was not finished with his attack.

"Are you not the same John W. Terrell who pleaded guilty to the crime of assault and battery on the person of Melvin Moore in Judge Wismer's court here in Bluffton in 1893?"

Sharpe objected, but this time his objection was overruled.

"I pleaded guilty to assault and battery on Melvin Moore," John said, his voice defiant.

"Do you not remember taking a club about four feet long and striking Melvin Moore across the head with it, knocking him unconscious?"

Again Sharpe objected, but he knew before he uttered his objection that it was futile.

"No, sir. It didn't happen that way."

Burns knew better than to ask for John's explanation. An experienced lawyer understands that if given the opportunity to explain, the witness undoubtedly would. So instead, he plowed on with other incidents.

"In the spring of 1903, didn't you commit the crime of adultery with Fred Hostettler's wife, and if you didn't pay Fred Hostettler a sum of money to avoid a prosecution for that crime?"

"Objection!" Sharpe did not need to say more than the word before Judge Smith sustained the objection. But again, the jury had already heard the accusation.

"Are you not the same John W. Terrell who committed the crime of assault and battery on the person of John Newhouse in the Township of Nottingham, and did you not plead guilty to that crime?"

Again, Sharpe objected, but this time the court ordered John to answer.

"We had a fight."

"You pled guilty then?"

"Yes, sir. But I don't remember the charge."

Burn sat down, his cross-examination finished. He had used his questions to destroy any favorable view of John Terrell. Instead, the jury now saw him as a philandering, hot-tempered atheist with a history of assaulting men.

Sharpe was promptly on his feet for redirect, speaking before Burns had even taken his seat. He would try to reclaim John's credibility and reputation, but it was a formidable task. "Mr. Terrell, tell the jury what Newhouse said to you caused the fight."

"He called me a son of a bitch."

"Tell the jury whether or not you both agreed to fight or if you just commenced to fight with him when he called you the name. Tell how it was."

"We both agreed to fight."

Regarding the Saturday night in Petroleum, John said that he took the gun only at the request of Mr. Stookey and that it was not loaded. "I brought it because he asked to borrow it for a belling."

Sharpe did not respond to the other incidents covered in cross-examination and announced he had no more questions. John stiffly arose from the witness chair, which he had occupied for more than four hours, and walked to his seat. He did not smile or show any emotion. Behind the prosecution table, a close observer could have seen Mrs. Wolfe silently mouth the word "Liar."

By that evening, John's testimony was the talk at every dinner table, restaurant, and drinking house in Bluffton. That evening's *Bluffton Evening News* ran a story with an oversized bold headline:

"IT GOT NIGHT; John Terrell's Mind Was Blank."[2]

27

Hundred-Dollar-a-Day Jibber-Jabber

Sharpe now turned to the final stage of the defense—a dozen paid expert witnesses, most from the state capital of Indianapolis, more than one hundred miles away. Most had never before stepped foot in Wells County.

In the early 1900s, before the days of fingerprints (first trial use in 1910),[1] blood types (first trial use in 1908),[2] ballistics (first trial use in early 1920s),[3] police crime labs (1923),[4] and chief medical examiners (1918),[5] and long before DNA (1986)[6] and related magic tools of crime scene investigators, expert witnesses were nearly unheard of. In the early 1900s, even courts in such metropolitan areas as New York, Philadelphia, and Chicago seldom saw expert witnesses. Never had there been a parade of expert witnesses in Wells County. And never had witnesses come at such a price.

Dr. H. H. Weir was recalled to the stand as the first expert witness for the defense.[7] He was different than those who followed. He diagnosed John Terrell as having "basilar meningitis or basilar congestion of the brain" caused by his fall off a corn wagon. Dr. Weir said that brain congestion meant that the brain was "too full."

In response to Sharpe's questioning, Dr. Weir explained, "The vessels involved were the sinuses in the base of the brain, lateral sinuses, and venous congestion. I had no evidence of arterial congestion at the base of the brain, but from his history and from the processes of the pain and from his insomnia, inability to sleep, and nervousness, darting pains in his head, my diagnosis was congestion of the base of the brain. I believe the condition was concussion of the brain, and the effect upon the blood vessels would weaken them, and the effect upon the head would make it permanent."

By 1905, devices for accurately taking a patient's blood pressure bedside existed. Not long after that, with growing knowledge of blood pressure, "congestion of the brain" found its way to the medical dustbin along with leeches and tapeworm diets. But in 1903, it was still an accepted medical diagnosis.[8]

The jury was no doubt confused by the onrush of unexplained medical terms. But no one attempted to explain the terms in words they could understand. And it was about to get worse.

Sharpe walked to the defense table and picked up a small stack of typed papers. It was a sixteen-page hypothetical question setting out the defense's version of the facts of the case and its medical conclusions,[9] concluding with the paragraph:

"Now, from the facts stated above, admitting them all to be true, you may tell the jury whether, in your opinion, the defendant was of sound or unsound mind at the time of the shooting and homicide?"

In the early 1900s, experts could give an expert opinion only in response to a hypothetical question that contained all of the facts upon which the question was based. Omission of such facts would prevent the expert from giving an opinion. It was a cumbersome procedure that remained in some state courts until well past the middle of the twentieth century.

Now modern rules streamline the procedure. Hypothetical questions remain an essential part of trials, but the process is simplified. If an opposing party believes critical facts have been omitted, it is left to cross-examination to bring this out.[10] But in 1903, the complicated cumbersome procedure was put on full display in John Terrell's trial.

Sharpe began reading the sixteen-page question. It would take him forty minutes to complete it. At the end of Sharpe's recitation, the prosecution stood and made its objection. "The question contains a very large number of facts that have not been testified to, and contains a large number of items and elements that were stricken out on motion by the court. The State objects for the further reason that it assumes facts which have not been proven, and concerning which there is no testimony whatsoever."

The court overruled the objection, and Dr. Weir answered the forty-minute question with a seven-word response. "I would consider him of unsound mind."

With Dr. Weir's answer, Sharpe concluded his exam.

The process would repeat itself by reading the entire hypothetical question, followed by the prosecution's objections, to each of the dozen expert witnesses. Repeated reading of the hypothetical question would consume nearly eight hours of trial time. The jurors' eyes glazed over, and their minds wandered as the lawyers droned on. They heard the exact words read over and over and over and over.

Eichhorn used Dr. Weir's minimum contact with John to undercut the physician's testimony. Dr. Weir had seen John only once, and that was in 1895. He prescribed him bromide of sodium for a headache and nothing else.

Eichhorn then moved his cross to Dr. Weir's compensation for his opinion in court.

"Are you being paid as an expert?"

Dr. Weir answered hesitatingly, "Yes, sir."

"What are you receiving for testifying?"

The witness shifted in his chair and avoided a direct answer. "There is no contract."

"Your compensation has been fixed?"

Again, Dr. Weir hesitated, shaking his head as he spoke. "There is no contract."

Eichhorn was experienced enough to know when a witness was being evasive. "Aside from the contract, has your compensation been fixed?"

Still, Dr. Weir refused to be direct. "It has been mentioned."

Eichhorn had milked Dr. Weir's evasion as far as he could. The jury was now leaning forward. If Dr. Weir wanted to hide it, then clearly the jury wanted to hear it.

Undoubtedly with a smile, Eichhorn made his question unavoidably direct. "What is it?"

"One hundred dollars a day."

There was a gasp around the courtroom. A dollar in 1903 was the equivalent of $35 in 2023. In 1903, the average farm laborer earned $1.45 per day. For six days of sunrise-to-sunset hard labor, he would earn less than $9 a week. That totaled about $450 for an entire year.

Earning $100 a day—nearly three months' wages in a single day—was unheard of. To the twelve ordinary farmers sitting in the jury box, it sounded like buying a man's testimony with an obscene amount of money.

Eichhorn poured water from the pitcher on the prosecution table into a glass. He took a sip, allowing the murmurs of outrage to spread through the courtroom. Only when prompted by Judge Smith did he continue.

When asked if the insanity or idiocy of John's relatives indicated unsoundness of mind, Weir responded in a less than definite answer: "I can't say it would. It might." The same was true of the head injuries John sustained. "I did not say that the falls produced his insanity. The falls might produce it."

Dr. Weir labeled John's unsoundness of mind as melancholia that was both intellectual and mental insanity. He described the combination of intellectual and mental insanity as involving "the cerebrum, manifested by multitudeness."

In the jury box, the twelve farmers exchanged looks. As children, none of them received more than a few months of education each year. Once they were old enough to work in the fields, their formal education stopped. They knew how to breed, raise, feed, and slaughter animals. They knew when to plant corn and beans and wheat, and when to harvest. And they could all calculate the price of their harvest to the penny. But they had no idea what Dr. Weir and attorney William Eichhorn were talking about.

Eichhorn was not oblivious to the fact that it would be difficult, if not impossible, for the jury of uneducated farmers to follow the technicalities of turn-of-the-century diagnosis of mental illness. The more technical the questions and the more obtuse the answers, the more likely the jury would dismiss the testimony as hundred-dollar-a-day jibber-jabber that was no more relevant to the trial than what was piling up in their stables to be shoveled once their jury duty was done.

Still, Eichhorn continued, showing the hours he had spent reading recent medical texts on insanity and mental illness. "Is there not stuporous melancholia and melancholia agitata?"

"Melancholia puerperal is either melancholia stuporous or agitata. There is also melancholia senile."

"What is the difference between melancholia stuporous or agitata?"

"In melancholia stuporous, it means what it says. The patient is stupid. He refuses to answer questions, refuses to look up when spoken to, refuses to go to their meals, go to bed, dress and clean themselves. In melancholia agitata, there is no accounting for what the patient may do in an agitated condition." Dr. Weir straightened his back and looked across at the jury, delighted at his opportunity to display his education and knowledge. The jury yawned back.

Eichhorn walked to the defense table and picked up three typed pages. This was his hypothetical question. It contained none of John Terrell's family history or any reference to his head injuries. It took just a bit over five minutes to read, concluding with, "I want to ask you whether, in your opinion, as a medical man, that person was of unsound mind when he did the shooting either at the road or at the doctor's office?"

Dr. Weir grimaced at facing the unexpected question. His answer was equivocal. "He might have been."

. . .

Dr. Frank B. Wynn followed Dr. Weir to the witness chair.[11] He testified to his impressive credentials, including two years of study in New York, Berlin, and Vienna and six years working in insane asylums and treating insane patients. Once his credentials were established, Sharpe read the forty-minute-long hypothetical question.

Dr. Wynn nodded after the recitation. "I believe he was of unsound mind. Might I be permitted to explain the conditions upon which I base that belief?"

The answer was no. Judge Smith sustained objections to each question Sharpe offered to elicit the basis of Dr. Wynn's opinion of insanity. The lawyer and the witness were frustrated, but there was nothing left to do but turn the witness over for cross-examination.

Eichhorn opened his cross by confirming that Dr. Wynn, too, was being paid the astonishing sum of $100 per day.

When asked by Eichhorn what type of insanity John Terrell suffered from, Dr. Wynn answered, "melancholia" and "certain peculiar spells which might resemble rather closely a form of epilepsy." When asked to "draw the line where sanity ends and melancholia begins," Dr. Wynn admitted difficulty. "If associated with a profound state of depression, simple melancholia may be without delusions. For instance, a person ordinarily of strong power and self-control giving way to tears, weeping as a woman would do."

Eichhorn looked toward the jury and produced a quizzical look on his face. "Sound persons cry when their feelings are hurt, don't they?"

"Some people do. We are all different."

"If a man once a month, on account of personal or family troubles, not delusions but real troubles, if he would go out on his premises and sit with his face in his hands and study for an hour, and do this once a month, or twelve times in a year, would that indicate such a state of intense dejection as would be a symptom of melancholia, a form of insanity?"

"I think if you did it twelve times, it could certainly indicate it. If it was done only once, I would think it indicated not altogether a normal frame of mind."

"Suppose he had been mixed up with another man's wife, and was threatened with prosecution and exposure unless he paid a considerable sum of money?"

Dr. Wynn rubbed his chin for a moment before he answered. "Well, that might worry him a good bit."

The banter between the lawyer and the doctor continued. They skirmished into the mid-afternoon about anger, frothing at the mouth, the impact of insanity of distant relatives related by marriage, and other nuances of mental illness. Meanwhile, the jury drifted off into drowsiness and inattention.

At the end of Dr. Wynn's testimony, the court ordered a short recess. Then the trial resumed.

Dr. Ernest C. Byer of Indianapolis was the third expert physician called. His qualifications were impeccable—a graduate of Bellevue Hospital Medical College in New York, postgraduate study in Munich and Paris, and eighteen years working at the Central Indiana Hospital for the Insane in Indianapolis.

Sharpe tried a different approach, asking questions in advance of the hypothetical about various abnormalities of the brain and the nature of those mental illnesses. But neither the prosecution nor the court would permit the change in tactics to elicit more information from the witness. Eichhorn objected, and Judge Smith sustained the objections.

Acknowledging that his strategy failed, Sharpe pulled out his now familiar sixteen-page hypothetical question and read for forty minutes. It is doubtful that any juror was now paying attention to this third reading of the sixteen-page question. In the end, Dr. Byer answered, "Of unsound mind."

Eichhorn pointed out that Dr. Byer was a lecturer at the Central Indiana Hospital for the Insane but did not treat patients. He reviewed John Terrell's various relationships to persons with insanity, then asked if that caused insanity.

"It might," Dr. Byer answered.

"And it might not?" Eichhorn responded

Dr. Byers nodded. "True. It might not."

"Do you think that the fact that it was reported to Mr. Terrell that his daughters had been mistreated by their husbands would tend to produce insanity?"

"It might," the doctor again answered.

Eichhorn followed with, "It might not?"

The doctor once again gave his equivocal answer. "It might not."

When Dr. Byer identified John as suffering from melancholia as a form of mental insanity, Eichhorn was quick to show off the extent of his preparation. "Do you know that mental insanity has been tabooed by all learned alienists in the country, and it is not regarded as a legitimate form of insanity?"

The witness reluctantly agreed. "Not as a distinctive form, that is correct."

When asked when John Terrell became insane, he identified a time when John was found "brooding and in tears at night" long before Melvin Wolfe rode by and taunted the old man.

"You think he was insane from that time onward?"

"Probably. That is a matter of opinion."

"On the day before the homicide, he was insane?"

"I believe so."

"Before he saw the victim pass his house, he was insane, in your opinion?"

"I believe so."

Eichhorn continued questioning about delusions and hallucinations and grieving and brooding paroxysms and suffused eyes. And the jury continued to stare blankly, seldom understanding anything being said. The crowd of courtroom onlookers waned as the hundred-dollar-a-day men droned on.

At the defense table, John Terrell turned his chair and fixed his gaze toward the back wall. As the testimony continued, John seemed to have little interest in the proceeding where his fate was being decided. Occasionally he stared at his hands, rubbing each finger in succession with his thumbs.

The afternoon dragged on with more of the same. Doctors George Fulton, Louis Severin, and E. R. Horton, all from Indianapolis, testified. After the hypothetical question was read, each testified that their opinion was that John Terrell was of unsound mind.

Eichhorn then cross-examined each, pointing out that they were receiving $100 a day for their testimony. He then bantered with each in a confusing battle of wits over melancholia, congested brain, and other maladies of the brain.

When Dr. Horton stepped down from the witness stand, Judge Smith determined that the jury had had enough for a Friday. Court was adjourned.

The following morning began with local Dr. John Dickason recalled to the stand.[12] Whether from a good night's sleep or the sight of a local doctor rather than one of the experts from Indianapolis, the jury seemed more alert. Dr. Dickason was not one of the hundred-dollar-a-day men. He was never asked the forty-minute hypothetical nor even for his opinion about John Terrell's sanity. Instead, Sharpe asked Dr. Dickason what he told John Terrell about his own experience with Melvin Wolfe.

Burns objected on the basis that whatever the answer was, it would not be a justification for murder. Judge Smith overruled the objection and signaled for Dr. Dickason to answer.

"Melvin told me that the old gray-headed bastard can pay for his bastard kid. He said that the kid belonged to Terrell himself."

"What did Mr. Terrell do in response to you telling him this?"

"He made no response. He just dropped his head and walked away."

Prosecutor Burns started his cross-examination, but he soon wished he had stayed seated and kept quiet. It was one of his few errors in judgment during the entire trial.

"Didn't you tell Terrell that Wolfe paid the bill?"

"I told him he hadn't. I told Terrell that Melvin's father paid the bill."

Behind the prosecution table, Jacob Wolfe grimaced.

"How did you come to run to Terrell with that statement, and what were you trying to do?"

Dr. Dickason showed his irritation at the question and its implication. "I wanted him to understand the feeling his son-in-law had for him."

Burns's follow-up was dripping with sarcasm. "Of course, you felt that would promote good feelings between them."

"No, sir. I thought it would put him on a basis where he could realize what kind of son-in-law he had to contend with."

Burns knew he had dug a hole, and he could only make it worse. He ended his cross-examination without further questions.

For the rest of the day, the defense continued its parade of doctors, most of them practicing in Bluffton: Dr. L. A. Spaulding,[13] Dr. L. Mason,[14] Dr. I. N. Hatfield,[15] Dr. Fred Metts,[16] Dr. H. W. Markley,[17] Dr. C. J. Blackman,[18] and Dr. T. J. Bolds.[19] It was like the defense lawyers had gone through the directory of the Wells County Medical Society and used it as a witness list.

The testimony ran the same course with each witness. First, Sharpe would extract the witnesses' qualifications, then one of the defense lawyers would read the sixteen-page hypothetical question. Newspaper reporters began timing how fast the lawyers could read the questions. The quickest time was thirty-two minutes, but late Friday afternoon attorney Robert Stine, to the relief of all, read the question in a remarkable twenty-four minutes, "hitting some of the big words at the rate of fifty miles an hour."[20]

The witness would only take a handful of words to answer: "Unsound. I would say unsound." "I think he was of unsound mind." "He was of unsound mind at the time of the shooting." "The conduct as a whole would indicate that he was of unsound mind." "Unsound."

Eichhorn then took front and center, verbally sparring over various mental illness terms and conditions. Meanwhile, John Terrell stared toward the back wall while the jury fought yawns and tried not to fall asleep.

Finally, on late Saturday afternoon, December 12, Dr. Bolds stepped down. The long and convoluted journey through the expert medical evidence had ended. Dr. Bolds was the last of the hundred-dollar-a-day men.

In reporting on the parade of expert witnesses, the local *Bluffton Evening News* cast doubt on the value of all the paid experts who testified for the defense.

Fifty years from now, taking the testimony of "experts" in important cases will be considered as we now consider the custom in feudal ages of testing of an accused's guilt or innocence by having him walk on hot plowshares. Now, even attorneys regard it as a very poor class of evidence, but they have used it for so long that it is more a matter of habit than necessity.

All the doctors subpoenaed for the plaintiff answer for the plaintiff when they are asked hypothetical questions, and all the doctors or experts of any other profession, subpoenaed for the defendant, answer his or her way when they are asked the question. The chances are if they forgot which side had called them, they would not know which way to answer the question.

Experts cost money—from $5 a day to $100 a day, the latter being the highest price ever paid for witnesses in this court so far as is known, and their testimony is worth far less than the ordinary kind.[21]

An exhausted Arthur Sharpe faced an equally exhausted Judge John Smith. "The defense rests." It seemed as if the entire room sighed in relief.

"Very good," Judge Smith said. "Mr. Burns, I assume the State will have some rebuttal witnesses."

"Yes, sir," Burns said. "We have quite a bit of rebuttal."

Judge Smith looked with irritation at the prosecutor. "Well, Mr. Burns, I cannot try your case for you, but for the sake of this jury, which has been most patient, I request that you take a good look at who is on your rebuttal list and decide whether they are indispensable for your case. I have business in my own court in Portland on Monday. We'll resume Tuesday morning at 8:30, and hopefully, we can get this case to the jury as soon as possible."

With that, Judge Smith banged his gavel to close the day's proceedings. An excruciatingly long second week was over in the longest trial in the history of Wells County. Yet, despite the fervent hopes of the judge, the lawyers, and most of all, the jurors, the case resolution was still more than a week away.

28

Rebuttal

On Tuesday morning Judge Smith reconvened court with just the lawyers present. For more than two hours, they dealt with various motions and arguments, some having to do with the testimony of the experts, others exploring the extensive jury instructions that Judge Smith would give at the conclusion of the evidence.

At eleven o'clock, the jury was summoned, and the third week of the trial began with the State's rebuttal. Between the prosecution and the defense, eighty witnesses would be called in rebuttal.[1] As opposed to the case in chief, the trial now moved briskly, with the jury sometimes hearing as many as six witnesses in a single hour.

Mary Wolfe, Melvin's stepmother, was the first to be called.[2] She glowered at John as she took the stand. Burns tried to get Mrs. Wolfe to testify about the sleeping arrangements at the Wolfe home, but Judge Smith sustained the defense's objection. She could only testify that after the shooting, none of the Wolfe family members spoke to John Terrell, nor did he speak to them. There was no cross-examination. Mrs. Wolfe huffed as she left the witness chair, never looking toward John.

Allen Boher was the next witness.[3] A fifteen-year resident of Nottingham Township, he knew both Melvin Wolfe and John Terrell. Prosecutor Burns questioned about what would become the three common targets during the State's rebuttal: John's sanity, his reputation, and his lack of belief in God and the Bible.

Boher testified that he had known John Terrell for eight or nine years and had several business dealings with him. From his experience, John was of sound mind. However, he had a bad reputation.

On cross-examination, Boher identified three people whom he heard say bad things about John before the shooting. "They said he didn't believe in the Bible, nothing of that kind. I heard he also had trouble with other men. He had a fight with John Shull. They had a racket at Oliver's saloon in Petroleum. And there was that matter with Melvin Moore."

Oscar Oliver, the owner of the restaurant in Petroleum, was recalled.[4] He testified about visiting John Terrell in jail on the Monday after the shooting. Thomas Fox and Dr. Landfair were also there. Oliver said John denied having a shotgun with him in Petroleum the night before the shooting.

Thomas Clevenger grew up with John in Randolph County and eleven years ago moved to Nottingham Township.[5] He had occasional business dealings with John but had not talked with him in the two years. Clevenger said that John was of sound mind in all their transactions.

Burns then turned to John's reputation. Clevenger testified that John had a bad reputation for being peaceable in Randolph County and Nottingham Township and a bad reputation for moral character.

The challenge faced on cross-examination was whether to let the reputation answer stand on its own and then argue it was not supported by evidence, or explore the basis of the opinion and run the risk of exposing the jury to more accounts of John's bad behavior. Sharpe chose the latter. He undoubtedly regretted his choice. Clevenger identified ten different individuals he had heard speak of John's bad reputation for being peaceable. He identified three preachers who said John's reputations for morals was bad, and "there were others. I just can't remember their names."

"What do you mean by his general moral character?"

"The general morality that he shows everybody is what I mean. My opinion is that a man's morals are made up when he believes there is an All Wise Being that rules this universe and that he serves Him."

"You mean a man's religion?"

"No, sir. There are several things. Generally speaking, that a man generally conducts himself in the right way when he is in religious services, and that he doesn't distribute literature through the country that is immoral."

Sharpe got Clevenger to agree that part of a moral reputation should include his truthfulness and whether he pays his debts, and Clevenger had never heard anything ill against John Terrell on those matters. But all Sharpe had accomplished was to pile more evidence in front of the jury about John's poor reputation in some quarters and his lack of belief in God or religion. In front of a God-fearing jury, truth and paying debts didn't seem to balance the scales against the Bible.

William Faulkner, a sixty-year-old farmer in Nottingham Township, knew John Terrell from when they grew up together in Randolph County.[6] They knew each other to "bid the time of day" when passing. "I judged him to be a man of sound mind." But when it came to John's reputation in the community for being a moral person, "I would have to answer it wasn't good. I would consider it bad."

On cross-examination, Faulkner explained, "if a man has trouble with his neighbors, I consider his reputation to be bad." Since Faulkner had heard of John having trouble with Melvin Moore and Landford Templen, he considered John's reputation bad, even though the problems were nearly twenty years ago.

Regarding moral character, Faulkner said derisively of John, "Don't belong to any church. Don't believe in God or heaven or anything else." Faulkner admitted that he had solicited John to join his church, but John refused.

"If he had joined your church, then would he not be, in your opinion, a man of good moral character?"

"Yes. If he would have lived up to the Bible."

Sharpe's cross-examination effectively exposed why Faulkner did not find John a man of good moral character. The problem was that in 1903 rural Indiana, most, if not all, of the men on the jury agreed with Faulkner.

Several more witnesses were called, testifying about their brief encounters with John Terrell and how he seemed sound of mind and cheerful in spirit. But their contact with the defendant was so minimal that it did not have any significant value as evidence.

In mid-afternoon, Burns called sixty-six-year-old Francis "Frank" Fisher to the witness stand.[7] He was a longtime neighbor of John, living only "thirty or forty rods, I guess" from John Terrell for the past twenty years. They talked several times a week, and Fisher considered himself and John friends. Fisher sat on the witness chair, uncomfortable at the prospect of answering questions in a way that would hurt his friend.

On July 12, Fisher was standing in his front yard when he heard two gunshots. He walked out into the road and saw three buggies headed north. Fisher's wife joined him and began walking toward the Terrell house. "As I walked down the road, I seen Mr. Terrell come out in a buggy and go north."

When the Fishers arrived at the Terrell house, the witness saw Lucy standing in the yard and George Harshman coming down the road from the other direction. Fisher was still at the Terrell house when, about three-quarters of an hour later, John returned, driving up to the front gate. As he got out of the buggy, Fisher heard John say to Lucy, "Your husband won't speak to you anymore. I fixed him.'"

A few minutes later, John came out of the house, now wearing his hat and coat. As he started to leave, John called to the Fishers, asking them to "stay with the folks."

Fisher testified that John had never complained to him about headaches, nor had he seemed downcast or depressed. "He was generally pretty cheerful—a cheerful kind of man."

"Based on your observation of Mr. Terrell at different times as you have testified, and having seen him on July 12 as you have detailed, from his manner and appearance, in your opinion during all the time you have known him and on the twelfth of July, 1903, was he a person of sound or unsound mind?"

Sharpe stood and objected, but it was of no use. The cat had long ago been let out of the bag. The question stood.

"I would think he was sound."

The courtroom was completely silent. Fisher was not someone with a grudge against John. He was not someone talking about reputation based on a fight nearly twenty years ago. This was not someone who had only a few business dealings with John. Fisher was a neighbor and friend who saw John several times each week. He saw John and spoke to him following the shooting. His testimony weighed heavily with everyone in the courtroom.

John remained stoic, looking only occasionally toward the witness chair. His only movement was the rhythmic rubbing of his fingers with the thumb of his right hand.

On cross-examination, Sharpe established that some ten years earlier, Fisher and John had a minor dispute over damage to crops, and more recently, a significant dispute over some oil from one of John's wells. Both resulted in Fisher paying John some money. But Fisher denied holding any grudge. Otherwise, Sharpe did little more than get Fisher to repeat the details of his encounters with John on July 12.

Frank Fisher's wife, Sarah, followed her husband to the witness chair.[8] She supported her husband's version of the event: hearing the shots, walking with her husband to Terrell's house, seeing Mr. Terrell drive out of the barn lot and head toward Petroleum, returning forty-five minutes later. She, too, heard John say to Lucy that her husband would not speak to her again.

A dozen local farmers and merchants followed the Fishers to the witness chair. All had no more than a handful of business dealings with John Terrell over the years. They stated that from their observations, John Terrell was of sound mind.

Amos King[9] and his mother-in-law, Lydia Kirkwood,[10] both testified that they saw John in his buggy stop just outside the King house, where Mrs. Kirkwood was visiting. Both heard John say, "I have killed the son of a bitch. He's deader than hell. He will never ruin any more girls." They also heard John apologize to Amos King, whose wife was ill. "He said he was sorry he had bothered anybody."

As the case moved toward the usual time for adjournment, Judge Smith announced that the court would take a short supper break, then return for an evening session. "I want to get this case done this week."

The trial resumed at six thirty and continued until nearly nine o'clock.[11]

Peter Ifer began the nighttime session. He was a neighbor who had known John ever since John moved to Wells County in 1880, but they were not close. "I conversed with him some little. Not very much." Despite their limited contact, Judge Smith allowed him to testify that John had a bad reputation and was of sound mind.

On cross-examination, Ifer agreed with Sharpe that he had never heard anyone question John's honesty or truthfulness. "His word was good."

But once again, Ifer equated bad reputation and moral character with religion. "A man would have to be virtuous and not tear down religious societies in any way. He was always fighting the church."

"Which church did he fight?"

"All of them. When they would get up a revival or anything. One time he scattered some literature from that Ingersoll fellow. I believe that wasn't just the right kind of stuff."

"You never heard John go into a church and interfere with the services, have you?"

"No, sir. I don't know as I ever did. But when he would sit through a service, afterward, he would always tackle the preacher for an argument."

Sharpe again established that the basis for the witness's opinion about John's bad moral reputation was his opposition to religious beliefs. But any time spent arguing about John's lack of religious beliefs seemed to work against John and his defense. For the twelve men in the jury box, all simple churchgoing farmers, equating lack of moral character with lack of religious beliefs likely seemed a perfectly reasonable opinion.

The State continued to call witness after witness who had occasional encounters with John, all of whom found him to be of sound mind.

. . .

The next day began particularly poorly for John's defense. Thomas Holtzapple, who at one time lived on the Terrell farm, was also in Petroleum the afternoon of the shooting. He was outside Dr. Saunders's office and saw John approaching. John said to him, "Stand back, Tom. I don't want to hurt anybody but that son of a bitch in there, and I'm going to kill him." Holtzapple gave his opinion that when he encountered John just before the shooting, John was of sound mind.

Cross-examination was limited. During the confrontation outside Dr. Saunders's office, Holtzapple noticed only that John's face was red but did not see anything unusual about his appearance. Holtzapple denied that, in the week after the shooting, he ever said John was crazy.

The next witness was Andy Books, the father of Will Books, John's son-in-law.[12] He was in Petroleum when he heard the gunshots that killed Melvin Wolfe. A short time after, he saw John leave Dr. Saunders's office.

Despite his family connection to John Terrell, Andy Books testified that John was of sound mind when he saw him shortly after the shooting. He also testified about John's reputation: "What I know of it is bad."

On cross-examination, Sharpe asked about John's appearance following the shooting.

"Why, about like a man that was mad."

Sharpe wanted to make sure the jury did not miss the answer. "I did not get your answer."

"I said like a person that was mad."

But bad news for John continued with the testimony of Byron Witmer. Witmer owned the mercantile store in Petroleum and one of the few telephones in town. He saw John riding in his buggy shortly after the shooting. John spoke directly to Witmer, asking him to call the sheriff. Witmer responded that he had already done so. Witmer then told John that he should go to Bluffton before Melvin Wolfe's family arrived in order to avoid any more trouble. He agreed, telling Witmer that he would go with Dr. Dickason.

Witmer described John as being "cool and apparently calm. His appearance was natural to me." In Witmer's opinion, John was of sound mind on the day of the shooting.

On cross-examination, Sharpe challenged Witmer's recollection. The best he could establish was that Witmer contradicted the testimony of Mrs. Dickason about what went on in her house. It would be a matter of who the jury believed—or whether it mattered.

George Bears, a twenty-one-year-old field hand who had occasionally worked for John, was the next witness.[13] He was in Petroleum on the afternoon of July 12 when he saw John drive by quickly, standing upright in his buggy, a shotgun in his hand. He then saw John go into Dr. Saunders's office and knock panels out of the interior door, then heard two shotgun blasts.

"What did you see next?"

"I saw him come out of the office. He extracted the shells from the gun and reloaded it. Then he says, 'I am going around to see whether I killed the son of a bitch.' And he went around to the rear window of the office and looked in."

Without hesitation, Bears said John was of sound mind.

On cross-examination, Bears described John's face as flushed, his hair standing on end, and his eyes "kinda wild."

Sharpe then asked the question that had to be bothering some on the jury. "You were an old acquaintance of his. Why did you not stop him?"

Bears gave a bit of a smirk. "I didn't have no business stopping him. It wasn't my place."

Sharpe continued to plow forward, eliciting little that helped John's case.

"When Terrell came out and loaded his gun, and went around the house, what was it he said?"

"He said, 'I am going around to see whether I fixed the son of a bitch.'"

"And you never said a word to him?"

"No, sir. Had no business saying anything."

Sharpe established the lack of bravery that afternoon of those standing around on the streets of Petroleum. But he did little else other than remind the jury of some of the worst testimony against his client.

Della Reed was again called to the witness stand.[14] The examination was short—only two questions. She denied that as she and Melvin rode by the Terrell house on the day of the shooting and that Melvin ever shook his fist toward John Terrell. She also denied that Melvin ever said to "hold up the little bastard."

There was no cross-examination.

The State followed up Della's brief testimony with several more witnesses who testified from their passing encounters with John that he was sane and had a bad reputation in the community.[15]

As the day was drawing close to the time to adjourn, Prosecutor John Burns stood. "The State rests."

Judge Smith turned to Sharpe. "Do you have any rebuttal?"

. . .

The rebuttal for the defense opened with a barrage of notable businessmen and longtime residents testifying that John Terrell had a good reputation in the community for truthfulness and honesty. The witnesses included prominent Bluffton lawyer Abram Simmons,[16] Studebaker Bank president Hugh Dougherty,[17] Wells County surveyor William Knuckle,[18] Wells County recorder J. H. Crum, druggist L. C. Davenport,[19] insurance agent W. W. Greek,[20] coowner of Studebaker Sale & Company James Sale, and the company bookkeeper Herbert Deam.[21] Other witnesses were longtime area farmers who also vouched for John Terrell's honesty and truthfulness.

Under cross-examination, several witnesses said they heard little, if any, conversation about Mr. Terrell's reputation and were basing their opinion on their business dealings with him. With other witnesses, the State did not cross-examine them at all.

With the end of the trial close, Judge Smith adjourned the case for the evening. The following morning, the Friday of the third week of trial, Sharpe addressed the court. "We have two more witnesses. They will be brief. The defense calls Lucy Wolfe back to the stand."[22]

A buzz went through the courtroom, but those expecting a replay of Lucy's earlier dramatic testimony were disappointed. She was called only to make a single, largely irrelevant point. Other witnesses had testified that when John arrived home after going to Petroleum, he told Lucy that her husband would not bother her any more. Lucy denied that her father said anything upon his return.

Cross-examination was not much longer. Burns tried to get Lucy to agree that she might not remember what her father said to her, but Lucy was adamant. "I know he didn't say a word to me."

"You could be mistaken."

"No, sir, I could not."

Her testimony completed, Lucy returned to her seat. Sharpe stood. "The defense recalls John W. Terrell."[23]

John shuffled to the witness stand. The days of sitting through the trial had taken a toll on how he walked. His face was haggard, his eyes downcast, but his jaw remained set. The questioning was brief. He denied ever making any statements that someone ought to shoot Melvin Wolfe.

Cross-examination challenged John about his memory of events in talking about Wolfe. John stuck to his testimony. While he did not recall all of his conversations about Melvin, he knew he did not threaten to shoot him.

With that, after three days of jury selection, fourteen days of testimony, and two night sessions, the evidence was done. All that remained were closing arguments and the verdict.

Outside the jury's presence, the judge and lawyers discussed instructions and closing arguments. "How much time do you want for closing?" Judge Smith asked.

"Eight hours," Burns said.

"Total for both sides?"

"For each side, your honor."

Judge Smith's jaw dropped. "Really?"

Sharpe joined in the request. "This is a long, complex case, your honor. We need that much time to go through all the evidence and then argue the points of law."

Judge Smith shrugged. He had never heard of sixteen hours of closing arguments in any case. But if the lawyers wanted that much time, he would not interfere. It would be up to the lawyers to keep the jury's attention and make their case.

"We'll start this afternoon."

29

A Speech to Hang Me

Since his arrest and all through the trial, John Terrell followed the early instructions from his then lawyer, Levi Mock. He did not talk with the press or business associates about his case. But as the trial moved to closing arguments, John could no longer resist. As he returned to the jail for dinner before the start of arguments, a local reporter yelled from across the street.

"Hey, John, what do you think about the closing arguments?"

For the first time, John yelled back. "That Eichhorn has it in for me. He always had ill will against me 'cause I never hired him as my lawyer. He will make a speech to hang me."[1]

Except for a few southern senators in the heyday of the filibuster and a couple of leaders in the old days of the Soviet Union, eight hours is generally regarded as too much for one person to speak. Consequently, the prosecution and defense teams divided the time they had been given. Prosecutor John Burns and his cocounsel William Eichhorn would begin and finish the arguments. The other two assistant prosecutors, who mainly had been quiet during the trial, doing research and organization work, would also get their opportunity to address the jury.

On the defense side, Arthur Sharpe would, as he had at trial, carry most of the responsibility. But Ralph Gregory from Muncie, the most experienced trial lawyer representing John, would also handle a large share of the closing. Robert Landfair and Charles DelaCour, John's business partner in the opera house, who sat silent during most of the trial taking notes and doing research, would also have an opportunity to address the jury, if for no other reason than to spare the vocal cords of the lead lawyers.

Contrary to modern trial procedures, the court allowed the sides to alternate presentations. Because the State carried the burden of proof, the prosecution would get the first argument and the last word, but in between, the court would have the parties alternate.

Court reconvened at one o'clock. Every seat was taken. But in a change from the testimony portion of the trial, Judge Smith allowed those unable to get a seat to pack three-deep around the edges and along the back of the courtroom. Latecomers were turned away, but they stayed outside in the corridors, hoping someone might leave and they could snag a seat. It was the biggest trial in the history of Wells County and everyone wanted a chance to see it.

William Eichhorn took his place, standing directly in front of the jury, and began his oration, seeking to convince the jury that John Terrell committed first-degree murder and deserved to spend the rest of his life in prison—or be hanged.[2]

As Eichhorn began to speak, the crowded courtroom fell silent as death. Like most experienced trial lawyers, Eichhorn began by effusively thanking the jury for their attentiveness and patience during the lengthy trial. More than a century later, this remains a common practice for trial lawyers. Like a carefully prepared teacher, Eichhorn went through the process of explaining that the State, not the Wolfe family, was the prosecuting party and that he was speaking on behalf of the citizens of Indiana. The trial was a serious proceeding in which the jury had to weigh the evidence and determine the innocence or guilt of John Terrell for a crime that would deprive him of his liberty or his life if he were found guilty. It was an effort to make Eichhorn sound like a reasoned, serious person whom the jury could trust. He was, after all, only seeking a fair determination under the laws of the state.

But with a thunderbolt, he went from fair-minded lawyer to what John Terrell had told a reporter he expected—a speech to hang him.

"I believe that Mr. Terrell murdered Melvin Wolfe with premeditation. The defendant waited in ambush, then shot Melvin Wolfe as he drove by. Then he pursued Mr. Wolfe as he was driven to a doctor. The defendant burst into the operating room where Mr. Wolfe lay helpless and intentionally shot Mr. Wolfe two more times, once in the back and a second shot into the dying man's head with the barrel only inches away, splattering blood and brains across the operating room. It was the most atrocious of all murders ever committed within the confines of Wells County and perhaps the entire state."

Everyone in the courtroom focused on Eichhorn except John Terrell. The defendant sat with his hands interlaced, resting on his stomach. His eyes were half closed. His face showed disinterest, never wavering, even as the prosecutor made his most personal attacks.[3]

Eichhorn explained the required element of premeditation was a "design conceived and deliberately planned and executed." However, it "does not mean days or weeks of study, but the act may follow the premeditation as rapidly as successive thoughts, as rapidly as picking up a gun and aiming it. Certainly as rapidly as a buggy ride from the Terrell house to Petroleum."

Eichhorn told the jury that there was no question about what happened on July 12. "While there are a few discrepancies on small matters—the exact words said, the precise time things happened—there is no dispute about the salient events. Mr. Terrell used his shotgun and purposely took the life of his son-in-law, Melvin Wolfe."

Eichhorn said that under the court's instructions, there was no legal justification for John Terrell's murder of Melvin Wolfe. And while the defendant had many peculiarities, none supported an insanity defense.

Without referencing notes, Eichhorn went through the litany of evidence of mental illness and deficiency in the Terrell family, finding none of it connected to John's acts. Nor were his claimed head injuries.

Next, Eichhorn turned with disdain to the medical evidence of insanity. Eichhorn had spent a good part of his nearly six months of trial preparation reading and studying the latest literature on insanity. His knowledge was so thorough that one newspaper observed, "Mr. Eichhorn was better posted on the question of insanity than were the experts." The reporter was not the only person who held that belief.

Eichhorn went through the expert testimony, always returning to the fact they were each paid the unseemly fee of $100 a day. "They were not brought all the way up here from Indianapolis and paid $100 a day by the defendant to come into this courtroom and tell you fine gentlemen of the jury that the defendant was as sane as you or I."

Eichhorn had been speaking for nearly three hours, but no one wavered in their attention to his eloquent oratory. But Eichhorn's most dramatic words were yet to come.

"This," he said, holding up the shotgun in front of the jury. "This is what the defendant carried around with him in his buggy on Saturday night before the shooting. This is what he was holding in his hand as he lay in wait in the side ditch by his home, waiting for Melvin Wolfe's buggy to come along. This is what he was waving above his head as he rode into Petroleum and yelled, 'God damn the man that stands between Wolfe and me,' and told Dick Risser to 'Get out of the way, or I will kill you, too.' This was what he was holding when he fired two shotgun blasts into Melvin Wolfe as he lay helpless on the operating table—one in the back and one in his head."

In a seat behind the prosecution table, Jacob Wolfe had remained quiet throughout the presentation. But now, great tears rolled down his face.

But Eichhorn was not done. He picked up the clothes Melvin was wearing at the time of the shooting and held them up for the jury to see. The holes showed where the steel balls from the shotgun had penetrated. The dried blood lay in huge patches on Melvin's trousers, shirt, and coat.

He described the shots that had ripped apart Melvin's clothes and body, how Melvin had suffered, how he had died in fear of the defendant. He concluded by reminding the jury of their duty to follow the law—to find John Terrell guilty of murder in the first degree and impose the sentence required by the law.

It was indeed a speech to hang John Terrell.

At the defense table, John sat unmoving and unmoved. His hands remained interlaced, resting on his stomach. His face did not change, not even a twitch, as Eichhorn described the crime or pleaded for the jury to take away John's liberty and perhaps his life.

After a break, Arthur Sharpe began his argument.[4] Although it had been some time since his last jury trial, Sharpe was polished. His style was smooth, his voice resonant, his approach reasoned, and his argument well structured. But his words did not resonate, nor did he not have the command of the room in the same way as Eichhorn.

He, too, began by thanking the jurors for their patience and expressed that he had no fear of the outcome because he knew the jury would "deal with the case as the law and evidence warranted."

As good criminal defense lawyers still do more than a century later, Sharpe emphasized that the burden of proof, even of proving John Terrell was sane, rested with the State. "The law presumes that a man is innocent until the contrary is fully proven. This applies even to sanity. And if there is reasonable doubt about any element, including sanity, then you must find that the State has failed to carry its burden, and John Terrell should be a free man."

Sharpe went into the concept of reasonable doubt at length, explaining what constituted a reasonable doubt and its importance in the law. He then went through the Terrell family history, arguing that the impact on John was more direct than claimed by the State.

He then turned to Melvin Wolfe and his treatment of Lucy and her father. While the court's instructions would tell the jury that provocation was not a justification for murder, Sharpe knew that a key to John's acquittal was convincing the jury that some men just need killing, and Melvin Wolfe was one of them, no matter what the law said.

At the defense table, John, for the first time in all the arguments, fully opened his eyes and seemed focused on the argument. Sharpe detailed Melvin Wolfe's mistreatment of Lucy and later the entire Terrell family. He reviewed all of the encounters between Wolfe and members of the Terrell family and then the final one when Wolfe yelled at John to "hold up the bastard."

"John had always cared for his family. Men had mistreated his daughters. Finally, it was too much, and his contact with reality snapped."

For the first time in his argument, Sharpe's voice filled with passion. "You gentlemen of the jury are not here only to determine the evidence and apply the law, but also to administer justice. As the Good Book says in Zechariah 7:9: 'Administer true justice; show mercy and compassion to one another.' There might come a time when, under the same provocation that Mr. Terrell had, you might be before the same bar of justice fighting for your life and liberty. As a matter of justice, as a matter of mercy, you must acquit him of these charges."

Sharpe had spoken for just over two hours. It was after six o'clock. Judge Smith adjourned for a supper break but announced that court would resume at seven thirty for a night session. He was determined that the case would be sent to the jury the next day.

The night session consisted of arguments by two lawyers who had remained largely silent during the trial. Deputy Prosecutor George Matlack,[5] a sharply handsome man with a receding hairline, large dark moustache, and heavy eyebrows, still in his early thirties, was given the role of attacking John Terrell without the reserve of an older lawyer.

"I cannot see any circumstances discussed that assuage in one iota the crime charged at Mr. Terrell's door." He set out all of John Terrell's actions on July 12 and said such showed "plans along the line of a fixed purpose." Matlack concluded, "These were not the acts of an insane man but rather a purposeful killer."

Matlack did not mention the gallows. He did not need to.

Robert Landfair,[6] the next defense lawyer to speak, had said even less than

Matlack during the trial. In his early thirties, he was the youngest lawyer participating in the trial. He was handsome with thick black hair, a moustache, and full eyebrows.

While Matlack was dynamic but sometimes overbearing in his approach, Landfair was polished and smooth, like a younger version of William Eichhorn. He focused on the legal excuses for killing another person—self-defense, protection of one's home, and insanity.

Landfair paused, drawing in the jury and showing an oratory skill far beyond his years. He was about to plant a seed that was nowhere in the instructions the judge would give to the jury. "There should be a fourth—the protection of the sanctity of a man's home and family. I refuse to believe that a jury could be found anywhere to convict a man who took a life when it was shown, as here, that he killed a person attempting to destroy the sanctity of his family."

Across the courtroom, there were murmurs of agreement.

Landfair sat down at 9:15 P.M. Judge Smith gaveled the end of the day's proceedings. Each side had used less than half of its allowed time. Arguments would resume on Saturday morning. Judge Smith determined that before the next day was done, the case would be in the hands of the jury.

Long before closing arguments resumed Saturday morning, every seat in the courtroom was taken, and the standing room was packed. John Rinehart continued the prosecution's closing arguments.[7] He was a stocky sixty-two-year-old Bluffton lawyer whose bearing reflected his German ancestry. His sandy hair, flecked with gray, was combed in a curl over his receding hairline. A thick bottle-brush moustache obscured his top lip.

Rinehart began by stating that he had known the Terrell family for more than twenty years and had "only the kindest of feelings toward Mr. Terrell and his family." But those expecting sympathy were soon disabused of the notion. Reinhart was the only prosecutor to expressly state that "the law demands the life of John Terrell."

Rinehart let the words hang in the air for a long moment before he continued. "This is not to vindicate the dead but to protect the living. This is a cardinal principle of law, necessary to the very existence of the law itself. Therefore, it is due to every citizen of Indiana that the rule in this case is enforced."

Reinhart pointed out that Melvin Wolfe was not the defendant and that "his judgment rests in a higher place than any earthly court." But the evidence before the jury showed that "Terrell acted as court, jury and executioner of Mel Wolfe." The defendant "deliberately went out and killed the man who was the object of his anger. That is not insanity. That is murder."

Rinehart made one mistake in his presentation. He took a personal swipe at one of John's lawyers, Charles DelaCour, "who, while he sits among lawyers, is in show business."

Immediately DelaCour was on his feet. Objections in closing arguments are rare, but DelaCour was angry. He rose to defend his reputation and status as a lawyer.

Judge Smith turned a stern chastising look toward Rinehart. Rinehart grimaced. He considered DelaCour a small-time show business huckster who had no business in a courtroom, but he also knew that his remark had crossed a line, at least in Judge Smith's eyes. "Your honor, I apologize for my over-exuberance. I withdraw my remarks. Please remove them from the record."

Rinehart renewed his argument, with much of its energy now drained from his words. After another ten minutes, he concluded.

There was a discussion at the defense table. After several minutes, Charles DelaCour stood and walked to face the jury.[8] "I did not come here today planning to make an argument. But as I sat being personally attacked, I changed my mind."

DelaCour defended not only himself but also the moral reputation and place in the community of John Terrell. Using his theatrical training, he eloquently painted John as an honest and successful farmer and businessman. He recounted that a parade of some of the county's leading citizens testified to John's honesty and reputation. It was only when Melvin Wolfe came into his life through his innocent youngest daughter that he found his sanity ebbing away. From the time of Wolfe's mistreatment of Lucy, an observer would see that John's actions from this point on gave every indication that he was of unsound mind.

"You are all parents. Look to yourself and how you would react should someone treat your innocent daughter as Mr. Wolfe treated Lucy. Would you maintain your sanity when you saw such treatment of your own daughter?"

After a dinner break, Charles E. Sturgis was the second of three successive defense lawyers to address the jury.[9] He concentrated on the insanity defense, detailing John's descent into an unsound mind into three layers: heredity, his head injuries, and the abuse of his three daughters by their husbands, particularly the mistreatment of his youngest and dearest, Lucy.

Sturgis was followed by Ralph Gregory, one of the most respected lawyers in eastern Indiana.[10] Gregory rose slowly, his hair unkempt and his long gray beard unfolding down his suit coat as he rose. The burden rested upon him to speak the last words to save John Terrell's life. It was the reason he was hired.

Gregory's voice resonated through the courtroom for two hours. He began with statistics regarding insanity and people of unsound minds. He then traced John's life from his birth in Randolph County to becoming a highly regarded farmer and businessman in Wells County. He spent much of the argument portraying John as a sympathetic person and one of the most important citizens of the county. He was hardworking, a good provider, a loving father to his children, and a caring husband to his wife as she dealt with the ravages of epilepsy.

Gregory recited the abuses each of John's daughters had suffered, then focused on Melvin's conduct toward Lucy. "Which one of us—which one of you—would know how you would react? Which of us could be sure we would not go insane and do the act that Mr. Terrell did? Do the right thing. Do what the law commands. Set this man free. Find him not guilty and send him home."

It was 6:15 P.M. when Prosecutor John Burns rose to give the final words for the prosecution.[11] He did not possess the aura of aged wisdom displayed by Ralph Gregory, the smooth presence of his cocounsel William Eichhorn, or even the feisty combativeness of Arthur Sharpe. Instead, he was a diminutive man with a smallish mouth and sharp nose, protruding ears, and black eyes that, behind his wireless spectacles, always seemed a bit crossed. His voice was thin and high-pitched.

But Burns had a sharp mind for facts and organization. His presentation skills were more like an effective lecturer than a fiery orator stoking passions. He had orchestrated the presentation of the State's case, and now it was up to him to guide the jury to the conclusion that would convict John Terrell of murder.

Despite the late hour, the courtroom was packed for this final act of the three-week trial.

Burns explained that the trial was not about mistreatment of John Terrell's daughters but about the "malicious, purposeful and intentional shooting and killing of Melvin Wolfe."

Pointing toward Jacob Wolfe, Burns said that the victim's father showed restraint and respect for the law throughout the trial. "He has not brought in a shotgun to this courtroom. He has not hidden in wait on the streets of this city waiting for Mr. Terrell to pass. Instead, he has sat here day after day, willing to abide by the decision of the law—the decision that you fine gentlemen of the jury will soon render." Burns contrasted Jacob Wolfe's behavior to that of the defendant who "took justice into their own hands."

As to the claim of insanity, Burns attacked the defense, saying that any link of John's actions to head injuries or mentally defective relatives was "nonexistent."

Burns turned, now pointing at John Terrell. At the defense table, John never raised his head, shifted his position, or even glanced toward Burns's accusing finger.

"What is John Terrell's defense? Is it accidental? Is it self-defense? No, gentlemen. It is that he was insane. But what is the basis of this claimed insanity? A non-existent link to distant relatives that were mentally deficient or lost their senses? But note that none of those persons were violent in their mental troubles."

Burns ridiculed the hundred-dollar-a-day experts as purchased testimony by one of the wealthiest men in the county. He encouraged the jury to believe "those good people of our county who saw John Terrell that day in Petroleum, who knew him, and said when they saw him that he was sane."

As the clock moved past eight o'clock, Burns brought the case against John Terrell to a close. "Gentlemen, we, the State, have shown that a murder was committed, that John Terrell was the murderer, and that Mr. Terrell was sane at the time the murder was committed. It is your duty under the law and the evidence to find John Terrell guilty of murder in the first degree."

There was dead silence as Burns returned to his seat. The burden the jury faced hung over the entire courtroom.

Judge Smith moved a stack of papers in front of him and adjusted his reading glasses on the end of his nose. Then, in a flat voice without modulation, he began reading the instructions to the jury. Each of the jurors focused on the judge, concentration showing on each face.

The pressure the lawyers had felt for the past three weeks faded. There was nothing more they could do. All the evidence was in. The arguments were made. The instructions had been settled, and all that remained was for Judge Smith to read them. For the first time since the trial started, the fate of John Terrell was no longer in their hands.

John Terrell sat as he had for much of the trial, his face stoic and unchanging. But the trial had taken its toll on him. A shroud of weariness passed over him. His face sagged, the lines showing deeper and darker than when the trial began.

Although no lawyer in sixteen hours of argument had mentioned it, Judge Smith instructed the jury that there were other options besides first-degree murder or acquittal.[12] He instructed the jury about second-degree murder, manslaughter, and assault and battery, all lesser offenses included in the first-degree murder indictment. The State did not argue those issues because it did not want the jury to compromise on the charge of first-degree murder. The defense did not mention it because they sought an acquittal based on insanity.

At 9:15, Judge Smith completed reading the instructions. Bailiff Adnah Hall led the twelve men from the courtroom to the room where they would determine the fate of John Terrell. As the door closed behind the jury, Judge Smith banged the gavel like a rifle shot, adjourning the court until the jury reached a verdict.

As the lawyers packed their bags and the crowd began to leave, Sheriff Johnston, as he had done each morning, noon, and night for three weeks, walked to John and put his ham-size hand on John's shoulder. He did not use handcuffs. Since John's arrest on July 12, he had never put handcuffs on his prisoner.

"Good luck, John," he said. The sheriff directed John through the crowd, guiding him with a hand on his shoulder and shouting, "Make way! Make way!"

Lucy stood, waiting for the crowd to leave before walking out. She did not want people she did not know, or even those she did, to come up and engage her in conversation. She just wanted to go back to the house of Sheriff Deputy Freeman Carlisle, where the Terrell family stayed during the trial. After the emotionally exhausting closing arguments, Lucy needed rest. But she did not expect sleep to come.

Lucy felt the tug of a hand on her arm and turned. There was Charles DelaCour, her father's partner in the opera house and one of his lawyers. "Can I speak to you for a moment, Lucy?"

Lucy looked around. The other lawyers were still gathered at the defense table, talking.

"It will just take a moment," DelaCour said.

"Very well, Mr. DelaCour, what can I do for you?"

"As you know, I have worked in the theater business much of my life. I have a theater management company, and I've done some acting, and now I'm working on getting the opera house built and up and running."

"Yes, sir. I know all about that. My pa has talked about it."

"I know Jacob Litt, the manager of McVicker's Theater. It's one of the biggest theaters in the country, right in downtown Chicago. Jacob got in touch with me and would like to make you an offer for you and your daughter to appear at the theater."[13]

Lucy was puzzled. "What on earth for? I ain't never stepped foot in Chicago."

"You're famous. People want to see you and meet you."

"Whatever for?"

"People like to meet people in the news, especially people like you. A woman wronged so badly that her father killed her husband. And a baby, too!"

Lucy's mouth dropped open.

"They'll pay you a handsome amount of money. Pay for your hotel and your food while you're there. They probably will even buy you a few new dresses at one of those fancy shops they have in Chicago. What do you think?"

It took Lucy another couple of minutes to understand what was being offered. "You mean they want me to just show up because of what happened to me? They want me to stand there like a carnival sideshow freak, like the fat man or the bearded lady? No thank you, Mr. DelaCour. I ain't interested."

DelaCour pulled Lucy closer and looked around to ensure they were not overheard. "I'll tell you, Lucy, I think you could get $300 for two weeks, maybe more.

Lucy hesitated. "I'll think about it." Then she added, "Once my pa gets out."[14]

It was shortly before ten o'clock when Sheriff Johnston had managed to weave his way to the jail with John. He shut the jail cell door behind John, both he and John expecting a long wait before they would hear from the jury.

30

Verdict

John awoke at 7:00 when the jail matron rattled his cell door with his breakfast. He ate sausages, eggs, and johnny cakes with sorghum, washed down with a half-pot of coffee. He was reading newspaper accounts of the trial when the sheriff came up the stairs and stopped at his door. It was 8:20.

"John, you need to get ready. The jury's back, and they have a verdict."

Twenty minutes later, John sat at the defense table, still wearing his overcoat with the collar buttoned up around his throat. Sheriff Johnston looked at him and wondered if he would soon have something else tight around his neck.

The jury had eaten breakfast, then shortly after 8:00, sent word they had reached a verdict. No one had expected a verdict until the afternoon at the earliest. Judge Smith sent out the bailiffs to inform the lead lawyers and Sheriff Johnston. By 8:45, when the jury walked into the courtroom, only half of the trial lawyers were present, but Burns, Eichhorn, and Sharpe were there. Only John's two oldest daughters made it to the courtroom for the reading of the verdict, and no one from the Wolfe family was present. A handful of people who heard that the jury was back sat scattered among the courtroom benches, but most of the seats were empty. Lucy was on her way but was delayed by trying to help her infirm mother. Catherine finally told her daughter to go on without her.[1]

John sat in his usual chair. But, as with most of the trial, his face did not reveal any emotion. Indeed, he did not seem to express any interest in the proceedings at all.

Judge Smith saw no reason to delay so more people could witness the event. Like the jurors, he wanted to get home. He banged his gavel, then turned to the jury. James M. Settlemyer, a fifty-eight-year-old farmer from Union Township in the northwestern corner of the county, handed a slip of paper to Bailiff Adnah Hall, who passed it to the judge.

Judge Smith read the paper, then looked up. Then, without using John Terrell's name, he announced, "Mr. Defendant, you will please stand up and listen to the reading of the verdict as the same is entered of record."

John stood, but he did not face the jury or the judge. Instead, he turned toward the back wall of the courtroom.

Judge Smith read loud and slowly so that no one in the courtroom would misunderstand the verdict. "In the matter of State of Indiana versus John W. Terrell: We, the jury, find the defendant guilty of murder in the first degree as charged in the indictment, and that he be imprisoned in the State Prison during life. Signed, J. M. Settlemyer, Foreman."[2]

Had there been a large crowd in the courtroom, or if the families of both the accused and the victim had been present, there undoubtedly would have been a commotion. But in the nearly empty courtroom, there was only mumbling. A few people dashed out of the room to spread the word of the conviction to everyone they knew.

John Terrell stood without any response. It was as if someone had just read the most recent price of corn rather than his condemnation to spend the rest of his life behind prison walls. Finally, Sharpe put his hand on the shoulder of his client. "We'll start working on the appeal today, John. We'll have a motion for a new trial on Judge Smith's desk before the week is out."

John stood silent, his face betraying no reaction or emotion. Behind him, his daughters Sally and Cinda sobbed.

Sheriff Johnston walked up to where John stood. "I'm sorry it turned out this way," he said. "I don't like doing this, but I don't have a choice." Johnston pulled out his handcuffs and, for the first time, placed them on John, keeping them loose so they did not pinch. Still, John remained silent, betraying no emotions.

Sheriff Johnston took John lightly above the elbow, guided him out of the courthouse, and headed toward the jail. A small crowd gathered to watch as they started down the front steps. John, showing his first awareness of those around him, reached up with his cuffed hands and pulled his hat down to shield his eyes and avoid the gaze of curious onlookers.

Lucy came running from along the street. She heard of the verdict from the shouts of a passerby. Tears flowed down her face. She met her father at the bottom of the courthouse steps and grabbed him in an intense hug. The sheriff did not intervene. Her words were hard to understand. "Can't," "Unfair," and "How could they?" escaped between her hurried breaths.

John patted his daughter on the head as best he could, hampered by the handcuffs. Finally, he kissed her on her cheek and softly said, "Don't cry, Lucy." Then he left and headed toward the jail.[3]

As they walked along the sidewalk, a local reporter walked up to John. "What do you think of the verdict?"

John's composure never wavered. "I can stand it. I can stand anything, but I feel sorry for my family."[4]

Outside the courthouse, news spread rapidly across the city about the "great surprise" verdict.[5] Many had expected an acquittal. Even those who thought the jury would return a guilty verdict expected the conviction to be on a lesser charge than murder, with a penalty of only a handful of years in prison. Few expected a judgment of life in prison.[6]

Prosecutor John Burns talked with local reporters. Prior to the John Terrell case, his most lauded accomplishment had been obtaining the conviction of a man who stole a horse harness from a Blackford County farmer.[7] Limited by statute to one term in office, he knew this would be his crowning accomplishment as prosecutor, the moment for which he would be remembered. Yet Burns was modest in his remarks, crediting his team of lawyers for presenting the evidence and the jury for reaching the right decision. He also had kind words for the defense lawyers. "They put up a tough fight for their client and made the State work very hard to get a conviction. But that is the way it should be." When asked about the life sentence rather than hanging, Burns's response was surprising. "I am glad that the verdict was no more severe. Had I been able to dictate to the jury, I should not have asked for a verdict of hanging. But the law required I leave that decision to them. And I believe they reached the correct one."[8]

There was no newspaper account of what John's lawyers thought in the wake of the verdict, other than that they would appeal. The fact that the jury deliberated for only a few minutes before reaching a verdict on the first ballot spoke loudly about the ineffectiveness of the defense's trial strategy.

In retrospect, the prosecution seemed to keep a sharp focus on its message of an angry father who meted out his own justice with a shotgun. On the other side, the defense often lost its way, along with the jury's attention, among meandering stories of mentally defective relatives, bumps on the head, and hundred-dollar-a-day medical jargon that no one in the courtroom could follow. Maybe there was a case to make for irresistible impulse, but it was lost among hour after hour of what the jury clearly considered useless nonsensical jabbering.

The defense also made a key strategic blunder in opening the door for reputation evidence, which showed John had engaged in other fights during his life. Perhaps more importantly to a rural Bible Belt jury, the judge allowed the prosecution to respond with evidence that John was not a moral person. He was a nonbelieving, antireligion atheist. This certainly reduced any sympathy the jury had for John due to the mistreatment of his daughters.

Did the last-minute withdrawal of Levi Mock, John's lead attorney, make a difference? It is doubtful. Clearly the trial strategy had already been established. The long line of expert witnesses and persons to testify about John's relatives had already been arranged before Mock withdrew. And the fact that the jury took less than fifteen minutes to decide the case showed that it was not a close decision, at least in the minds of those twelve men.

John returned to his cell. He spent most of the afternoon standing at the jail cell window looking out through the bars at the opera house, which was nearing completion. He directed the sheriff that he did not want any visitors, even his family.

On the streets, the verdict was all anyone talked about. Some fervently said the jury was right, while others maintained it was a miscarriage of justice and that any man would have done precisely what John Terrell did to defend his family.

By late afternoon, the *Bluffton Evening News* was on the streets, selling as many copies as could be printed. The headline was in the largest size type the newspaper owned: "IMPRISONMENT FOR LIFE"

The news story reported that the jury reached its verdict on the first ballot. After a dozen hundred-dollar-a-day men, none of the twelve jurors thought John Terrell was insane. None thought he was innocent. There was not even a single vote to convict him of a lesser crime.

It took four ballots to determine the punishment. None of the jurors voted for the death penalty. From the outset, eleven voted for life in prison, with one holdout voting for a lesser sentence. But after three 11–1 ballots, the last man yielded, and the life sentence was imposed.[9]

Late that afternoon, Sheriff Johnston brought John's supper and a copy of the newspaper in case John wanted to read it. John placed his tray on his desk, then looked at the front page, its headline screaming back at him. He handed the newspaper back to the sheriff.

"It's pretty strong," was all he said.[10]

Part IV

Into Madness

When life itself seems lunatic, who
knows where madness lies?

MIGUEL DE CERVANTES SAAVEDRA,
DON QUIXOTE

A mad man is punished by his own madness.

JOHN W. TERRELL V. STATE,
APPELLANT'S BRIEF, 68,
INDIANA SUPREME COURT

31

The Man Is a Lunatic

The verdict convicting John Terrell was not the last news before Christmas out of the Wells County Circuit Court. The day after John Terrell was convicted, Judge Vaughn filed a Petition for Disbarment against John Terrell's lawyer and business partner Charles DelaCour. The petition accused DelaCour of having "willfully misrepresented to the court his qualifications" for admission to the Wells County Bar and having "secured his admission by fraud."[1]

According to Judge Vaughn, who filed the petition himself, DelaCour falsely represented that he was a graduate of the University of Michigan Law School and licensed to practice law in Michigan. DelaCour was given five days to respond.

Falling so closely behind news of the Terrell verdict, the story grabbed headlines across the state from Fort Wayne to Indianapolis.[2] The *Muncie Morning Star* led page 1 with the headline, "ONE OF TERRELL'S ATTORNEY'S CHARGED BY COURT WITH FRAUD."[3]

DelaCour (French for "of the court") was distraught over the allegations, but ever a showman, he met with reporters to profess his innocence. He explained that his birth name was Charles DelaCour, but his adopted father's name was Cline. Since he provided the money needed for college, DelaCour registered as Charles Cline out of respect for his adopted father. The name on his diploma is Cline, but he has gone by DelaCour throughout his business life.[4]

By mid-afternoon, DelaCour was on his way to Michigan to retrieve the necessary documents to prove he was a lawyer. DelaCour returned just after

Christmas and on December 28 filed his response, along with a copy of his diploma, class graduation photo, and license to practice law in Michigan.[5] The following day, Judge Vaughn entered an order dismissing the disbarment proceedings and fully exonerating DelaCour of any wrongdoing.[6]

The five days between the verdict and Christmas was even less joyous for the Terrell family than it was for DelaCour. The Terrell family visited John daily except for Catherine, who was in bed ill with both the grippe and depression at her husband's fate. His lawyers also were regular visitors, but John had sent word that he didn't want to see his business associates. The truth was, few of them wanted to see John.

There was scattered talk in the community of seeking a pardon for John after he had served two years in prison, but Prosecutor John Burns announced that he would fight any such petition. He promised to go to Nottingham Township, where both John and the Wolfe family lived, and round up a group of men to go before Gov. Winfield Durbin to personally oppose any such petition.[7] Even jury foreman James Settlemyer got involved, telling the *Bluffton Banner* that he would join in the fight against a pardon, "and we'll get the rest of the jurors also."[8]

There was one bright spot in John's first week after his conviction. The 125 young women ("girls" as the newspaper called them) who worked at the Boss Manufacturing mitten factory were known for the huge holiday dinner they hosted before Christmas each year. Shortly before the feast was served, a committee of the women took a Christmas dinner to John in the Wells County Jail. It seemed that even though the twelve men of the jury found him guilty, the young women of the mitten factory appreciated John's defense of his daughter.

The newspaper described the meal: "A tray was heaped full of choice viands,[9] and Terrell had one of the best dinners ever served in the city." John gave a gracious thank-you to the women who brought his meal, which a reporter noted was probably "as much or more emotion" than he had showed since his arrest.[10]

On Christmas, John's daughters tried to make the day as cheerful as possible, bringing a large dinner of John's favorite foods, but he ate very little and said even less. At his request, the family shared the meal with the other men spending the holiday in jail. By mid-afternoon, the family cleaned away all the dishes and headed home. Lucy stayed a bit longer, but by four o'clock, John was by himself.

Twenty-year-old Bert Earl was a good-natured young man who worked in the oil fields and had known John Terrell for several years. He also had the misfortune of having a fondness for alcohol and a penchant for getting in trouble when drinking. Since November 21, when he decided to celebrate Thanksgiving early by helping himself to several turkeys belonging to a local farmer, he occupied one of the cells across from John.

At about seven o'clock Christmas Day, after the jail matron had cleared away the supper dishes, the jail was mostly quiet. Some men reflected on how they ended up in jail on Christmas.

Bert was lying on his cot, his eyes closed, when he heard some strange mumbling. He opened his eyes and saw John Terrell standing at the bars of his cell, his eyes fixed, talking to himself. He began making sweeping gestures with his hands. But try as he might, Bert could not understand John's words. It was like when he attended a backwoods church with a cousin, and people started talking but not in any language he had ever heard. His cousin called it speaking in tongues, but Bert thought they were all crazy. He wondered the same about John.[11]

On the last day of the year, John's lawyers filed a seventy-seven-page bill of exceptions and motion for a new trial. It detailed an astonishing list of 287 claimed errors ranging from not disqualifying certain jurors, allowing or disallowing certain testimony, and giving erroneous instructions to a typographical error in the indictment, filling in the year so that it read "18903" rather than 1903.[12] Judge Smith promptly overruled the new trial motion but withheld making a formal entry on the docket. Under court rules, the record of an appeal must be prepared within sixty days of the ruling on the motion for new trial. Because of the length of the trial, it would be impossible for the court reporters to prepare the transcript within the allotted time if Judge Smith promptly denied the motion. Consequently, Judge Smith indicated that he would formally overrule the new trial motion at the beginning of the next term in February, giving the shorthand recorders an extra thirty days. Because of this situation, Judge Smith also indicated he would not pass sentence on John Terrell sooner than February.[13] Judge Smith sent notice that he expected to be back in Bluffton about February 11 and would hear argument on the motion at that time. After that, he would hold the required sentencing hearing.

When Arthur Sharpe visited John with a copy of the pleading, John seemed uninterested. He refused the copy Sharpe brought for him. As the lawyer sat trying to converse with his old friend, John seemed unfocused and disinterested. He grunted an answer now and then but, for the most part, sat silent, staring off past Sharpe, never making eye contact.

Sharpe heard gossip in taverns, restaurants, and on the street that John Terrell would never go to prison. "He'll hang himself before he goes to prison. You just see," some wag at a local restaurant said so loudly that Sharpe could hear him across the room.

Though he would never say it out loud, after seeing John in his cell, Sharpe thought the man might be right.

As the dark and cold of January wore on, John Terrell withdrew into himself. His family noticed as they sat watching John stare blankly past them for long hours. John responded less and less to their accounts of Catherine's struggles with her illness, his grandchildren's latest accomplishments, and his son Jake's news that he and Minnie Kirkwood were getting married at the end of the month.[14]

John began taking some financial steps. In early January, he sold 115 acres in Jackson Township for $8,500.[15] He then settled the lawsuit over legal fees with Levi Mock, who represented John until shortly before the trial. Soon afterward, John sold his interest in the opera house to his son-in-law John Schott for $10,000. As a local newspaper noted, "Mr. Terrell is selling all of his property as fast as possible and converting it into ready cash."[16]

John's lawyers met with him at least twice a week to give an update on the pending motion for a new trial and tried to keep up his spirits. Each week, he withdrew more and interacted less. Arthur Sharpe became concerned enough that he stopped by Sheriff Johnston's office.

"Jim, I'm worried about John. He doesn't seem, well, he doesn't seem all there."

The sheriff took his feet off the desk and leaned forward. "I noticed. John ain't eating much, and he ain't taking care of himself. Ain't keeping himself clean."

Sharpe nodded in agreement. "He smells."

"It's getting so bad the other inmates are complaining," Johnston said. "And they ain't ones to keep themselves fresh as a daisy."

"So, are you going to do anything?"

"I don't know what I can do, Arthur. The man is convicted of murder. He's going to get a life sentence. I feel sorry for him, but there's not much I can do. I can't make him eat, and I'm sure as hell not gonna give him a bath."

"How about having one of the inmates keep an eye out and let you know what's going on when you're not around?"

Sheriff Johnston rubbed his chin. "Maybe I can get one of the boys back there to do that. Let me think about it."

"Just keep me informed on how he's doing," Sharpe said, his voice reflecting genuine concern for his longtime friend.[17]

. . .

On February 8, John's break from reality seemed complete.[18] Sheriff Johnston went to John's cell in what had become a routine of daily trips to check his well-being. "So, John, you've not been eating much, and you don't look well. How are you feeling?"

John, who had been sitting in his chair, lunged toward the bars, startling the sheriff. "I want to get this thing on a paying basis," he said, his manner frantic. "We got to get it on a paying basis."

Johnston stepped back. "What thing, John?"

"This railroad! This here damned railroad."

"What railroad, John?"

"This interurban. We got to get it on a paying basis. Yes sir. I built it, and I own it, and we need to get it on a paying basis."

Inmates in surrounding cells complained about John's ramblings until all hours of the night, talking of owning the Muncie, Hartford City, and Fort Wayne Railroad. He babbled about owning bonds of the City of St. Louis and rattled on and on and on about what percentage interest the railroad needed to pay him for his bonds.

Sheriff Johnston talked to John's lawyers and family. They told him that John had no stock in a railroad nor any bonds for the City of St. Louis.

More disconcerting than his ramblings was his conduct. Except for an occasional handful of rice or a bite of an apple, John stopped eating altogether. He did not touch his meals nor the occasional pies and cakes brought by his family. John was never a heavy man, but the weight loss on his broad frame was becoming apparent. He was pale and drawn, his skin turning gray.

A man who always cared about his grooming, he quit bathing. The issue became more troublesome, particularly to other inmates, when he started urinating in his clothes as he stood rambling at the cell bars. Sheriff Johnston noticed that John no longer used the jailhouse toilet. It was not his usual practice to track the bowel movements of inmates, but it became apparent that John was not having any.

By February 9, John had gone ten days without a bowel movement. Sheriff Johnston called Dr. Edwin R. Horton, a fifty-five-year-old Bluffton physician who acted as the jail doctor. He had known John Terrell for a few years, although he never served as his physician. Dr. Horton was shocked by what he found.[19]

John was in filthy dungarees that smelled of urine. He furiously paced across his cell. When they called out to him, he stopped for a moment. The doctor could see John's hands. They were red, scraped, and swollen. There were abrasions and bumps on his head. John's eyes showed no recognition of either man, although he knew both.

Dr. Horton spoke, but John turned away and resumed his rapid pacing.

"That's all he's been doing," a voice said behind them.

Charles Smith, a twenty-two-year-old inmate jailed on a charge of bastardy, had occupied one of the cells across from John for nearly six months. "He's been doing all of that," Smith said. "He's gone loco."

"What's he been doing?" Dr. Horton asked.

Smith snorted. "Just what you're seeing. And he stinks. He pisses hisself like some baby. Won't take a bath. And the last couple of weeks, he's been pacing all day and all night, mumbling as he goes. Don't make no sense. And he don't seem to sleep at all. And you see those bumps and cuts?"

Dr. Horton nodded.

"He's been climbing up those cell bars like a monkey. And he gets up near the top and bangs the bars with his hands and his head. I don't know how he does it, hitting his head like that. You'd think he'd knock hisself out."

"When did all this start?" Dr. Horton asked.

"Not long after the trial, right after the first of the year. Now he don't eat. Don't take care of hisself. Hell, he don't even know people anymore."

Dr. Horton watched John for several more minutes, then turned to the sheriff. "I want to get Dr. Cook to look at him this afternoon. I don't deal much with this and don't know anything about all that stuff at trial, but I think this man has gone insane."

That night, Dr. Horton's thoughts that John had gone insane were reinforced. Shortly after ten o'clock, several inmates woke to a smell of smoke. It took a couple of minutes before the reality hit that the jail was filling with smoke. "Oh, hell!" Bert Earl yelled out from his cell. "That crazy John is burning the whole goddamn jail down."

A pandemonium of yells rang out. The words "Fire!" finally caught the attention of Freeman Carlisle, serving as the deputy on jailhouse duty that night. Carlisle took his time until he, too, smelled the smoke making its way downstairs. Carlisle ran up the stairs, grabbing a bucket of water that Sheriff Johnston kept on each floor, just in case someone fell asleep while smoking.

"Oh, shit!" he yelled as he saw a stream of black smoke rolling out of John's cell. "What have you done, old man?"

Carlisle unlocked the door and flung it open. John sat on the floor, the door to his safe standing open. In front of him, fire licked over the top of a tin basket meant for waste paper. Carlisle threw the bucket of water into the tin basket, extinguishing the flames, the black smoke turning white.

"Jesus Christ, John. You nearly burnt the whole jail down."

John didn't move. His gaze did not stray from the tin basket. The smoke cleared, revealing the burnt remnants of large-denomination currency— twenties, fifties, even hundreds. In his whole life, Carlisle had never seen a hundred-dollar bill. Now he was looking at the burnt remains of perhaps a dozen. There were also the remnants of bills of sale, contracts, and even a deed.

"Oh, John, what on earth have you done?"

The old man kept sitting on the floor, staring off at a spot only he could see.[20]

The next day, the news of John's condition broke in the *Bluffton Evening News*:

JOHN TERRELL RAVES IN HIS CELL A MANIAC

John W. Terrell, under conviction in the Wells county jail of the murder of his son-in-law, now paces the corridors of the jail a raving maniac. For some time, Terrell has been showing evidences of insanity and he has been carefully watched.

The denouement came last night when Mr. Terrell lost the last shred of reason and became a maniac in every sense of the word. During the nighttime, he entered his safe where he keeps his private papers and took from the hiding place several valuable papers, the exact contents of which are unknown....

This morning Drs. Cook and Horton were called to the jail in attendance upon him. Dr. Horton stated that beyond doubt John Terrell was now a person of unsound mind and not only that, but he was stark raving crazy....

Lucy Terrell filed a petition with Magistrate M. W. Walbert, the same man who held John Terrell's arraignment on murder charges. He held an inquest on February 10 but after researching the law, determined that he had no jurisdiction and refused to issue a report.[21]

With the news of John's slide into insanity, he was again the topic of nearly every conversation throughout the county. "It's all horse manure," a local farmer summed up. "He's got money, and he's just trying to scam everybody." Others thought the pressure of the trial and impending imprisonment had finally caused the old man to lose touch with reality.[22] It was a controversy that would continue until the day John Terrell died.

Reports of John's condition continued to worsen. Dr. Horton and Dr. Spaulding were able to get John to take an opiate, inducing his first sleep in over a week. But still he ate almost nothing, talked to no one, and did not recognize his family members. He was growing so thin and gaunt that friends and Sheriff Johnston worried that if there was not a change, John would die within days. The local newspaper reported that "Those who have seen him say that a look at him will convince the most incredulous that there is no shamming on Terrell's part."[23]

But not all were convinced. Deputy Prosecutor George Matlack vowed that the prosecutor's office would do all in its power to show that John was still of sound mind and only "shamming" his insanity.[24]

Thirty miles away in Portland, the county seat of Jay County, Circuit Judge John Smith, the special judge in the Terrell murder trial, saw the reports of John's insanity in the local paper. He knew this would add complexity to what should be the routine formality of pronouncing a life sentence for a man convicted of first-degree murder.

If Judge Smith had not long ago decided that nothing in the murder case of John Terrell was going to be simple, it was made clear when he received a phone call from Indiana governor Winfield T. Durbin about the Terrell case.[25]

It was impossible for anyone who read the state's leading newspapers not to be aware of the John Terrell case, including Governor Durbin. The murder and trial had been prominently covered in Indianapolis newspapers, which the governor intently read.

The issue of insane inmates was something of interest to the governor. Just over a year earlier, Governor Durbin, in his Biennial Message to the Indiana General Assembly, had noted "an embarrassing condition at the Indiana Prison because of the number of insane inmates, with no place for detention except in the prison cells." In his message, he proudly announced that the problem of these insane convicts was "solved" by the construction of a special unit at the state prison. He did not need the highly publicized case of John Terrell making a mockery of his announced accomplishment.[26]

The governor encouraged Judge Smith to use every means to keep John Terrell from being sent to prison if he was as incapacitated and insane as reported.

The governor's call to Judge Smith followed a call to Wells County sheriff Robert Johnston. The governor probed Sheriff Johnston on John's condition and if the situation was as bad as reported in the press. When informed that John's condition was as bad as reported, Governor Durbin responded that an insane man should not be sent to prison and that local officials "should be very careful in such matters."[27]

Neither Judge Smith nor Sheriff Johnston likely were pleased with the governor intruding into the work of the courts. Local newspapers were outraged when they learned of the call. One commented, "It is the general consensus of opinion that the governor is considerably overstepping himself."[28]

But the phone calls were only the first steps in Governor Durbin's involvement in the John Terrell case.

Judge Smith arrived in Bluffton on February 18, a week later than expected due to the birth of his newest son.[29] The planned purpose of the hearing was the defense motion for a new trial and sentencing of John Terrell. Judge Smith had already signaled that he would deny the new trial motion, but the defendant's declining condition raised questions about how the case would proceed.

When Judge Smith walked into the courtroom at 1:30, he immediately noticed that one person was missing—John Terrell. Before any business was transacted, Judge Smith made clear that the defendant should be present.[30]

John's lawyers, Arthur Sharpe and Charles Sturgis, both said they did not think it was possible. Sharpe explained that John was not physically or mentally in condition to be in court. "He is unable to walk and has not his right mind."

The judge noted that he was sympathetic to the defendant's condition, but he insisted that John be present. When Sturgis suggested that the court could visit John in jail, the judge bristled. "I do not feel it the duty of the court to visit the prisoner in jail," Smith said, then issued an order that the defendant be brought to court.

While arrangements were being made for John to be transported to the court, Sharpe presented the court with a Suggestion of Insanity Occurring Since Verdict,[31] accompanied by seven affidavits, including three from local doctors, three from inmates in the jail, and one from Sheriff Johnston.

William Eichhorn, speaking for the prosecution, opposed allowing the Suggestion of Insanity to be filed. "There is no provision of state law allowing the filing of such a suggestion or providing what the court should do with it."

Judge Smith allowed the Suggestion to be filed. He then spent time reading through the submission while waiting for John Terrell to arrive. The affidavits detailed John's aberrant behavior over the past several weeks, including not eating, not sleeping, banging his head on his cell bars, not recognizing family and friends, talking incoherently, and not having a bowel movement for nine days.

It was near 3 P.M. when John Terrell was brought before the court. It was the first time he had been seen in public since his trial, and his appearance sent a palpable shock through the courtroom. He walked with an encumbered gait, his left leg dragging behind. The sheriff and a deputy held him upright, directing him to a seat.

Judge Smith was struck by the appearance of John Terrell. The man who had always been clean and well dressed sat as a shell of a man, his clothes rumpled and hanging loosely on his frame, showing the effects of a rather dramatic weight loss. His eyes were glazed and unfocused, and his arms flailed in endless circles. It was evident that he did not understand his situation.

With John in place, Judge Smith moved quickly to the Motion for a New Trial. He promptly denied it without allowing argument.

Under normal procedures, he would have proceeded to imposing the life imprisonment sentence imposed by the jury, but he didn't. Instead, he announced that it was not proper to pass judgment on the defendant when clearly the proper place for him was in an asylum. Perhaps surprisingly, the lawyers on both sides agreed. The question was, how could it be lawfully done?

After extensive discussions of how to deal with the situation, Judge Smith requested that the lawyers research the matter and bring him their suggestions when court resumed the next morning.

On Friday morning, February 19, following a night of research, the court ordered a special jury immediately empaneled to determine whether John Terrell was insane. A panel of twelve men was quickly assembled and by late morning, a second trial began, this time solely on the issue of John's current mental state.[32]

Dr. Edwin R. Horton and Dr. Leander Spaulding testified. Both recounted John's behavior and the alarming deterioration of his physical health. Dr. Goodin made his opinion clear. "The man is a wreck, not only mentally but physically as well. I honestly believe that he will not be alive two months from now."

"What is your opinion as to Mr. Terrell's current mental state? Is he sane or insane?"

"Whether he was insane when he did the shooting is more than I can say, but there is no doubt about it now. The man is a lunatic."

Sheriff Johnston testified about John's increasing detachment from reality and deteriorating physical condition. He said there was no doubt that John had "just gone plumb crazy."

Following Sheriff Johnston, three inmates described their observations of John's outlandish behavior. Each said he "had no mind."

On Saturday morning, February 20, the jury returned and deliberated only three minutes before reaching its decision. "We, the jury, find that the defendant John W. Terrell, since the verdict returned in the case of State of Indiana vs. John W. Terrell, has become, and is now, insane. John K. Beatty, Foreman."[33]

John Terrell was insane. The question now was what to do with him.

Judge Smith was still unsure of the long-term answer, but he announced his short-term order. He withheld sentencing and remanded John to the custody of Sheriff Johnston. Before doing so, Judge Smith called the sheriff in front of the bench. He impressed upon Sheriff Johnston that John was not a well man and that the sheriff had to make arrangements for medical care and to keep a close watch on his prisoner.[34]

The nearby *Huntington Herald* ran a story summarizing the fate of John Terrell:[35]

> Even the worst enemies of John Terrell could not have wished him the fate that has befallen him. Nine months ago, he was a prosperous farmer worth $35,000 or $40,000, had a good home and had every prospect of spending his old age in luxury and peace.
>
> In one short hour, all this was wiped out by the slaying of his son-in-law, Melvin Wolfe, to avenge the wrongs to his daughter, Lucy, and insults to himself. Since that act, justice has taken from him liberty for life. The loss of his liberty has caused him to part with his property and had broken up the home, and he had been deprived, perhaps mercifully, of his reason.
>
> John Terrell has always been an atheist, and unless his belief has changed materially, his hopes for a future life are as dark as the prospect for a happy life on earth. . . . Compared to what has befallen him, a death sentence would have been much more preferable to the sentence he received.

But for John Terrell, the worst was yet to come.

32

Confined until Cured

While Judge Smith and the lawyers considered what to do with John, the Terrell family made its own decision. On March 15, Lucy signed a petition prepared by Charles Sturgis to declare John insane. The one-page document was simple and made no mention of the criminal case.[1]

"Said John W. Terrell is now a person of unsound mind and is incapable of managing his own estate. Wherefore petitioner prays the court for the appointment of a guardian of the person and estate of said John W. Terrell."

The previous November, Judge Edwin Vaughn had thought he had rid himself of John Terrell and his problems with the appointment of John Smith as special judge to hear the murder trial. But as he sat at his desk looking at the one-page filing, it occurred to Judge Vaughn that John had become his proverbial bad penny. The judge looked at his calendar and wrote a note to his bailiff to set the matter for a jury trial on May 18.

Yet another jury would determine if John Terrell was of unsound mind.

While Prosecutor John Burns had delivered a closing argument against John Terrell with hopes of a life sentence rather than hanging, it was not so with Deputy Prosecutor George Matlack. He and John Rinehart took only minor roles in front of the jury during the trial, but they had been the most strenuous in their arguments, trying to convince the jury that John Terrell should go to the gallows.

Now Matlack seethed. John was fooling them all—the sheriff, the doctors, a jury, and maybe even the judge. Matlack believed that John was again trying to get away with murder, and if he did nothing, Terrell would succeed.

On the last day of March, Matlack caught the interurban to Marion, a booming industrial city thirty-five miles southwest of Bluffton, where his friend A. E. Gibson was the managing editor of the *Marion News-Tribune*. Matlack had an idea to expose what he was sure was the scam John Terrell was pulling on the court and the entire Wells County community. Matlack thought Gibson could help.[2]

Matlack explained his scheme to Gibson. "I want to get a good detective or maybe a reporter. Someone who knows how to observe people and who can be trusted. I want the person to get thrown in jail and see what's going on with John Terrell."

Gibson was intrigued by the idea and sensed a big news story. But he wasn't willing to get a reporter thrown in jail. "Let's go over and talk to Police Chief White. He might be able to help."

After Matlack explained his plan, Chief Bert White was enthusiastic. He promised to find a good man for the job.

The following Saturday, Matlack returned to Marion, where Chief Bert White introduced him to Harry Linville, a detective in the Marion Police Department. "This is your man," White said. The three men discussed the operation and put the plan in motion.

The following Monday, Linville disguised himself as a tramp and rode the evening Clover Leaf train to Bluffton. He quickly found a dingy tavern along the railroad tracks in a shoddy section of Bluffton. Linville drank several beers but exaggerated the effects, becoming loud and annoying several customers. He left the tavern at about eleven o'clock, swaying as he walked toward downtown, loudly singing the bawdiest songs that he knew.

It wasn't long before a Bluffton officer walking his beat spotted Linville and quickly arrested him for being drunk and disorderly. The next morning, Linville was brought before Bluffton mayor John Mock, son and partner of Levi Mock. Mock's responsibilities as mayor included acting as a justice of the peace, and he promptly sentenced Linville to nine days in Wells County Jail.

Linville was disappointed that he was placed on a different floor in the jail than John Terrell. For four days, he tried to catch glimpses of Terrell through rivet holes and cracks in the wood floor of his cell. Linville chatted with the jail nurse and tried to listen to conversations whenever John was visited by his lawyers, doctors, or family. He could not hear the conversations well enough to discern what was said. Finally, on Friday afternoon, after four days in jail, Matlack retrieved Linville from his cell and again took him to Mayor John Mock, where he explained the situation and asked Mock to release Linville.

"Did John Burns know about this stunt?" Mock asked, his tone sharp.

"No, he didn't."

"And Sheriff Johnston didn't know either, did he?"

"No, sir. I thought it was best to keep this quiet."

"I guess you did. You just took it upon yourself to go behind the prosecutor's back and snoop on Sheriff Johnston and his jail. I'm going to make sure the prosecutor knows what you did. You're lucky I'm going to let Mr. Linville out of jail, and don't order him locked up for another thirty days. And you with him."

Later that day, Prosecutor Burns sent word to Matlack's law office that he wanted to speak to him. In all his time working with Burns, Matlack had never seen him so angry. "Sheriff Johnston is probably the most popular elected official in this county. Now I'm not running for another term as prosecutor, but I may want to run for something else, and I don't want Jim Johnston telling all his supporters not to vote for me because I can't be trusted."

Matlack sat across from Burns, his own anger growing. But he remained silent.

"I have to work with the sheriff!" Burns was now nearly shouting. His face glowed red. "We see each other every day. In case you haven't noticed, I have to prosecute everyone he or his department arrests. And now you pull this? How am I supposed to look him in the face?"

Matlack spoke through clenched teeth. "That John Terrell is scamming everybody into thinking he's crazy. I thought this was the best way to get the goods on him."

"Get the goods? That's hogwash! None of your detective's statements are worth anything in court. I read his notes. He wasn't even on the same floor as John Terrell. He heard whispers, but he didn't know what was being said. Hell, he doesn't even know who was talking. When he sees John, it's through a rivet hole. If you ever do something like this again, I'll find another lawyer to serve as deputy prosecutor."

George Matlack walked out of John Burns's office. He was livid. After thinking on it for several nights, Matlack sent word to Linville. The detective took an early morning train to Bluffton. With Linville's notes in hand, Matlack and Linville walked into the office of the *Bluffton Banner*. They had a story to tell. Matlack knew in his bones that John Terrell was faking, and with the help of the *Bluffton Banner*, he was going to make sure the rest of the county knew too.

On April 20, half of page three of the *Bluffton Banner* was taken up with a single story about the detective spying on John Terrell in the Wells County Jail with the headline: "A DETECTIVE WATCHED TERRELL AT THE JAIL"

But the editor at the *Banner* wasn't entirely committed to the story, so he included a disclaimer: "The Banner has no apologies or brags to make in its interest in the matter, but believe it has simply gone on proper lines to get the news. The Banner has no comments to make. The facts are presented here, and the reader can draw his own conclusions."[3]

The article reported Linville's observations by date and time. He described a darkened jail cell where John Terrell was housed. His daughter, Lucy, was a frequent visitor, bringing meals to him. He heard Lucy tell the jailhouse nurse that John had not eaten much, but Linville reported that, contrary to reports of the elderly man not eating and losing weight, he would always "eat and drink heartily" and always had an empty plate.

Linville was on a separate floor than John, but on the first night, about 2:30 A.M., "I heard a man walking through the corridor, and by looking through a rivet hole in the iron floor, I recognized John Terrell. He was walking erect and looked very sane. He stroked his head occasionally and sometimes twisted his mustache."

On the second day, Linville "learned from one of the inmates that Terrell's daughter, Mrs. Books [Lucinda], came to see him, and she had a talk with her father." The inmate told Linville that he pretended to be asleep. Mrs. Books looked in at the inmate and satisfied herself that he was sleeping. She "then went into the corridor and got a stool and went into her father's cell and held a whispered conversation with him. Someone came into the residence part of the jail, and Lucy, who was in the jail part, called out to her sister, 'Lucinda, come out of there.' And Mrs. Books rushed out into the corridor."

Later that same day, John's wife visited the cell and "brought a basket of eatables and other stuff." Linville reported that "I listened very closely and heard a seemingly whispered conversation," although he admitted that the jailhouse nurse was talking to Linville at the same time, and "the nurse made so much noise I could not hear very well."

Very early on Friday morning, Linville had his most prolonged encounter with John Terrell. He saw John walking through the jail corridor, apparently a regular nighttime occurrence. He observed John banging his head, swinging his arms wildly, and rolling on the floor, all of which Linville attributed to be a show "for my especial benefit."

"I tried to engage him in a conversation, but he would not answer me. He sat looking wildly about, opening and closing his eyes. He would not look directly at me, but cast his glances four or five times to the side, and looked in every other direction."[4]

The article heightened the debate about John's sanity but changed few minds. Linville was never called to testify at any of the proceedings on John Terrell's sanity. Ultimately, the article had no impact on events other than the volume of arguments held in taverns, in restaurants, and around pickle barrels in general stores throughout the county.

In early 1904, Governor Durbin began his fourth and, under the Indiana Constitution, last year in office. He started receiving letters and petitions to pardon John Terrell, followed by petitions opposing a pardon.

Governor Durbin was a Civil War veteran who returned to service in the Spanish-American War and a successful businessman. In the era of Teddy Roosevelt's presidency, Durbin had a sparkling progressive Republican reputation. He was responsible for establishing the first juvenile court in Indiana. He promoted a statewide highway system to take advantage of Indiana's centralized location and the burgeoning new automobile industry.[5] In the wake of a smallpox epidemic, he pushed through legislation to improve the effective use of quarantines, stating, "The health of our people should be paramount to all other considerations." In light of the increasing use of guns in crimes, he pushed for restrictions on the sales of firearms that could be concealed.

Most of all, Governor Durbin was known for enforcing Indiana's 1901 Anti-Lynching Law, aimed primarily at groups known as "White Caps," responsible for most of the sixty-eight lynchings that occurred over the past half-dozen years, mostly in southern Indiana. Durbin implemented his power under the law, removing one sheriff who did not provide sufficient protection for a prisoner who was lynched. Nearly overnight, the lynchings stopped. From 1902 until August 7, 1930, when two Black men were lynched in Marion on the courthouse square, there were no lynchings in Indiana. There have been none since.[6]

When news reached Durbin that a jury found John Terrell had gone insane after his conviction and that the judge was withholding sentencing for the time being, Durbin's interest in the case magnified. So, too, did the letters and petitions he received demanding and opposing a pardon for the convicted man.

In the third week of April 1904, Durbin and Attorney General Taylor had one of their regular lunches in the dining room at the Columbia Club on Monument Circle. Durbin told his attorney general that he was concerned about the case. "What's bothering me is that I stood in front of the legislature not long ago and bragged about how the problem of insane inmates was solved. So, if this Terrell fellow gets sent up to Michigan City and it doesn't work out up there, I'm going to have a lot of egg on my face."

"You're not running for re-election, so does it matter?"

"It does to me. I understand that the judge set the case for sentencing before the month is out. I want you to do some research about what I can do if he goes ahead and sentences this Terrell fellow. I want a recommendation from you."

"When do you need it?"

"End of the week."

On Thursday, April 28, Judge Smith reconvened the lawyers at the Wells County Courthouse for a sentencing hearing. John Terrell was carried "like a dead man feet first" into the courtroom by two deputy sheriffs.[7] They placed him in a chair a few feet from the defense table. The jailhouse nurse and Dr. Cook sat next to him. Throughout the ninety-minute proceeding, John sat motionless, head nodding, eyes closed.[8]

Once again, Arthur Sharpe presented a Suggestion of Insanity Occurring Since Verdict and filed a Motion in Arrest of Judgment. Judge Smith promptly overruled them without argument. It was obvious that he had already made up his mind.

Judge Smith somberly announced his decision.[9] "I've heard all these arguments before, gentlemen. I've researched this issue every way I know how, but I cannot find a clear answer to what should be done when a person goes insane after conviction but before sentence. I have decided that, without any law saying otherwise, I must go forward with sentencing. That is what I'm going to do. Defense motions are overruled."

Judge Smith turned toward John Terrell and, as required, asked the defendant if he had anything to say before sentencing. John remained speechless, slumped in his chair, his eyes closed, his mouth hanging open.

Sharpe stood up. "Your honor, this man is incapable of responding. He is clearly of an unsound mind. He has no sufficient mind to understand what is going on. Because of his insane condition, I object to passing sentence at that time."

"I understand, Mr. Sharpe. Your motion is overruled. We will proceed with sentencing." Judge Smith read from a sheet of paper in front of him. "Court renders judgment on the verdict of the jury. It is therefore ordered, adjudged and decreed by the court that the defendant, John W. Terrell, for the offense by him committed, be confined in the State Prison of Indiana during life. The Sheriff of Wells County is hereby charged with the due execution of the foregoing judgment."

John showed no indication that he understood the judge's words or even heard them.

Word reached Governor Durbin late Thursday that John Terrell had been sentenced to life in prison and would soon be transported to the state prison in Michigan City. The following morning, he met with Attorney General Taylor in the governor's office.

"Will, what do you think I should do?"

"Nobody will fault you for letting the case run its course in the courts," Taylor said. The answer was not well received. Taylor leaned forward in his chair. "The sheriff up there could be taking him to the State Prison as early as Monday, so if you're going to do something, you need to do it now.

Durbin shook his head. "I don't want to send an insane man to prison, but I'm not going to pardon him, either."

Taylor nodded. "We could parole him to the asylum, with the condition that if regains his sanity, he gets sent back to prison."

The governor sat in silence for a moment, thinking. Finally, he spoke. "I like that idea. What do I need to do?"

"First thing is call up the head of the asylum over in Richmond and get him to agree to take Terrell. If he does that, notify the sheriff so he doesn't load Terrell up to take him to Michigan City."

Governor Durbin nodded. He picked up the phone and had the operator call the East Haven Asylum in Richmond. His phone conversation with Dr. Samuel Smith, superintendent of East Haven Asylum, was short. It was unlikely that a man appointed to his position by the governor would refuse his request. After he hung up, Governor Durbin reached into a drawer and pulled out a sheet of official stationery. He handwrote a message to be sent by telegram to Sheriff Johnston:[10]

Indianapolis, April 29

To: Sheriff Wells County

Acting on the advice of the Attorney General, I will tonight send you an order for the removal of Terrell to Richmond Insane Hospital where I have made arrangements for immediate admission when proper lunacy proceedings have been had.

Winfield Durbin, Governor.[11]

The next day, in late afternoon, a courier from the governor's office arrived in Bluffton by train. He carried a formal typed order signed by the governor, which he delivered to Sheriff Johnston.[12] The order stated: "I herewith enclose the necessary document authorizing you to take John W. Terrell to the Eastern Indiana Hospital for the Insane, that he may be there confined until cured, and, when cured to be taken to the State Prison, unless otherwise ordered by me."

Governor Durbin's order was not well received in all quarters. The *Fort Wayne Sentinel* ran a front-page story that was more an editorial. Headlined "Governor's Power Doubted," the newspaper stated that "the power of the governor is only to pardon and not to interfere with the execution of the orders of the judiciary."[13] Likewise, the *Jeffersonville Evening News* headline declared, "A STRANGE CASE: Convicted Murderer, John W. Terrell, the Subject of Executive Interference."[14]

But not all comments were critical. The *Indianapolis Star* quoted an editorial in the *Huntington Journal:* "Taking life is an extremely serious matter, but Terrell did the world a great service when he put the young hoodlum out of it."[15]

Despite the controversy, Governor Durbin's order was unchallenged in the courts by Judge Smith or Prosecutor Burns.

Three weeks after the governor's order sending John to the insane asylum, the guardianship proceeding filed by Lucy was tried in Judge Vaughn's court with a twelve-man jury. Two of John's daughters, Lucy and Sally, testified, as did Dr. Leander Spaulding, Dr. Samuel Godin, and several jail inmates. The jury was out for five minutes before returning a verdict that John Terrell was of unsound mind and required the appointment of a guardian.[16] It was the second jury that had found John Terrell had gone insane after the verdict in his murder trial.

Judge Vaughn appointed a local businessman with the peculiar name of Pleasant Stanley as guardian with control of John's assets.[17]

If Governor Durbin thought he was done with the John Terrell matter when he issued the order sending him to the East Haven Asylum in Richmond, he was wrong. As Durbin's term as governor was winding down, petitions to grant or deny a pardon to John Terrell inundated his office.[18] One prepared by John's attorneys carried over four thousand signatures. Countering that petition were letters prepared by Prosecutor John Burns and signed by prosecuting attorneys from several surrounding counties.[19]

Every day letters arrived pleading for a pardon because John had only done what any upstanding father would do. These were countered by letters that said John was lucky he was spared the rope and should never be let out of prison.

On January 3, 1905, less than a week before he left office, Governor Durbin notified Arthur Sharpe that he would not pardon John Terrell.[20] Any reprieve would have to come from the new governor, Frank Hanly. But the incoming governor was a prohibitionist who believed that forgiveness rested with the Almighty, not the governor.[21]

John's only hope for freedom now rested with the Indiana Supreme Court.

33

Reversal of Fortune

Insane asylums in the early 1900s were houses of terror, nothing short of hell on earth. Mental illness was treated with the same fear and lack of understanding as leprosy. Psychiatry was in its infancy, practiced by the oddly named "alienists," who sought to observe and care for patients suffering "mental alienation."

The hell of mental asylums was exposed to the nation in 1887 through an inexperienced but determined young woman reporter named Nelly Bly. Working for Joseph Pulitzer's *New York World*, Bly feigned insanity and was admitted to the notorious Blackwell Insane Asylum for Women. Her articles, headlined "Ten Days in a Madhouse," detailed filthy conditions, inedible food, ice-water baths, and vicious nurses who choked, beat, and harassed patients.[1]

Mental institutions were human warehouses of emotional suffering beyond comprehension. Doctors could do little besides diagnose patients with melancholia or mania, then look away. There were no antidepressants, anti-anxiety medications, stimulants, antipsychotics, or mood stabilizers. Instead, there were straitjackets, bed restraints, and locked padded cells. Once admitted, three-fourths of the inmates were destined to live out their lives in institutions.[2]

Still, the Eastern Indiana Hospital for the Insane in Richmond, more commonly called East Haven, was better than most, reflecting some of the reforms since Nelly Bly's articles. It was built in 1890 on 390 acres.[3] Much of the asylum was so beautifully landscaped that area citizens often picnicked on its grounds. Most inmates resided in cottages rather than oversized central dormitory rooms.[4] The institution had its own orchestra and a baseball team.

Patients roamed the day rooms, babbling incoherently. Some could not sleep and spent the night pacing. Others screamed out. Yet others were subject to fits and violence and kept in locked cells. On the whole, if forced to make a choice, most people would choose prison over a mental hospital.

On May 3, 1904, Sheriff Johnston and Deputy Carlisle boarded the train with the jailhouse nurse and John Terrell. Upon arrival at East Haven, Dr. Samuel Smith, the superintendent, gave John an examination, completed the admission process, and assigned him to a locked room on the second floor of the men's cottage.[5] It was where he would spend the next four and a half years.

John's incarceration in the Eastern Indiana Hospital for the Insane did not quiet the Wells County community debate about whether he was insane or scamming people to avoid prison. In December 1904, the *Bluffton Banner* reported on an unnamed woman from Wells County who had spent several months in the East Haven Asylum. She said John Terrell was participating in all the social activities at the asylum and was sane.[6]

The story set the gossip in Wells County ablaze with reports that John was of sound mind and had pulled off a scam to keep himself out of prison. The *Muncie Morning Star* tracked down the woman and interviewed her for a more extended account. Mrs. Jesse Day was ordered to East Haven in April, just before John Terrell was sent there. She remained for six months before returning to her home in Nottingham, not far from the Terrell farm.

Mrs. Day's interview with the Muncie paper did not leave a clear picture of John's sanity. She saw John at the weekly dance in the hospital's ballroom. It was the only place where she saw John. The newspaper reported their interview with Mrs. Day.

"About five weeks after he arrived, I saw John Terrell at one of the weekly dances in the ballroom. The first three times he attended, he did not dance. He sat very quietly, speaking to no one. About the third or fourth week, I saw him dancing with one of the attendants. He never danced with any of the patients. He did not seem to know much about dancing. He was very awkward. He drugged [sic] both his feet, shuffling them over the floor rather than walking."

"Did Terrell seem to enjoy the dances?"

"No. He seemed to look wild out of his eyes and not know where he was or what he was doing."

"Did Terrell talk to anyone?"

"I never heard him talk except to ask one of the attendants to dance with him."

"How did he look?"

"He was very pale and much thinner than when I knew him in Nottingham Township. He had a peculiar look out of his eyes. Something like an idiot. Rather wild. He seemed lost and did not know what to do."

"In your opinion, is Terrell insane?"

"He's not right. I think he could come home, but if they did not watch him, he will kill himself."[7]

The saying "out of sight, out of mind" seemed to apply to John Terrell in 1905. His name seldom appeared in local newspapers. But not so with the Bluffton Opera House, originally named the Terrell Grand Opera House. To the delight of theater manager Charles DelaCour, John's former lawyer, the theater opened to the public on April 6, 1904, with a performance of "Our New Minister."[8]

But by the middle of 1905, the shared dream of John Terrell and Charles DelaCour was in shambles. In mid-June, William Eichhorn, the same lawyer who prosecuted John Terrell, filed suit against the Bluffton Opera House Company on behalf of Wiley Brothers Construction Company for unpaid bills and to enforce its lien.[9]

DelaCour was removed by the Wells County Circuit Court as manager, and local businessman Frank Ehle was appointed receiver. On July 6, the court ordered DelaCour to turn over all bookings he had made as manager, ending DelaCour's relationship with the opera house.[10] By October 1, the court approved the receiver's sale of the theater for $16,000, less than half of the original cost of construction.[11]

His business partner in an insane asylum and his theater sold by creditors, DelaCour vanished from Bluffton later that summer. The only word of his whereabouts came a few months later in a small article in the *Muncie Morning Star.*

DYING IN THE FAR WEST BAD LEMONADE IS BLAMED

Bluffton, Ind, Nov. 4.—Word has been received here that Charles DelaCour, a former attorney of this city and partner of John Terrell, the opera house builder and murderer of his son-in-law, is fatally ill in California from two operations he has recently had performed in an endeavor to restore his health.

A year or so ago, DelaCour, while in a restaurant at Warren, Ind., drank a lemonade that was supposed to have chemical poison in it, and to this the doctors ascribe his illness that is expected to prove fatal.[12]

But Charles DelaCour's illness wasn't fatal. Whether he was poisoned or whether it was a story planted by a showman to dupe his creditors remains a matter of speculation. DelaCour relocated to southern California where in 1907, he announced plans for a new twelve hundred–seat theater in downtown Los Angeles.[13]

The drought on mentions of John Terrell in area newspapers changed dramatically on Thursday, November 2, 1905. News flashed through Wells County like a wild brush fire, leaving the entire citizenry in shock. The Indiana Supreme Court, in a unanimous decision, reversed John's conviction and quashed his indictment.[14] The reason: a typographical error that misstated the year as "18903" rather than 1903.

An Indiana statute provided that "No indictment or information shall be deemed invalid, nor shall the same be set aside or quashed . . . For omitting to state the time at which the offense was committed . . . nor for stating the time imperfectly, unless time is of the essence of the offense."

The State argued that the law was clear; a simple scrivener's error in putting the date on the indictment form was not a reason to set aside a three-week trial resulting in a conviction.

The supreme court disagreed, applying what even lawyers might consider an ultrafine technicality. Relying on an 1888 decision, the Indiana Supreme Court held the statute was inapplicable where the date stated in the indictment was "an impossible date." The court held, "Had the legislature intended to cure a statement of an impossible time in an indictment, it would have declared its purpose in express and positive language."[15]

The Indiana Supreme Court acknowledged that by deciding the case based on an extremely technical procedural issue—indeed, a single typographical mistake—it did not need to address any of the dozens of thornier legal issues argued on appeal. However, it did not acknowledge that by virtue of its decision, the state supreme court considerably lightened its own workload. The justices did not need to comb through the extensive procedural record, avoided reading nearly 2,500 pages of trial testimony, did not need to analyze the legal correctness of 34 jury instructions nor evaluate hundreds of evidentiary rulings.

News of the reversal spread in headlines across the state. John Terrell was a free man. Except he wasn't.

After the 1904 election, the legal landscape in Wells County and the surrounding counties changed. Prosecutor John Burns and Judge John M. Smith returned to private practice. But that did not mean they lost interest in the Terrell murder case. On the contrary, both were angry when they read the supreme court's opinion, finding that all their work had been for naught. So, too, was William Eichhorn, who called up John Burns at his law office in Hartford City. "Did you see the Supreme Court decision in the Terrell case?

"I read it."

"I bet that as soon as that old man discovers he'll be free, as soon as the doctors say he's sane, he'll be saner than you or me."

"I think he's smarter than that. He'll gradually get better and be out just before spring planting. But maybe we can do something. Do you know Ashley Emshwiler, the new prosecutor?"

"Sure," Burns said. "His office is just down the street from me."

"If I came over there, would you go with me to meet with him? I want to convince him that he needs to re-indite [sic] that son-of-a-bitch."

On November 28, the Wells County grand jury reindicted John Terrell for the murder of Melvin Wolfe.[16] That afternoon, Judge Vaughn issued a bench warrant. He arranged for the sheriff of Wayne County, where the asylum was located, to make the sixty-mile trip to Bluffton, where Judge Vaughn handed the sheriff the murder warrant from the second indictment.[17] Judge Vaughn gave clear directions to the sheriff. "Serve this on Terrell and take him into custody the moment he is released from the asylum."

But John Terrell wasn't released. He continued to occupy a room in the male cottage at the Eastern Indiana Hospital for the Insane. And in Bluffton, lawyers continued to squabble over the second indictment.

Once every two or three months, Lucy would make the trip by train to Richmond to visit her father. It was an exhausting trip that would take most of the day. She would arrive in time to have supper with John, then spend the night in a nearby boardinghouse. The next day, she would return to the hospital and visit him until after dinner, then catch the afternoon train back to Bluffton.

Occasionally, one of her sisters would make the trip with Lucy. At Thanksgiving, her mother would try to make the trip if her epilepsy and pernicious anemia permitted. But mostly it was just Lucy.

A reporter would see Lucy on the streets of Bluffton while she was shopping. Invariably, it would lead to a small story in the following week's newspaper. Lucy generally dismissed inquiries about her father by saying he was still in the same condition—no better, no worse. If asked about the case, she refused to answer. "I don't talk about that," was all she would say.[18]

Any news about John remained worthy of attention in the local papers. On one occasion, a Bluffton reporter caught Lucy in a men's store, buying new clothes for her father. She suspected that the shopkeeper had sneaked into the neighboring saloon and used the telephone to tip off the reporter, something for which the shopkeeper would expect the reporter to compensate him after Lucy left.

The story provided a glimpse of John's life at East Haven. Lucy was buying clothes for her father because of his substantial weight increase. Now weighing 210 pounds, he required trousers with a forty-eight-inch waist. But more troubling was Lucy's revelation that her father now was "troubled considerably" by heart disease.[19]

In November 1906, Charles Sturgis was elected as the new judge of Wells County Circuit Court.[20] However, even before he was sworn into office, Sturgis let everyone know that he would disqualify himself from the John Terrell matter because he had served as one of John's lawyers. So as Sturgis took office, one of his first acts was to appoint highly regarded Judge Richard K. Erwin from adjoining Adams County as special judge.[21]

With a new special judge handling the case, the squabbling and positioning among the lawyers began anew. John was now represented by Jay Hindman and R. W. Stine. The lawyers were with the firm formerly known as Sturgis and Stine, but after Sturgis's election, ethics rules required that Sturgis's name be removed from the firm. The State was nominally represented by elected prosecutor Ashley Emshwiler from nearby Hartford City; however, the strategy for the case was still guided by former prosecutor John Burns and attorney William Eichhorn.[22]

Not long after Judge Erwin took control of the case, John's lawyers filed a motion to dismiss the indictment because it had been returned by a regular grand jury rather than a special grand jury as required by statute. Technicalities had won dismissal of the first indictment, so the defense team was confident that they could be successful again. After all, the Indiana Supreme Court had sent the message that it would abide by the most technical requirements in criminal indictments—at least in the case of John Terrell.

Judge Erwin set the hearing for April 17, 1907. For two hours, he listened to the lawyers argue about the most minuscule aspects of procedure set out in Indiana's criminal statutes. When the lawyers finished, Judge Erwin addressed them.

"It is a fixed principle in all states that an insane man cannot be put on trial. I'm going to put everything on hold and not rule on anything further until

I decide for myself whether Mr. Terrell is sane or insane. To that purpose, sometime soon, I will visit the asylum in Richmond. Until I do, I don't want any of you gentlemen filing more motions."[23]

Judge Erwin put off the trip for six months, but finally, in October, he made the trip to the Eastern Indiana Hospital for the Insane. He visited John in a visitor's room in the main building. John sat on a chair while guards stood on either side. Judge Erwin thought John looked well and, if anything, a little plump.

"Well, John," Judge Erwin began, "how are you today?"

John glared up at the judge. "I'm the best man in town, and I can lick anyone."

"I guess that's so," Judge Erwin said.

John looked over the judge, his eyes roaming from head to foot, then back. "Well, you look pretty rough. Maybe I better take that back."

The judge attempted to talk to John for half an hour but did not get any answers that made sense. His talk was disconnected from reality. At the end of the half hour, Judge Erwin had enough. He had reached his conclusion.

Following his return home, he did not wait for his next court appearance to make his decision known. "Mr. Terrell is viciously insane," he told a waiting reporter. "His case, as far as the re-trial is concerned, is indefinitely postponed."[24]

34

The Way the World Ends

John's confinement in the East Haven Asylum did not prevent him from raising a furor. He did exactly that in early February 1908 as he approached four years in the asylum. A letter from John Terrell appeared in the *Bluffton Banner* accusing the Eastern Indiana Hospital for the Insane and its superintendent, Dr. Samuel Smith, of inhumane treatment.[1]

I have done everything I could to get back and have it settled. I would rather be taken to Michigan City and hung that [sic] to have to die here. I know how people die in here. Have seen poor, weak, sick, helpless men beaten, choked and stamped to death. This was a regular slaughterhouse until this fall.

I reported one Christian attendant and he was fired. I served notice on the rest. The attendants here now is all OK.

Smith is sore at me. He is a very religious man, being a strict Presbyterian. He thinks the Presbyterian God will punish me in his hell forever, so he reasons that he has a right to torment me. I am sure the doctor intends to keep me here the rest of my life. The doctor would be glad if the grave would close over me and cover this up.

I hope Governor Hanly can see this letter. If he knew the truth, I believe he would have my case investigated."

In the letter, John claimed he was sane and kept at the asylum against his will. He also maintained that he was denied visitation with his family and that his isolation was part of Dr. Smith's scheme to inflict as much punishment on John as possible.

The letter started a firestorm. The debate over whether John Terrell was insane or faking, which had quieted for some time, erupted again throughout Wells County and the state. Those who had always thought John was scamming everyone with his claim of insanity pointed out that the letter was coherent, literate, and could never have been written by a madman. But of course, they also had to admit that if he was sane, the assertions of inmates being choked and beaten had to be given some credibility. On the other side, if the accusations were accurate, didn't that show that John Terrell had regained his sanity?

Reporters hounded Lucy and the rest of the Terrell family. They demanded to know John's status and whether he wrote the letter, but the family refused to respond. Lucy speculated that someone may have used John's name to gain notoriety.[2]

The Terrell family demanded an immediate investigation. Lucy caught the next train to Richmond, seeking to meet with Dr. Smith. She was determined to find out whether her father was now sane and whether he was being abused at the institution. If Dr. Smith's answers were unsatisfactory, she planned to go directly to Indianapolis and meet with Governor Hanly.

Meanwhile, reports came out that at least some of John's statements were inaccurate. Members of the Terrell family had visited John throughout his confinement at East Haven. Judge Erwin had visited the previous October, concluding that John was "viciously insane." The previous year, Bluffton newspaperman Fred Rinehart, brother of the assistant prosecutor who argued John should be hanged, convinced asylum administrators to allow him to interview John. But Rinehart concluded that John was still "undoubtedly insane."[3]

Another visitor was William Sellers, a Bluffton resident who worked in Richmond for a time. He claimed to have visited John early in 1907, before either Rinehart or Erwin. During that purported conversation, Sellers claimed John was rational and talked of an upcoming visit he expected from his son Jake. Of course, Sellers did not know whether Jake was actually planning a visit. However, Sellers let others know that he thought Terrell had cleverly fooled Rinehart and Judge Erwin.[4]

Dr. Smith vehemently rebuked the allegations of John's letter and his claim of sanity but otherwise kept quiet. The accusations of an insane convicted murderer did not seem to carry much credibility. As the *Richmond Palladium* summarized: "The charges made by Terrell are considered the outgrowth of a diseased mind and are not believed."

. . .

Governor Hanly did not wait for a visit from Lucy. Upon seeing press reports of John Terrell's letter, he immediately contacted Amos Butler, secretary of the Board of State Charities. The governor directed the board to send someone to the Eastern Indiana Hospital for the Insane and investigate John Terrell's claim as soon as possible. While the investigator was there, he should also meet with John to determine if he was now sane. The next day, Rev. Francis H. Gavisk, a Jesuit priest, was on his way to Richmond.[5]

Father Gavisk was a good-humored, well-respected priest in Indianapolis, active in both church and secular affairs. He was fifty-one, with a broad face and chest. If not for his clerical garb and collar, he looked more like a brick mason than a scholarly priest.[6]

Father Gavisk met briefly with Dr. Smith and was given a copy of John's letter, which had been published in numerous Indiana newspapers. Dr. Smith reached into his desk drawer and pulled out a stack of six other letters.

"You should see these, too," Dr. Smith said, offering the stack to the priest.

Gavisk took the proffered letters. "What are these?"

"Six letters Mr. Terrell wrote to his daughter Lucy that we deemed unfit for mailing. The oldest was written about a year after his admission here. The most recent was about two months ago, just after Thanksgiving. If you read through these, you'll better understand what we are dealing with."

Gavisk pulled his spectacles from inside his frock. He began reading. The letters were incoherent ramblings, all except the last, which, in places, made some sense. The letters were filled with blasphemous denunciations of religion and the faithful. Several contained denunciations and accusations of indecent conduct made against his lawyers.

After reading through them, Gavisk put them back on the desk. He asked to see John.

Dr. Smith led Father Gavisk to a small room in the men's cottage. A few minutes later, an attendant brought John Terrell into the room. Two guards stood just outside the door, available if needed.

John took his seat and looked around suspiciously, not greeting anyone. Dr. Smith introduced Father Gavisk as a member of the Board of State Charities and told John he could talk with complete freedom. Dr. Smith then stepped back and stood against the wall.

"Good day, John," Gavisk said to John. "How are you today?"

"You're a priest, ain't you?" John spoke slowly, almost stuttering.

"I am."

"Well, you can't be a good man if you're a priest."

"I try to be a good man."

"Ain't nobody a good man that believes all that religious bunk." John continued to speak slowly, but his tone became friendlier. Sometimes incoherent, he denunciated God, Christ, religion, preachers and priests, church members and lawyers. His language was profane and obscene, which seemed to delight him. But he remained calm, never getting excited or working himself into a frenzy.

Gavisk tried to direct John to other topics—weather, health, family—but John would not be dissuaded. He kept bringing the conversation back to religion and how preachers and churchgoers were crooks and fools.

Only when Gavisk asked about food at the asylum did John's attention change from religion. "Food's good," he said, pointing at his expanding waistline. "And I get plenty."

"How are they treating you?"

"Oh, I'm treated well. So are the other patients. I ain't got nothing to complain about except Dr. Smith won't let me go home."

"Why do you want to go home?"

"Well, my family is sick. And I have a lawsuit in Bluffton that I need to get settled. I need to do it myself. I ain't gonna have lawyers around no more. I'm gonna defend myself. Everybody says I'm crazy. Even my daughter Lucy said so. But I ain't. People become crazy 'cause of religion. I ain't never been so crazy as to believe in religion."

On the train heading back to Indianapolis, Father Gavisk wrote his report to Governor Hanly. His conclusion was clear. "The impression I received from my interview with Terrell is that he is insane. I am of the opinion that Dr. Smith's course in keeping from the patient all visitors other than members of his family and those having business relations with him is best, both for the patient and for the public."[7]

The hubbub over John's letter and his sanity quickly subsided after Father Gavick's report. Two magistrate inquests, two juries, and an inspection by a respected judge and a priest had all found John Terrell insane.

As 1908 passed, word spread that John Terrell was doing better. At times, he appeared rational and began talking with relatives in a cogent manner.[8]

Not so when Lucy and Jake visited the asylum on September 16. John looked more physically fit than he had in years. He still complained of heart palpitations and occasional chest pain, but his skin looked healthy from being in the sun. The attendant told Lucy that her father had taken up the game of croquet and spent endless hours on the manicured lawn of the asylum playing the game with other inmates.[9]

John sat with Lucy and Jake and talked at length. John looked engaged in their conversation for the first time since the trial nearly five years earlier. John recognized both of them immediately and discussed how their lives were going. He was now regularly reading all the newspapers he could get his hands on and talked about some recent items he had read. John talked about his home and the farm and asked how the harvest was going. "I want to go home," he said finally.

"We'll see what we can do, Pa," Lucy said. "We'll see."

On Monday, October 12, 1908, Dr. Smith announced to shocked Richmond reporters that after four years and five months as an inmate, John Terrell, the most infamous patient ever at the Eastern Indiana Hospital for the Insane, would be discharged. However, he would not be freed immediately. Instead, he would be held for the Wells County sheriff to serve the warrant for John's second indictment for the murder of Melvin Wolfe.

One of the reporters asked point blank: "Is Terrell completely cured?"

That had been the specific condition contained in Governor Durbin's order, which initially placed John in the asylum. The order preceded the Indiana Supreme Court's decision reversing John's conviction.

Dr. Smith answered slowly, carefully choosing each word. "I can simply say that his condition at this time does not warrant further confinement in this institution." Beyond that, Dr. Smith would not comment.[10]

News began to filter around Bluffton that John was being released from the East Haven Asylum. Levi Monk, the six-foot, ten-inch dean of Wells County lawyers, heard the rumors in the courthouse and asked a local reporter for confirmation. The reporter checked with the county judge, sheriff, and clerk, none of whom would confirm that John was being discharged. He then telephoned Lucy, but she had no news of the impending release.

Earlier in the day, the judge, prosecutor, and sheriff had received word from Dr. Smith that he was discharging John. After a quick discussion, they decided not to spread the information until the sheriff traveled to Richmond to take John into custody and return him to the Wells County Jail. But after Levi Mock heard the news, there was no keeping it quiet.

At six o'clock the following morning, Sheriff William Addison Lipkey, known to his friends as Adam, and his son-in-law, Deputy Charles Pierce, boarded the interurban to Hartford City en route to Richmond. A butcher by trade, the fifty-five-year-old sheriff did not look forward to bringing his old friend, John Terrell, back to Bluffton only to put him in a cell. The health of his fifty-one-year-old wife, Mary, was weighing on him even more. She had been suffering from heart ailments for several years and recently was stricken with pneumonia and confined to bed. Before the month was out, she would be dead.

Sheriff Lipkey and Deputy Pierce arrived at the Richmond train station in late morning. Wayne County sheriff Linus Meredith was waiting for them. They wasted no time driving to the asylum.

Dr. Smith had them wait in his office while he fetched John. Sheriff Lipkey had already decided that he would not mention the warrant or the indictment he had in his pocket. He wanted to avoid all possible trouble and would not read them to John until they were in Wells County.

After several minutes, Dr. Smith brought John into the office. He was wearing a dark suit that fit his expanded size. Sheriff Lipkey last saw John during his trial nearly five years before. John seemed fit, although obviously much heavier. His hair was thinner, his face older and more drawn, but overall, Lipkey was surprised at how well the old man looked.

"How are you, John?" Lipkey said, smiling and extending a hand to his old friend.

John did not speak or respond to the outstretched hand. Instead, his eyes shifted about the room as if he was suspicious of some trick.

"I'm Bill Lipkey. I'm sheriff now. You remember me, don't you?"

John slowly shook his head, suspicion evident in his gaze. "No," he said. He said nothing more.

Sheriff Lipkey and Deputy Pierce led John from the superintendent's office and out of the asylum, where the car was waiting. They directed John into the backseat, and the two Wells County officers took their place on either side of him. The Wayne County sheriff drove. As they headed toward the train station, John's eyes were wide and constantly moving. It may have been his first ride in an automobile.

Lipkey talked at length to John, trying to engage him in conversation and make him feel at ease. He told John of all the changes that had taken place in Bluffton while John was away. He also talked to him about how his family was doing and events that had happened with neighbors. John did not say anything in response.

The entourage arrived at the train station, and Lipkey ushered John into a nearly empty passenger car. A few minutes later, the train pulled out of the station.

. . .

At 3:40 Tuesday afternoon, October 13, 1908, the Union Traction interurban car from Hartford City pulled to a stop on West Washington Street across from the Wells County Jail. John Terrell, in the company of the sheriff and his son-in-law deputy, disembarked. Only a handful of people stood on the street, staring curiously at John but offering no greetings. The Terrell family knew John would be arriving in Bluffton that afternoon, but they were not yet in town.[11]

Sheriff Lipkey led John past the opera house that John had been instrumental in building. John seemed not to recognize it, and when someone asked if he remembered the opera house, he shook his head. Levi Mock, unmistakable with his long white beard, untamed white hair, and six-foot, ten-inch frame, came across the street. He was the first to greet John. John just stared blankly at the giant man.

"Don't you remember me?" Mock asked.

John stared for a long moment, then said, "Can't say as I do." Then after another moment, he added, "You are Dr. Carter."

Mock gave a small smile but did not respond.

John stared for another moment, then added, "You know I have been away for a long time."

A reporter standing nearby yelled out, "How do you feel?"

John puffed out his chest. "I am the best man on earth. This morning I tipped the scales at 300 pounds!"

While John had gained weight over the past few years, he was closer to 220 pounds and certainly nowhere near his claimed 300 pounds.

"How about that letter in the newspaper that said it was from you? Did you really write that?"

John's face went blank. He was silent for a long time, then finally answered flatly. "I write all the time." That was all he said.

As Sheriff Lipkey led John into the jail, the sheriff's six-year-old granddaughter ran out from the residence side of the jail. For the first time, a smile broke across John's face. He muttered something, leaned down, and gently brushed the girl's cheek.

Someone asked John if he remembered the jail. He answered, "No," never taking his eyes off the girl.

Finally, Sheriff Lipkey took John by the elbow and led him to his cell.

The Terrell family arrived shortly after John was placed in his cell. The sheriff opened the cell door so the family could hug the old man. As Lucy and her father hugged, they both broke down in tears. John recognized the family members who had regularly visited him at the asylum. But when friends started showing up later that evening, he did not remember any of them. When they left, all shared the opinion that John remained insane.

. . .

Three days after John was transported back to Bluffton and locked in the Wells County Jail, District Prosecutor Ashley Emshwiler arrived from Hartford City for a meeting with Wells County Circuit Court judge Charles Sturgis and Sheriff Lipkey. There was one question on their agenda: what do we do with John Terrell? But despite their best efforts, they could not come up with a solution.[12]

Three weeks after John's return to the Wells County Jail, Lucy appeared before the Wells County commissioners with a request that the county provide an attendant or a nurse to supervise John's care. The commissioners walked over to the jail to see John and talked to the sheriff. They returned to the courthouse and unanimously denied the motion. The president of the commissioners addressed Lucy. "Now, Mrs. Wolfe, if you can get the court and the prosecutor to agree, we wouldn't have any problem if your pa was released to live at home, as long as your family paid for the deputies that would be needed to keep an eye on him."[13]

At about the same time that Lucy was making her futile request, Judge Erwin sent notice to the Wells County Circuit Court that he would no longer serve as special judge in John's case.[14] The case fell back into the lap of the sitting judge, Charles Sturgis. But since Sturgis had served as one of John's lawyers at trial, he could do nothing other than appoint a new special judge. With nothing happening in the case, there was no urgency.

As 1908 drew to a close, Judge Sturgis, on December 28, appointed Delaware County judge Joseph G. Leffler as the new special judge, the fifth judge in the case.[15] But Leffler's stay was short, and on February 1, he informed the Wells County Circuit Court that he could not serve. Judge Sturgis promptly appointed Grant County Circuit Court judge H. J. Paulus as the sixth and final judge to serve in the case.[16]

As Thanksgiving approached, Sheriff Lipkey admitted to a local newspaper, "I'm at a loss to know what course to pursue."[17]

Following Judge Paulus's appointment, John's lawyers filed multiple motions to dismiss, arguing that technical flaws in the second indictment required that the case be dismissed. Finally, in late May, Judge Paulus arrived in Bluffton to hear the motion and any other matters the attorneys wanted to discuss. The attorneys argued the motions for two hours. Judge Paulus listened patiently, but as soon as the lawyers finished, he denied the motion to dismiss.

"Any further matters we need to discuss?"

Jay Hindman, forty-seven years old and dashingly handsome, rose. In ten years, after relocating to Modesto, California, he would be dead, a victim of the 1919 Spanish flu pandemic.[18] But for now, the handsome trial lawyer from Hartford City had only one thing in his thoughts.

"Your honor. Defendant moves that the court set bond for John Terrell so he can be released from the Wells County Jail. Mr. Terrell has been in the custody of the State, in one way or another, for six years. After his release from the Eastern Indiana Hospital for the Insane, he has spent the last six months in the Wells County Jail. Two juries have found him insane. An inspection by a priest acting on behalf of the governor and another by one of the most respected jurists in this state, the Honorable Judge Richard Erwin, both found Mr. Terrell insane. And since he has returned to Bluffton, all of his friends and business associates who have visited him in jail have all left with the same conclusion. He is still quite insane."

Hindman continued, "As we know, this court cannot put an insane man on trial. So, what is to be done? Is this court to continue to hold Mr. Terrell in the Wells County Jail for the rest of his life because he has not become sane? That is not justice. That is not the law. He needs to be released to his family to be looked after and cared for, upon setting a reasonable bond, of course."

Hindman sat down. Judge Paulus looked toward Prosecutor Ashley Emshwiler, who consulted in whispers with John Burns seated next to him. After several minutes, Emshwiler rose.

"The State must object to this as it does not wish to be on records as assenting to the granting of release on bond but has no other comment at this time."

The courtroom went utterly silent. Judge Paulus removed his spectacles, placing them on the bench before him. He leaned back in his chair and stared at a far corner of the courtroom, thinking but not saying a word. After several minutes, he leaned forward and put his glasses back on.

"This case has suffered from inaction for far too long. You are right, Mr. Hindman. We cannot continue to keep an insane man in jail, hoping he will become sane. And until he does become sane, we cannot place him on trial. The court grants your motion. Mr. Terrell may be released to the custody of his family upon posting a bond in the amount of $15,000."[19]

With that, Judge Paulus hit his gavel. "We are adjourned."

After six years, John Terrell was on the verge of being a free man—provided his family could post a bond of $15,000, the equivalent of more than $500,000 in 2023.[20]

Before shooting Melvin Wolfe, John Terrell was one of the wealthiest men in Wells County. He owned farms, business properties, oil wells, and an opera house. He rented property, loaned money, and took notes and mortgages. If he needed $15,000, he could walk into any bank in Bluffton and walk out ten minutes later with the cash in hand.

But six years later, the opera house had gone into receivership and been sold, his farm equipment had been sold, the oil wells were nearly dry, and he had sold much of his property. The remainder was conveyed to his wife. He had not been around to run the farms or his businesses. Most significantly, lawyers had taken over $30,000 for six years of legal fees.[21]

Arrangements were completed for the necessary bond. No one told John he was being released, unsure how he might react. When Lucy, Jake, and Hindman arrived, Lipkey retrieved John from his cell and delivered the news. "John, you're going home."

John didn't react. There was no smile, no joy, no excitement. The old man continued to stare out, his eyes seemingly unfocused. It was as if Lipkey had told him he was having boiled beef for dinner.

Lucy greeted her father with a huge smile and a hug. John returned the hug, but he was no different than any other day since he had returned to the jail. Jake put his hand on his father's shoulder. "Let's go home, Pa."

No one in the Wolfe family was present. Shortly after the news that John was being released made the newspaper, a reporter asked Jacob Wolfe for his reaction. "I ain't got nothing to say about it. That man will have to answer to God for what he done, even if he don't answer to the law."

So, on Monday, May 31, shortly after ten o'clock, John Terrell climbed into the backseat of a car, Lucy sitting beside him. They headed south on what formerly was called Bluffton-Camden Pike but was now designated Indiana Highway 1.

Thirty minutes after leaving Bluffton, they passed through Petroleum, where John had shot Melvin Wolfe in Dr. Saunders's office six years earlier. Only a few minutes later, they were at the Terrell house. Catherine Terrell, looking frail, stood on the porch. She was crying with one hand to her mouth, the other waving.

John Terrell was home.

John's release did not remove him and his family from the public eye. Throughout 1909, every time Lucy or Jake traveled to Bluffton on business or to shop, they would be approached by townspeople and reporters asking about their father's condition. These were not caring inquiries. The following day, stories would appear reporting that John Terrell continued to be sullen and uncommunicative despite being at home. Newspapers quoted friends as saying they did not think he would ever regain his sanity.[22]

In August 1909, the *Hartford City Telegram* reported, "The aged man is kept at home and does not express any desire to leave the old farm, being content to sit in the yard and smoke his pipe or walk through the barnyard."[23] Two years later, when Jake finally took John into Bluffton for the first time since his release, the event was reported in newspapers from Fort Wayne to Muncie.[24]

After the summer of 1909, more than a year passed before John Terrell's name again appeared in local newspapers. On October 17, 1910, Pleasant Stanley, the oddly named businessman appointed as John Terrell's guardian in 1904, filed a final report. Every last cent of John Terrell's estate had been spent, including more than $30,000 in attorney fees and court costs.[25]

John Terrell, at one time one of the wealthiest men in Wells County, was penniless.

Stanley noted that John's family was providing his food and care, so there was no need to continue the guardianship. The next business day, Judge Sturgis, who at one time had been John's lawyer, dismissed the guardian.

Two weeks before Christmas in 1911, John gave the newspapers good cause to put him on the front page again. Domestic discord had again come to the Terrell home, but this time it involved Jake, now twenty-seven, and his wife Minnie Kirkwood Terrell, now twenty-four. Minnie moved in with her brother in Petroleum, not far from John's daughter Sally, and filed for divorce.

While John was visiting Sally, he walked away and ended up in a house next to where Minnie was staying. He wandered through the house, calling out for his daughter-in-law and mumbling threats about what he would do when he found her. The neighbor went to get Sally, who retrieved her father, then immediately took him back home. But the neighbor also told Minnie.[26] The result was headlines that John "Again Becomes Wild."[27]

Minnie called the sheriff, now Freeman Carlisle, who, like most Wells County politicians, had been a friend of John. The last thing Carlisle wanted was to be put in the position of his predecessors of having an insane man sitting in his jail.

Sheriff Carlisle went to the Terrell farm. John sat on the porch as he often did, puffing away on his pipe, mumbling to himself, and staring aimlessly across the now barren fields. John's three daughters were there, as was his wife Catherine, although she was confined to bed. Lucy and Sally were waiting at the front door.

"Hello, Freeman," Sally said. "We were expecting you. Come in and have a seat. Would you like some coffee?"

"Hello, Mrs. Books," Carlisle said and stepped into the parlor. He sat on a stuffed chair while Lucy, Sally, and Cinda sat across from him on the davenport. "John got into Hollis Fletcher's house, looking for Minnie and making all kinds of threats. Now Minnie is ranting up and down and wants John arrested."

"I'm sorry," Sally said. "I just turned my back for a minute, and Pa was gone. I didn't know where he went."

"We won't let it happen again," Lucy added.

Carlisle nodded. "I don't want to put John in jail. Frankly, I don't want to deal with it. But he can't be running around threatening people. I don't think he's a problem out here on the farm, but you're gonna have to watch him closer any time you have him off the farm."

"We understand," Lucy said.

"Anytime he's off the farm, one of you will have to be with him, and I mean right with him. If this happens again, I'll have to arrest him."

"We understand," Sally said.

"You tell your menfolk that they need to lock up the guns. I can't risk him getting something in his fool mind and going after Minnie or someone else. I'll come back in a few days and check on everything."

The Terrell family kept their word. Occasionally they took John into Bluffton, but one of the family always made sure he was never out of their sight. So, for nearly five years, John's name disappeared from the newspapers.

The marital stress between Minnie and Jake eased, and she moved back with Jake and dropped the divorce proceeding. They remained married until Minnie's death from cervical cancer in 1926 at age thirty-nine.[28] Jake never remarried.

On November 11, 1914, Catherine's long battle with epilepsy and pernicious anemia that had left her bedridden for much of the past decade finally ended. She died at home with her family around her.[29] John understood the parting but did not shed any tears. "Well, she's gone. Guess we better get her buried," was all he said, standing over his wife's still-warm body.

Catherine was buried in Union Cemetery among the rolling hills and woods about a mile outside Windsor in Randolph County. It was the final resting place for her parents and nearly all of the expansive Terrell family since brothers Wesley and Drummond Terrell first set foot in Indiana in 1827.

John was at the funeral with his entire family. His father, William, now eighty-five, was feeble and seemed to no longer recognize his son or anyone else. The elderly man had difficulty walking to the gravesite near the crest of the hill at the east edge of the cemetery. Two years earlier, John's half brother, Grant, was appointed guardian for their father. In two months, William, too, would be dead.[30] So, too, would be Will Books, the thirty-three-year-old second husband of Lucinda Terrell; he died two days before Christmas from consumption.[31]

The extent that John's actions hovered over his entire family was no more evident than in February 1916, when Lucy remarried. Although it had been nearly thirteen years since Lucy became a widow, the events of July 12, 1903, still shadowed her.

Lucy and her new husband, Florence Johnson, from Muncie, anticipated the publicity that would attend their wedding. Knowing that even the issuance of a marriage license would draw attention, they eloped to Kentucky, where they were married on February 12, 1916. Only after they returned to Indiana and set up housekeeping in Muncie did they make their marriage public.

Still, newspapers across the state noted the marriage. The *Fort Wayne Sentinel* story was typical.

MARRIAGE RECALLS MURDER

Lucy Terrell-Wolfe, daughter of John W. Terrell of Petroleum, arrived home Wednesday from Muncie and announced to her friends that her marriage to Florence Johnson of Muncie took place last week in Kentucky. The couple eloped, telling no one of their intentions.[32]

Even though Lucy moved from the Terrell farm to Muncie with her new husband, she continued to take turns with her sisters in looking after their father. Then in October, John visited, planning to stay for several weeks.

On Monday morning, October 16, 1916, Lucy was in the kitchen washing the breakfast dishes when she heard her father make a noise, then heard a crash. She dashed to the front parlor where her father had fallen, upending a side table and a reading lamp. He lay motionless on the floor. She ran to him and knelt. His face was contorted in pain, one hand over his chest. His skin was turning a smoky gray.

At age sixty-three, John Terrell was dead.[33]

More than thirteen years after shooting Melvin Wolfe and seven years after being released from jail, news of his death spread rapidly through headlines in newspapers from Fort Wayne to Evansville. The *Muncie Morning Star* was the first to announce the news on a front-page banner headline.

JOHN W. TERRELL SUCCOMBS HERE

With the death at 9 o'clock this morning of John W. Terrell, 63, at the home of a daughter, Mrs. Lucy Terrell Johnson, in Muncie, Ind., there was written the final chapter in one of the most noted criminal cases in Wells County and the state of Indiana, a case in which John Terrell, in 1903, shot and killed his son-in-law Melvin Wolfe.

Two days later, John was laid to rest in Union Cemetery next to his wife and only a few feet from his father. Forty feet south, under an eroding soapstone marker, was his mother, whom he never knew. While John was an unrepentant atheist all his adult life, his daughters still insisted on a funeral at the Union Church, where both his father and grandfather had preached.

A small notice of the burial was published in the *Muncie Morning Star.*[34] Of the hundreds of news stories about John published over the past thirteen years, it was the only one that did not mention the murder of Melvin Wolfe.

Epilogue

One hundred twenty years after events, the question still remains. Was John Terrell really insane or was he just shamming everyone? It really is a two-part question.

When it comes to the shooting, there is no question that John killed Melvin Wolfe in a sensationalistic way that drew the attention of newspapers across the nation, including the front page of the *New York Times*. He was undoubtedly angry, livid, outraged, and in a blind fury.

More than a century later, there is no one around to interview, not even anyone who knew any of the principals involved. The closest I had was my father, now gone more than fifty years. He never mentioned John Terrell to me, nor did any of my other relatives. It was something I stumbled on while doing genealogy research in those long days of the early pandemic. However, on at least one occasion, my dad told one of my sisters about his "crazy" uncle whom he met once while in his early teens. Unfortunately, my sister is now in a memory care unit, the details of that discussion locked away in the inaccessible recesses of her mind.

What remains are 2,500 pages of sworn testimony and hundreds of somewhat less reliable—and at times unreliable—news stories. They disclose a very troubled man who saw his two older daughters abused, then abandoned by roustabout husbands. The youngest, Lucy, was used and discarded by a womanizing rake who had already impregnated one young woman, and who afterward, to one degree or another, tormented the Terrell family.

John took his vengeance, but was that insanity?

John's lawyers were well-regarded, capable men. They served as judges, prosecutors, and legislators. Each of them, upon their death, was lionized as a giant of the legal profession and their community. They filled the court record with more than a dozen experts testifying in incomprehensible terms about brain congestion and melancholia puerperal that was either stuporous or agitata, each concluding that John Terrell was of unsound mind.

The problem was that the jury of uneducated farmers understood none of it. What they did understand was that John Terrell was paying these doctors $100 a day for their opinions, an obscene amount in 1903 rural Wells County.

With the benefit of hindsight, the mistake John's lawyers made was in losing focus on two factors: who they were trying to convince and the concept of irresistible impulse. As for the former, the jury was lost in the endless droning of hypothetical questions and hoodoo medical jargon used by the expert witnesses of the time. The jurors were hopelessly lost in the discussion of brain congestion and melancholia puerperal. Perhaps more importantly, they didn't care. What they heard had absolutely no connection to those twelve men and their life experiences as farmers. That was made clear by the rapid verdict.

The second factor was the defense team's failure to focus on the concept of irresistible impulse. In 1903, irresistible impulse was unquestionably established as an aspect of the insanity defense in Indiana. But at trial, the defense focused on a general "unsound mind." None of the experts opined on the idea that someone could become so overcome by rage or emotion that it was impossible to resist the urge to commit a crime—a murder. Yet, that was the law in Indiana at the time. Unlike blood congestion and melancholia, it was a concept understandable to a jury of men, most of whom likely had daughters. But it was never the focus of the defense.

So, was John insane? Under today's law, no. Today not a single state recognizes irresistible impulse as a form of insanity that excuses criminal conduct. But in 1903 Indiana, from a perspective of 2023, I think yes, the evidence established that John Terrell was insane at the time of the shooting, suffering from an irresistible impulse. It at least merited more than ten minutes of discussion by a jury eager to get home after three weeks of courthouse confinement. However, after forty years of practicing law, I know that not every jury gets it right—at least right as I see it.

What about after the trial when John was in jail, and later an asylum, acting as a madman? Was John Terrell really insane, or was he faking, shamming everyone to avoid prison? The truth is, I don't know. Not for certain.

In jail, John pissed himself and shit himself. He banged his head on the bars of his cell and pounded the walls until his hands were like raw meat, but he never showed pain. He just kept doing it. He didn't recognize his children or friends, and he spoke in incoherent gibberish like a Holy Roller speaking in tongues.

Regardless of John's state of mind when he killed Melvin Wolfe, his conduct descended into the abyss of insanity following his conviction in December 1903. He didn't die until 1916. Who could play insane for more than a dozen years, never having a meaningful conversation with anyone? Never slipping up, not even once, to reveal his lie, to reveal he was sane?

Was prison worse than an insane asylum in the early 1900s? What was more frightening—being in a cell surrounded by criminals and bullying guards or being in an asylum of lunatics and turnkeys who did God knows what to inmates, knowing that no one would take the word of a crazy person?

Even after he was released from the asylum, was John's life any better? Was he ever truly free? After all, the murder charges against John remained pending, dismissed only after his death.

The situation brings to mind the exchange between Dr. Faust and the devil in Christopher Marlowe's *Doctor Faustus*. When Faust asks Mephistopheles why he is out of hell, the devil responds, "Why this is hell, nor am I out of it."

In the end, the prison John created with his own mind was far greater than any walls ever built by the state. Did it really matter if his insanity was the product of uncontrolled demons or a calculated fabrication? Would not the latter be its own form of insanity? In either case, as John Terrell's brief to the Indiana Supreme Court concluded, "a madman is punished by his own madness." So, too, is his family.

Notes

Prologue

1. *Muncie Morning Star,* Oct. 17, 1916, 1.

1. Ambush on a Sunday Afternoon

1. Events detailed in this chapter are drawn from the transcript testimony and specifically the testimony of Lucy Terrell Wolfe, Clarence Turner, Della Reed, Lemuel Bouse, Frank Fisher, and Sarah Fisher. The conversation in Melvin Wolfe's buggy is a creation of what might have been said given events of the day.

2. Raining Money

1. The first producing oil well in Indiana was located near the small town of Keystone in Wells County, about eight miles north of John Terrell's farm in Nottingham Township, which became the center of oil production. See "News from the Oil Fields; Nottingham an Oil Center," *Muncie Morning Star,* July 17, 1900, 3. It was part of the Trenton Field. It reached its peak production between 1904 and 1906 and thereafter sharply declined. By 1910, the oil wells were largely exhausted. Indiana Department of Natural Resources, Division of Oil and Gas, "History of Indiana's Oil and Gas Fields," og-OilGas_in_Indiana.pdf.

2. Wells County was not named for the oil wells that dotted the county in the late nineteenth century. Rather, when the county was organized in 1837, it was named for frontier military scout and spy Capt. William Wells, who served under Gen. "Mad" Anthony Wayne. See State of Indiana, Wells County, https://www.in.gov/core/mylocal/wells_county.html. See also Joshua Shepherd, "Williams Wells," Warfare History Network (Apr. 2016), https://warfarehistorynetwork.com/article/william-wells/.

3. *Transfer Book, Nottingham Township,* Wells County (Ind.) Auditor's Office (1880) (hereafter *Transfer Book*). Drummond continued to live with John Terrell for five more years until his death in 1885. "Drummond Terrell," Death Certificate, Indiana Department of Health, Delaware County, 1885.

4. Oil wells in the Indiana oil boom averaged nine hundred feet. Indiana Department of Natural Resources, Division of Oil and Gas, "History of Indiana's Oil and Gas Fields," og-OilGas_in_Indiana.pdf.

3. The Vandergriff Boys

1. *Transfer Book* (1893).

2. "The Oil Fields: Operators More Than Pleased with the Prospects," *Fort Wayne Journal-Gazette*, May 6, 1896, 4.

3. Sarah "Sally" Terrell testimony, in *John W. Terrell v. State of Indiana*, Indiana Supreme Court, No. 20474, Trial Transcript, Indiana State Archives (1904), 1033 (hereafter Transcript).

4. Wells County Clerk, Marriage Records; Transcript, Lucinda Terrell Books testimony, 1053; *Ben Vandergriff v. Lucinda Vandergriff*, Huntington County Clerk, Cause No. 7609, Sept. 18, 1899.

5. See Transcript, Testimony of David Kelly, R. 544.

6. A search of the records of the Wells County Clerk revealed more than a dozen lawsuits filed in the 1890s by John Terrell against various persons, mostly for collection of debts owed or enforcement of mortgages or mechanics liens.

7. Transcript, Testimony of Lucinda Terrell Books, R. 1053.

8. Transcript, Testimony of Sarah "Sally" Terrell Schott, 1012; Marriage Records of Wells County Clerk.

9. Transcript, Testimony of Sarah "Sally" Terrell Schott, 1012.

10. Transcript, Testimony of Sarah "Sally" Terrell Schott, 1012–15.

11. Transcript, Testimony of Sarah "Sally" Terrell Schott, 1026.

12. Transcript, Testimony of Lucinda Terrell Books, 1055–61.

13. Transcript, Testimony of Sarah "Sally" Terrell Schott, 1033.

4. The Cad of Wells County

1. Sarah Terrell Vandergriff filed for divorce against Jacob Joseph Vandergriff on January 13, 1888, in Wells County Circuit Court, No. 6011, which was granted. Records of Wells County Clerk. Ben Vandergriff filed for divorce against Lucinda Terrell Vandergriff on September 18, 1899, in Huntington County Circuit Court, No. 7609, which was granted on October 3, 1899. Records of Huntington County Clerk.

2. 1900 US Census, Nottingham, Wells County, Indiana, District 0152.

3. 1900 US Census, Nottingham.

4. Transcript, Testimony of Sarah "Sally" Terrell Schott, 1039; Transcript, Testimony of John Terrell, 1322–23.

5. Transcript, Testimony of Samuel Gherrett, 2112.

6. Known as "The Great Agnostic," lawyer, author, and speaker Robert Ingersoll challenged organized religion. Between 1880 and his death in 1899, he regularly drew crowds of several thousand to his talks. He attacked the Bible and blamed religion for much of the hypocrisy and injustice in the world. Frank Smith, *Robert Ingersoll: A Life*, foreword by Gordon Stein (Amherst, NY: Prometheus Books, 1990).

7. Transcript, Testimony of William Faulkner, 1911–12.

8. John W. Tyndall and O. E. Lesh, *Adams and Wells Counties Indiana: An Authentic Narrative of the Past* (Chicago: Lewis, 1918), 540–41, 562–63.

9. Ancestry.com, "Hannah Louisa Lacey Wolfe," Dec. 24, 1844–Sept. 27, 1887, Brubeck Family Tree, https://www.ancestry.com/family-tree/person/tree/77751850/peson/30408493783/facts?_phsrc=qsr10&_phstart=successSource.

10. Ancestry.com: "Mary Jane Wimer," Death Certificate No. 21, Wells County, July 12, 1843–May 15, 1915; "Leo Melvin Wolfe," Death Certificate No. 21, Indiana State Board of Health, Wells County, July 12, 1903; "Della Reed Wilson," Death Certificate No. 20904, Wells County, June 1, 1951.

11. Chloa Alice Blair gave birth to Gladys May Wolfe on February 28, 1901. In 1904, Chloa married a local farmer, Simon Holloway. While Gladys retained the legal name of Wolfe, she was referred to as Gladys Holloway. See photo from *Bluffton News-Banner,* May 10, 1915, listing Gladys as one of the Holloway children. On September 17, 1964, Chloa and Simon Holloway celebrated their sixtieth wedding anniversary. *Bluffton News-Banner,* Sept. 24, 1964. On Father's Day, June 17, 1956, Gladys (now Gladys Penrod) wrote a handwritten tribute to her grandfather, her stepfather, and her birth father, Melvin Wolfe. I was given access to Gladys's handwritten note by Gladys's grandson, Geoffrey Penrod, and his wife, Nicole.

12. Ancestry.com, Marriage Record for Sarrah [*sic*] Terrell to John Schott, Sept. 4, 1901, FHL Film Number 002318977.

13. Ancestry.com, Marriage Record for Lucinda Terrell to William Books, Sept. 12, 1901, FHL Film Number 002318977.

5. He Promised

1. Transcript, Testimony of Lucy Terrell Wolfe, 932–33.

2. See Transcript, Testimony of Lucy Terrell Wolfe, 963–64.

3. Jacob Wolfe's great-uncle was James Wolfe, the English general who, although fatally wounded, led the British victory over the French at the 1759 Battle of Quebec. John W. Tyndall and O. E. Lesh, *Adams and Wells Counties Indiana: An Authentic Narrative of the Past* (Chicago: Lewis, 1918), 563. See also "Jacob Wolfe Descendent of General Wolfe," *Bluffton Banner,* Dec. 2, 1903, 4.

4. Tyndall and Lesh, *Adams and Wells Counties Indiana,* 562.

5. See Transcript, Testimony of Lucy Terrell Wolfe, 964–65.

6. Wolfe's Den

1. The accounts of this chapter are drawn from the testimony of Lucy Terrell Wolfe and John Terrell at her father's trial. Transcript, Testimony of Lucy Terrell Wolfe, Direct Exam, 937–46; Cross Exam, 968–80; Redirect Exam, 1002–3; Testimony of John Terrell, Direct Exam, 1231–36.

2. Erick Trickey, "Inside the Story of America's 19th Century Opiate Addition," *Smithsonian Magazine,* Jan. 14, 2018. See also David Courtright, *Dark Paradise* (Cambridge, MA: Harvard Univ. Press, 2001).

3. Trickey, "Inside the Story." See also James Nevius, "The Strange History of Opiates in America," *Guardian,* Mar. 15, 2016, theguardian.com/commentisfree/2016/mar/16/long-opiate-use-history-america-latest-epidemic.

4. See Elizabeth Gray, "Losing Sorrow in Stupefaction," *Nursing Clio,* Aug. 18, 2022, https:nursingclio.org/2022/08/18/losing-sorrow-in-stupefication-american-womens-opiate-dependency-before-1900/.

7. Fraudulent Marriage

1. The account of Lucy's return home is drawn from the transcript testimony of Lucy Terrell Wolfe, John Terrell, Catherine Terrell, Lucinda Terrell Books, John Books, and George W. Harshman.

2. Transcript, Testimony of Lucinda Terrell Books, 1063–64, 1075–80.

3. The *Muncie Star* listed Levi Mock at "six feet six inches in his stocking feet," in an article showing a photo of Mock towering over two businessmen who were barely over four feet tall. "Leading Counsel for Murderer John W. Terrill [*sic*]," *Muncie Morning Star,* July 23, 1903, 1. However, Larry E. Mock, Levi's great-grandson, who still carries on the Mock name and practices law in Bluffton, stated that Levi's height was near six feet, ten inches, and one newspaper listed Mock's height at six feet, eleven inches. "Long and Short of It," *New Albany (IN) Public Press,* Feb. 21, 1900, 7.

4. Records of Wells County Clerk show that the Mock firm represented John Terrell in more than a dozen lawsuits filed between 1892 and 1903.

5. *State ex rel. Lucy Wolfe v. Melvin Wolfe,* Complaint for Fraudulent Marriage, filed May 13, 1902, in the Wells Circuit Court (Records of Wells County Clerk).

6. Certificate of Death, Adams County, No. 10965.

7. Transcript, Testimony of Lucy Terrell Wolfe, 977.

8. *State ex rel. Lucy Wolfe v. Melvin Wolfe,* Wells Circuit Court, No. 10071 (1902), Records of Wells County Clerk, Order Book Index No. 7659.

9. Records of Wells County Clerk in case of *State ex rel. Lucy Wolfe v. Melvin Wolfe,* No. 10071 (1902).

8. "Bye, Oh, Baby"

1. Transcript, Testimony of Lucy Terrell Wolfe, 1000.

2. See Transcript, Testimony of Lucy Terrell Wolfe, 952; Testimony of Sarah "Sally" Terrell Schott, 1030–31.

3. Transcript, Testimony of Lucy Terrell Wolfe, 952.

4. Transcript, Testimony of John Terrell, Offer to Prove, 1345.

5. Transcript, Testimony of Lucy Terrell Wolfe, 951.

6. Transcript, Testimony of Lucy Terrell Wolfe, 950; Testimony of Jacob Terrell, 1139; Testimony of Catherine Terrell, 1249.

7. Alfred G. Robyn, "Bye, Oh! Baby!" (New York: William A. Pond, 1890).

8. See Transcript, Testimony of Jacob Terrell, 1136.

9. Transcript, Testimony of Jacob Terrell, 1136.

10. Transcript, Testimony of John Terrell, 1340–41, 1343, 1355.

9. "God Damn the Man That Comes between Me and Wolfe"

1. Transcript, Testimony of Lucy Terrell Wolfe, 961.

2. Transcript, Testimony of John Terrell, 1308.

3. Transcript, Testimony of Lucy Terrell Wolfe, 961, 1030–31, 1052; Testimony of John Terrell, 1307–8.

4. Transcript, Testimony of John Terrell, 1308.

5. Transcript, Testimony of Lucy Terrell Wolfe, 954.

6. Transcript, Testimony of John Terrell 1310; Testimony of Lucy Terrell Wolfe, 955.

7. Transcript, Testimony of Della Reed, 301–2.

8. Transcript, Testimony of Della Reed, 303–4, 314–16.

9. Transcript, Testimony of Della Reed, 305.

10. Transcript, Testimony of Dr. J. E. Saunders, 419–21; Testimony of William Kirkwood, 358–59.

11. Transcript, Testimony of J. M. Hopkins, 332–33.

12. Transcript, Testimony of William Kirkwood, 356–57.

13. Transcript, Testimony of J. M. Hopkins, 336, 346.

14. Transcript, Testimony of Della Reed, 306; Testimony of William Kirkwood, 357.

15. Transcript, Testimony of William Kirkwood, 373.

16. Transcript, Testimony of Clarence "Dick" Risser, 347.

17. Transcript, Testimony of Dr. J. E. Saunders, 423; Testimony of William Kirkwood, 368–72.

18. Transcript, Testimony of Dr. J. E. Saunders, 428–32.

19. Transcript, Testimony of Dr. J. E. Saunders, 424–28; Testimony of Harry Kirkwood, 469–70.

10. "He Killed My Boy"

1. Transcript, Testimony of Emma Oliver, 531.

2. Transcript, Testimony of Dr. J. E. Saunders, 423–25.

3. Transcript, Testimony of Dr. F. M. Dickason, 478–80.

4. Transcript, Testimony of Dr. F. M. Dickason, 478.

5. Transcript, Testimony of Byron Witmer, 2127.

6. Transcript, Testimony of Emma Oliver, 531.

7. Transcript, Testimony of Dr. F. M. Dickason, 479–81, 483, 492–505.

8. Transcript, Testimony of Ida Dickason, 512–26.

9. Transcript, Testimony of Dr. F. M. Dickason, 503–4.

10. Transcript, Testimony of Sheriff J. R. Johnston, 439–40.

11. Transcript, Testimony of Coroner James A. McBride, 212.

12. See Transcript, Testimony of Jacob Wolfe, 209–10.

13. "Light for Bluffton," *Indianapolis News*, July 31, 1903, 7; "Bluffton Electric Light Co. Files Articles," *Muncie Morning Star*, Aug. 1, 1903, 2.

14. Transcript, Testimony of William Kirkwood, 407–10.

15. "Plea of Not Guilty Entered by Terrell," *Muncie Morning Star*, July 15, 1903, 1.

16. Transcript, Testimony of Jacob Wolfe, 210.

17. Transcript, Testimony of Jacob Wolfe, 210–11.

11. Headlines across the Nation

1. David R. Spencer, *The Yellow Journalism: The Press and America's Emergence as a World Power* (Chicago: Northwestern Univ. Press, 2007), 1–2.

2. Lewis H. Lapham, "Notebook: The Consolations of Vanity," *Harper's Magazine*, Dec. 1997, 11.

3. Lapham, "Notebook," 11, 17.

4. Lapham, "Notebook," xi–xii.

5. My search for stories on the murder in newspapers on July 13, 1903, returned with stories in more than 650 newspapers: 587 in newspapers.com and another 77 in newspaperarchive.com.

6. "Shot While Lying on an Operating Table," *New York Times*, July 13, 1903, 1.

7. "Got Him," *Boston Globe*, July 13, 1903, 5.

8. "Killed on Surgeon's Table," *New Orleans Times-Democrat*, July 13, 1903, 2.

9. "Slays His Son-in-Law on Operating Table," *Champaign Daily News*, July 13, 1905, 4.

10. "Wealthy Farmer Shot Son-in-Law," *Austin American-Statesman*, July 13, 1903, 1.

11. "The Patient Was Shot Dead," *Pittsburgh Press*, July 13, 1903, 4.

12. "Kills Victim, Defies a Mob," *Minneapolis Star-Tribune*, 1.

13. "Bent on Having Man's Life's Blood," *Nashville American*, July 13, 1913, 1.

14. "Kills a Son-in-Law," *Nebraska State Journal*, July 13, 1903, 1.

15. "Killed Him on Operating Table," *Butte (MT) Miner*, July 13, 1903, 2.

16. "An Indiana Feud and Its Results," *Davenport Democrat*, July 13, 1903, 1.

17. "Killed His Son-in-Law," *Bangor (ME) Daily News*, July 13, 1903, 1.

18. "Most Persistent Murderer," *Sioux City Journal*, July 13, 1903, 1.

19. The Associated Press story that appeared across the nation was as follows:

BLUFFTON, Ind., JULY 12—John Terrell, a wealthy farmer living near Petroleum, nine miles north of the city, killed his son-in-law, Melvin Wolfe, this afternoon, firing both barrels of a shot gun into his head as Wolfe lay on the doctor's operating table to have his leg amputated, necessitated by a wound from Terrell's gun fired a short time before.

Four years ago, Wolfe married Terrell's daughter. Wolfe deserted the girl, leaving her with a child in her arms.

A suit was brought to compel him to support his wife.

It is claimed Wolfe had twice driven past the Terrell home, shouting insulting remarks and shaking his fist at Terrell. The third time he drove past, Terrell jumped from some bushes along the roadside and fired with a double-barrel shot gun.

The first charge shattered Wolfe's right leg. The second barrel missed. Wolfe was hurried to the office of Dr. Saunders at Petroleum and placed on the operating table to have the leg amputated.

While a crowd stood around watching the doctor, Terrell came up from his home in a buggy, broke in the doors of the doctor's office, drove the crowd out at the point of his gun, and with the remark, "I am after him and I am going to get him yet," fired both barrels into his son-in-law's head. He was terribly mutilated.

At the time he fired, the young man was only half-conscious. Terrell got into his buggy, loaded up his shot gun and pointed it at the mob that had hastily formed, held it at bay, and drove to the sheriff's residence. He is in jail.

20. "Sexual Weakness. Any man who is running down through night losses or drains by day, and is lacking in ambition and confidence, is invited to consult me either in person or by mail free of charge. The World's Acknowledged Specialist in Private Nervous and Chronic Diseases. Dr. Linn, Main Street, Corner North Division, Buffalo, N.Y.," *Buffalo Enquirer*, July 13, 1903, 3.

21. "$100 Reward for Any Case of Stricture, Varicocele, Hydrocele or Nervous Debility That We Cannot Cure in 8 Days." Offered by the Rowe Medical Company, 60 Niagara Street, Buffalo, NY, *Buffalo Enquirer,* July 13, 1903, 3.

22. "Blood Poison Cured to Stay, Cured Forever. There is no human disease, hereditary or contracted, that requires prompter or more heroic treatment than specific or contagious poison in the blood." Offered by E. D. Porter, MD, Porter Medical Co., 333 Main St., Buffalo, NY, *Buffalo Enquirer,* July 13, 1903, 3.

23. "Slain While Surgeon Was Using Knife," *Buffalo Enquirer,* July 13, 1903, 3.

12. No Sorrow for the Deed

1. Levi Mock was such an imposing figure that two weeks before John Terrell shot Melvin Wolfe, Mock was featured in a tongue-in-cheek article on page 1 of the July 1, 1903, issue of Huntington, Indiana's *Daily News-Democrat* titled: "Uncle Levi Abroad." The article stated: "Judge Levi Mock, of Bluffton, the Jumbo of humanity, was in the city Saturday. As he came up town he stopped to scratch his chin on the court house spire and incidentally shook hands with Judge Headington through a third story window."

2. See "Terrell, Who Murdered Son-in-Law," *Muncie Morning Star,* July 14, 1903, 1.

3. Official Register of the United States, Containing a List of the Officers and Employees in the Civil, Military, and Naval Service, vol. 2, 1905, 110.

4. "Famous Murder Trials," *Evening News,* July, 1903, 1.

5. See "Petroleum Tragedy Shocks the Community," *Fort Wayne Gazette,* July 14, 1903, 1.

6. "Plea of Not Guilty Entered by Terrell," *Muncie Morning Star,* July 14, 1903, 1.

7. "Terrell Has Waived Preliminary Trial," *Indianapolis News,* July 14, 1903, 4; "Terrell, Who Murdered Son-in-Law," 1.

8. "Terrell, Who Murdered Son-in-Law," 1.

9. "Plea of Not Guilty Entered by Terrell," 1.

10. "Plea of Not Guilty Entered by Terrell."

13. Jailhouse, Opera House, and Charles DelaCour

1. See "Plea of Not Guilty Entered by Terrell," *Muncie Morning Star,* July 14, 1903, 1.

2. "Terrell Will Pay for Repairs," *Muncie Morning Star,* July 16, 1903, 1.

3. "Member of Good Family," *Indianapolis News,* 13. The article pointed out that his father, William Terrell, was a Methodist minister in Windsor and that his brother, Grant Terrell, was a prosperous Delaware County farmer. Grant is my grandfather.

4. "Dr. Saunders Gets License," *Bluffton Banner,* July 15, 1903, 8.

5. See "Plans for Opera House Were Submitted Today," *Bluffton Banner,* June 24, 1903, 8; "Prospects Are Brighter," *Bluffton Banner,* July 1, 1903, 1; "Seat Sale for Opening," *Bluffton Banner,* May 7, 1903, 6.

6. "DelaCour Presents Proof of Graduation," *Indianapolis Journal,* Dec. 29, 1903, 1. See also University of Michigan, Law Class of 1886, Class Photo, image No. 109.

7. "Benefit Entertainment for Carnegie Library," *Muncie Morning Star,* May 7, 1994, 6.

8. "New Theater Projected," *Indianapolis Journal,* Feb. 8, 1902, 6.

9. "Plans for Opera House Were Submitted Today," 8; "Looks Like Real Stuff," *Bluffton Banner*, July 15, 1903, 2.

10. "Bluffton Will Have a New Grand Opera House," *Fort Wayne Daily News*, Nov. 12, 1903, 1.

11. "Terrell, Who Murdered Son-in-Law," *Muncie Morning Star*, July 14, 1903, 1.

12. "Financing His Fortune," *Sunday Sentinel*, Sept. 22, 1903, 9.

13. "Terrell to Incorporate Opera House Today," *Indianapolis Star*, Sept. 1, 1903, 5.

14. "Opera House Contract," *Bluffton Banner*, Sept. 9, 1903, 9.

14. Shadow of the Gallows

1. Transcript, 1–2; "How an Indictment for Murder Reads," *Bluffton Banner*, Sept. 16, 1903, 1.

2. "John W. Terrell Pleads Not Guilty," *Bluffton Banner*, Sept. 23, 1903, 1.

3. "Financing His Fortune," *Sunday Sentinel*, Sept. 22, 1903, 9.

4. That would be the equivalent of $1.8 million to $3.6 million in 2023 dollars, according to the CPI Inflation Calculator, https://www.officialdata.org/us/inflation/.

5. CPI Inflation Calculator.

6. John Terrell's daily schedule as set out in the "Financing His Fortune" article was as follows:

6 A.M. Breakfast

6:30–7 A.M. Exercise—walking from one side of his cell to the other

8 A.M. Stenographer arrives and takes dictation for an hour

9 A.M. Callers—purely business. Two hours of oil men, financiers & bankers call to transact business

11 A.M. Friends and relatives visit

Noon—Dinner

1 P.M. Consultation with architect and contractor regarding status of construction of Opera House

2 P.M. Surveys work done on building during morning. For 2 hours, supervises directly the work from his cell window.

5 P.M. Consults with his lawyers

6 P.M. Supper

7. "Financing His Fortune," 9.

8. "Financing His Fortune," 9.

9. "Financing His Fortune," 9.

10. "Financing His Fortune," 9.

11. "Financing His Fortune," 9.

12. "To Lay a Cornerstone," *Indianapolis Journal*, Oct. 20, 1903, 2.

13. "Opera-House Corner Stone Laying," *Indianapolis News*, Oct. 20, 1903, 15.

15. The Cusp of Trial

1. *Complaint on Account, Levi Mock, John Mock, George Mock v. John W. Terrell*, Wells Circuit Court, No. 7988, filed Nov. 6, 1903, for "services in prepairing [*sic*] his defense in the case of the State of Indiana against John W. Terrell, on a charge of murder in the first degree from July 12th 1903 to October 10th, 1903. $500." Records of Wells County Clerk. See also "Mock and Sons Have Retired from Terrell Case," *Bluffton Banner*, Nov. 18, 1903, 3; "John Terrell Sued for Attorney Fees," *Bluffton Banner*, Nov. 18, 1903, 8.

2. "John Terrell Sued for Attorney Fees," 8.

3. "Will Move to Town," *Bluffton Banner*, Nov. 11, 1903, 5.

4. "Bluffton Will Have a Grand New Opera House," *Fort Wayne Daily News*, Nov. 12, 1903, 4.

5. "Terrell Case Set for November 30," *Bluffton Banner*, Nov. 30, 1903, 5.

6. Affidavit for Change of Judge, *State of Indiana v. John Terrell*, Wells County Circuit Court, No. 1204, Records of Wells County Clerk.

7. "Circuit Court News," *Bluffton Banner*, Nov. 25, 1903, 5.

16. Twelve Men Tried and True

1. *The Terrell Murder Trial: Complete History of the Crime, Trial and Conviction of John W. Terrell* (Bluffton, IN: Banner Book Concern, 1904), 4–5; "Terrell Trial on at Bluffton," *Fort Wayne Gazette*, Dec. 1, 1903, 1.

2. "Local Lawyers to Attend Rites," *Muncie Sunday Star*, Mar. 29, 1931, 26.

3. See "Terrell Jury Is Yet Incomplete," *Fort Wayne Sentinel*, Dec. 1, 1903, 1.

4. For a detailed account of the voir dire of potential jurors on the first day of trial, see *Terrell Murder Trial*, 5–6.

5. In the preceding forty years, no fewer than twenty-five men had been found guilty of murder by Wells County juries, yet not a single one had been sent to the gallows. "Death Penalty Unpopular in Wells County," *Indianapolis Morning Star*, Dec. 1, 1903, 5.

6. *Terrell Murder Trial*, 6.

7. *Terrell Murder Trial*, 8–9.

8. "The Terrell Trial: Jury in Famous Murder Case Not Yet Secured," *Fort Wayne Journal-Gazette*, Dec. 2, 1903, 1.

9. *Terrell Murder Trial*, 9.

10. *Terrell Murder Trial*, 9.

11. *Terrell Murder Trial*, 11.

12. "The Terrell Trial: Jury in Famous Murder Case Not Yet Secured," 1.

17. The State's Case Begins

1. *Terrell Murder Trial*, 11.

2. Transcript, 203–11.

3. Transcript, 212–22.

4. Transcript, 223–59.

5. *Terrell Murder Trial,* 14.

6. Transcript, 230–71.

7. Transcript, 272–97.

18. Della's Story

1. Transcript, Testimony of Della Reed, 298–331.

19. Three Times Dead

1. Transcript, Testimony of J. M. "Hop" Hopkins, 332–44.

2. Transcript, Testimony of Clarence "Dick" Risser, 345–54.

3. Transcript, Testimony of William Kirkwood, 355–79.

4. Transcript, Testimony of Oscar Oliver, 380–86.

5. Transcript, Testimony of Merle Stine, 387–90.

6. Transcript, Testimony of Frank Kelly, 391–98.

7. Transcript, Testimony of Harry Kirkwood, 406–12.

8. Transcript, Testimony of Jacob Wolfe, 413–15.

9. Transcript, Testimony of Jacob Wolfe, 414.

10. Transcript, Testimony of Jesse E. Saunders 416–36.

11. Transcript, Testimony of Sheriff James Johnston, 439–41.

12. Photo that still hangs on the wall of the Wells County Circuit Court office.

20. In Defense of John Terrell

1. *Terrell Murder Trial,* 21–23.

2. Michael L. Perkin and Heather Ellis Cucolo, *Mental Disability Law: Civil and Criminal,* 3rd ed. (New York: Lexis/Nexis, 2017), sec. 14–3.2.

3. "APPL Practice Guideline for Forensic Psychiatric Evaluation of Defendants Raising the Insanity Defense," *Journal of the American Academy of Psychiatry and the Law Online* 42 (Dec. 2014): 53–576.

4. Rudolph J. Gruber, *The Insanity Defense* (Port Washington, NY: Associated Faculty Press, 1984), 10.

5. Gruber, *Insanity Defense,* 21–28; Perkin and Cucolo, *Mental Disability Law,* n12, sec. 14–2.2; Thomas Maeder, *Crime and Madness: The Origins and Evolution of the Insanity Defense* (New York: Harper & Row, 1985), 23–36; Grant H. Morris, *The Insanity Defense: A Blueprint for Legislative Reform* (Lanham, MD: Lexington Books, 1975), 11–12.

6. See *Kahler v Kansas,* Appendix, 140 S. Ct 1021, 1051 (2020). However, opposition to the insanity defense has resulted in four states abolishing the defense, while others have adopted a "guilty but mentally ill" verdict. See Paul S. Appelbaum, MD, "*Kahler v. Kansas:* The Constitutionality of Abolishing the Insanity Defense," *Psychiatry Online,* Nov. 10, 2020, https://doi.org/10.1176/appi.ps.202000707.

7. Perkin and Cucolo, *Mental Disability Law,* n12, sec. 14–1.2.3; Frank R. Freeman, "The Origin of the Medical Expert Witness," *Journal of Legal Medicine* 22 (2001): 349, 368–73.

8. Freeman, "Origin of the Medical Expert Witness," 368–73.

9. Perhaps the most well-known example of irresistible impulse was in Otto Preminger's 1959 Academy Award–nominated film *Anatomy of a Murder,* based on the 1958 novel by former Michigan Supreme Court justice John D. Voelker writing under the pen name of Robert Traver.

10. *Bradley v. State,* 31 Ind. 492, 507 (1869).

11. See, *Plake v. State,* 23 N. E. 273, 121 Ind. 433 (1890); *Conway v. State,* 118 Ind. 482, 21 N. E. 285 (Ind. 1889); *Goodwin v. State,* 96 Ind. 550 (Ind. 1883). The irresistible impulse rule was heavily criticized. See Gruber, *Insanity Defense,* 46–47 (summarizing criticisms). Nevertheless, irresistible impulse remained a part of Indiana's insanity defense until it was removed from the insanity defense by statute in 1984. Ind. Code sec. 35-41-3-6 (1984). By 1990, not a single state used the irresistible impulse test. See *Benefiel v. State,* 578 N. E. 2d 338 (Ind. 1991).

12. *Terrell Murder Trial,* 23.

13. Transcript, Testimony of Ida Clark, 463–66.

14. Transcript, Testimony of J. M. Hopkins, 467–77.

15. Transcript, Testimony of Dr. John Dickason, 478–511.

16. Also called woodbine, gelsemium was a root used to treat migraines, asthma, and other breathing problems.

17. Veratrium was a white poisonous alkaloid mixture mainly used to treat rheumatism and neuralgia.

18. Transcript, Testimony of Ida Dickason, 512–25.

19. Transcript, Testimony of Emma Oliver, 527–44.

20. In the early years of the twentieth century, railroads that traveled in a straight flat route were termed *air-line railroads.* In 1913, *Webster's Dictionary* offered the definition: "Air line, a straight line; a bee line. Hence Air-line, adj; as, air-line road." See en-academ ic.com. See also "President Uses Silver Spade," *Indianapolis Star,* Sept. 9, 1906, 15; "Electric Air Line Is Not Being Built as Promised," *South Bend Tribune,* Feb. 20, 1906, 6.

21. William Henry Eichhorn Death Certificate, No. 17087, Wells County, May 27, 1948.

22. Transcript, Testimony of David Kelly, 545–51.

21. Hold up the Bastard

1. Transcript, Testimony of Dr. Saunders, 552–64.

2. Transcript, Testimony of William Eberly, 565–70.

3. Transcript, Testimony of Dr. Charles Caylor, 571–88.

4. Transcript, Testimony of Daniel Fetters, 597–600; Testimony of Isaac Smith, 601–3; Testimony of Thomas Fetters, 604–6.

5. Transcript, Testimony of Lemuel Bouse, 607–33.

6. Transcript, Testimony of Louisa Terrell, 634–55.

7. George Wesley Terrell served in the Indiana 124th Regiment, Company H. H. E. Tucker, *History of Randolph County* (Richmond: Eastern Indiana, 1967. First published 1882 by A. L. Klingman [Chicago]), 286. He died at age twenty-three on March 24, 1865, after being wounded at the battle of Wyse Fork, North Carolina, only sixteen days before Robert E. Lee surrendered to Ulysses S. Grant at Appomattox Courthouse on

April 9. George Terrell is buried in the New Bern, North Carolina, National Cemetery, under the designation "G. C. Terrell," Grave Marker No. 3039, https://www.findagrave .com/memorial/65165084/george-c.-terrell.

8. Transcript, Testimony of D. S. Terrell, 656–79.

22. The Heavens Will Pass Away

1. *Terrell Murder Trial*, 31.

2. Transcript, Testimony of William Terrell, 683–711.

3. William Wesley Terrell is my paternal great-grandfather.

4. "Terrell Weakens," *Fort Wayne Journal-Gazette*, Dec. 6, 1903, 1.

5. Mary Ann Thornburg Terrell is my paternal great-grandmother.

6. According to the Randolph County Historical Society's interview with me, such arrangements were not uncommon in the 1800s among families in rural Indiana.

7. John W. Tyndall and O. E. Lesh, *Biographical and Historical Record of Adams and Wells County, Indiana*, vol. 2 (Chicago: Lewis, 1887).

8. Transcript, Testimony of Mary Ann Thornburg Terrell, 712–18.

9. Transcript, Testimony of Delford McClain, 730–35; Testimony of Nathanial Bouse, 719–29; Testimony of Ezra Deering, 744–48; Testimony of George Harshman, 749–56;

10. Transcript, Testimony of Bert Stookey, 757–63.

11. Belling was a once-common practice associated with taunting newly wed couples. After the wedding, friends and neighbors would gather outside the newly-weds' house. When the lights were turned off, the assembled crowd would make as much noise as possible, including shooting off guns. "Belling Once Common Practice," Southwest Franklin County Historical Society, Grove City, OH, Jan. 27, 2021, http:// grovecityohhistory.org/belling-once-common-practice.

12. *Terrell Murder Trial*, 36.

13. "Terrell Weakens," 1.

14. "Terrell Weakens."

23. Lunatics and Idiots

1. *Terrell Murder Trial*, 36.

2. Transcript, Testimony of Dr. Nelson T. Chenowith, 764–79.

3. Transcript, Testimony of William Cecil, 780–99.

4. Transcript, Testimony of William Fitzpatrick, 800–819.

5. Transcript, Testimony of Charles Dudley, p820–37.

6. Transcript, Testimony of Jeremiah Smith, 838–57.

7. Transcript, Testimony of Cinda Halstead, 858–66.

8. Transcript, Testimony of William Terrell, 867–81.

9. "Many Members of Family Proven to Be Insane," *Bluffton Evening News*, Dec. 11, 1903, 1.

10. Transcript, Testimony of Ross Thompson, 897–909.

11. Transcript, Testimony of George Harshman, 910–29.

24. Lucy's Story

1. *Terrell Murder Trial,* 42.

2. Transcript, Testimony of Lucy Terrell Wolfe, 930–1011.

3. *Terrell Murder Trial,* 42.

4. *Terrell Murder Trial,* 42.

25. Atheist and Believers

1. Transcript, Testimony of Sarah Terrell Schott, 1012–52.

2. Transcript, Testimony of Lucinda Terrell Books, 1053–87.

3. Casey Cep, "Why Are Americans Still Uncomfortable with Atheism?," *New Yorker,* Oct. 28, 2018.

4. President McKinley died eight days later on September 14, 1901.

5. Cep, "Why Are Americans Still Uncomfortable with Atheism?," 1.

6. R. Laurence Moore and Isaac Kramnick, *Godless Citizens in a Godly Republic* (New York: W. W. Norton, 2018).

7. Cep, "Why Are Americans Still Uncomfortable with Atheism?," 1.

8. John Locke, *Letter on Toleration* (1689).

9. Barb Amandine, "A History of Atheism, Religion, Civic Belonging, and Collective Identity in the United States," www.brewminate.com; https://brewminate.com/a-history -of-atheism-religion-civic-belonging-and-collective-identity-in-the-united-states/.

10. Leigh Eric Schmidt, *Village Atheists: How America's Unbelievers Made Their Way in a Godly Nation* (Princeton, NJ: Princeton Univ. Press, 2016), 260, quoting "Freedom of Unbelief Denied," *Truth Seeker,* Apr. 23, 1904. Schmidt attributed the coining of the phrase "village atheist" to an 1808 review of British clergyman George Crabb's poem "The Parish Register" in the *Monthly Review.* Schmidt, *Village Atheists,* 14.

11. Jud Campbell, "Testimonial Exclusions and Religious Freedom in Early America," *Law & History Review* 37 (2019): 479.

12. Thomas Raeburn White, "Oaths in Judicial Proceedings and Their Effect upon the Competency of Witnesses," *American Law Register* 51 (1903): 373, 444n41. For an extensive discussion of easing oath requirements for nonbelievers by caselaw and statutes, see Campbell, "Testimonial Exclusions," 456–74. It was not until the 1940s that every state granted atheists the right to testify. See Jonathan Belcher, "Religion-Plus-Speech: The Constitutionality of Juror Oaths and Affirmations under the First Amendment," *William & Mary Law Review* 34 (3rd ed., 1940): 286, 293, citing sec. 1828. It was not until 1965 that the Maryland Supreme Court struck down the requirement that jurors swear an oath demonstrating a belief in God. *Schowgurow v. State,* 213 A.2d 475 (Md. 1965).

13. Transcript, Testimony of Fred Goss, 1088–1109.

14. In private, Ingersoll referred to himself as an atheist. Smith, *Robert G. Ingersoll.*

15. Smith, *Robert G. Ingersoll.*

16. See "After Pagan Bob," *Evansville Journal,* Apr. 15, 1896; "Prayed for Bob," *Huntington Daily Democrat,* Nov. 29, 1895; "Saturday Night. The Editor's Reverie," *Hamilton County Ledger,* Oct. 20, 1893; "Ingersoll on Which Way," *Marshall County Independent,* Jan. 11, 1895; "In His New Lecture Col. Robert G. Ingersoll Assails Christianity,"

Huntington Daily Democrat, Nov. 29, 1895; "God of the Bible and the Book Itself Defended by Dr. J. P. D.," *Logansport Pharos Tribune,* Apr. 15, 1894; "A Sermon," *Muncie Daily Times,* May 22, 1894; "Ingersoll Attacked," *South Bend Tribune,* Feb. 6, 1895.

17. Transcript, Testimony of Emanuel Caves, 1110–18.

18. Transcript, Testimony of John Schott, 1119–30; Testimony of William Books, 1209–31.

19. Transcript, Testimony of Jacob Terrell, 1131–49.

20. Transcript, Testimony of Cassius White, 1150–57.

21. Transcript, Testimony of Frank Kirkwood, 1185–90.

22. Transcript, Testimony of Henry Stanley, 1191–93.

23. Transcript, Testimony of Dr. Charles L. Landfair, 1158–87.

24. Transcript, Testimony of Catherine Terrell, 1232–71.

25. "It Got Night; John Terrell's Mind Was Blank," *Bluffton Evening News,* Dec. 10, 1903, 1.

26. John's Story

1. Transcript, Testimony of John Terrell, 1293–1356.

2. "It Got Night; John Terrell's Mind Was Blank," *Bluffton Evening News,* Dec. 10, 1903, 1.

27. Hundred-Dollar-a-Day Jibber-Jabber

1. Francine Uenuma, "The First Criminal Trial That Used Fingerprints as Evidence," *Smithsonian Magazine,* Dec. 5, 2018, https://www.smithsonianmag.com/history/first-case-where-fingerprints-were-used-evidence-180970883/.

2. Brandy Schillace, "Forensics on Trial: America's First Blood Test Expert," *Crime Reads,* Aug. 28, 2020, https://crimereads.com/forensics-on-trial-americas-first-blood-test-expert/.

3. "The History of Forensic Ballistics—Ballistic Fingerprinting," *Incognito Forensics Foundation,* https://ifflab.org/the-history-of-forensic-ballistics-ballistic-fingerprinting/.

4. "America's First Crime Lab," *Los Angeles Almanac,* https://www.laalmanac.com/crime/cr720.php.

5. Charles Norris and Alexander Gettler, Crime Museum, https://www.crimemuseum.org/crime-library/forensic-investigation/charles-norris-alexander-gettler/.

6. "Killer Breakthrough—the Day DNA Evidence First Nailed a Murderer," *Guardian,* June 7, 2016, https://www.theguardian.com/uk-news/2016/jun/07/killer-dna-evidence-genetic-profiling-criminal-investigation.

7. Transcript, Testimony of Dr. H. H. Weir, 1357–92.

8. See Gustavo C. Román, MD, FACP, "Cerebral Congestion: A Vanished Disease," *Archives of Neurology* (Apr. 1987): 444–48.

9. The first recitation of the defense's extended hypothetical question is set out at Transcript, 1360–76. It reappears no less than twelve times, taking in excess of two hundred pages of the transcript of proceedings.

10. See William A. Papenbrock, "The Expert Witness and the Hypothetical Question," *Western Reserve Law Review* 13 (1962): 755, https://scholarlycommons.law.case.edu/caselrev/vol13/iss4/9.

11. Transcript, Testimony of Dr. Frank B. Wynn, 1393–1449.

12. Transcript, Testimony of Dr. John Dickason, 1595–99.

13. Transcript, Testimony of Dr. L. A. Spaulding, 1600–1641.

14. Transcript, Testimony of Dr. L. Mason, 1642–73.

15. Transcript, Testimony of Dr. I. N. Hatfield, 1674–96.

16. Transcript, Testimony of Dr. Fred Metts, 1697–37.

17. Transcript, Testimony of Dr. H. W. Markley, 1738–62.

18. Transcript, Testimony of Dr. C. J. Blackman, 1763–81.

19. Transcript, Testimony of Dr. T. J. Bolds, 1782–1839.

20. "What Dr. Dickason Said to Terrell," *Bluffton Evening News,* Dec. 12, 1903, 1.

21. "What Dr. Dickason Said to Terrell."

28. Rebuttal

1. See Index, Record on Appeal, *John W. Terrell v. State of Indiana,* Indiana Supreme Court, Cause No. 20474, Indiana State Archives.

2. Transcript, Testimony of Mary Wolfe, 1840–42.

3. Transcript, Testimony of Allen Boher, 1843–73.

4. Transcript, Testimony of Oscar Oliver, 1874–79.

5. Transcript, Testimony of Thomas Clevenger, 1885–99.

6. Transcript, Testimony of William Faulkner, 1900–1912.

7. Transcript, Testimony of Francis "Frank" Fisher, 1925–35

8. Transcript, Testimony of Sarah Fisher, 2098–2111.

9. Transcript, Testimony of Amos King, 2003–19.

10. Transcript, Testimony of Lydia Kirkwood, 2020–28.

11. "Night Sessions Brings Terrell Murder Trial Near Its Close," *Bluffton Evening News,* Dec. 17, 1903, 1.

12. Transcript, Testimony of Andy Books, 2303–14.

13. Transcript, Testimony of George Bears, 2146–72.

14. Transcript, Testimony of Della Reed, 2315–16.

15. Transcript, 2401–4.

16. Transcript, Testimony of Abram Simmons, 2380–81.

17. Transcript, Testimony of Hugh Dougherty, 2391–92.

18. Transcript, Testimony of William Knuckle, 2382–83.

19. Transcript, Testimony of L. C. Davenport, 2384–85.

20. Transcript, Testimony of W. W. Greek, 2376–79.

21. Transcript, Testimony of Herbert Deam, 2386–87.

22. Transcript, Testimony of Lucy Terrell Wolfe, 2437–40.

23. Transcript, Testimony of John Terrell, 2441–44.

29. A Speech to Hang Me

1. "He Will Make a Speech to Hang Me; John Terrell, in Conversation with a News Reporter, Charges That W. H. Eichhorn Has Personal Malice against Him and Will Try to Give Him Severest Penalty Known to Law," *Bluffton Evening News,* Dec. 18, 1903, 1.

2. "He Will Make a Speech to Hang Me." See also "Some of the Best Speeches Ever Made in the County Are Delivered in the Terrell Trial," *Bluffton Evening News*, Dec. 19, 1903, 1; *Terrell Murder Trial*, 77–79.

3. "He Will Make a Speech to Hang Me."

4. *Terrell Murder Trial*, 79–80.

5. *Terrell Murder Trial*, 80.

6. *Terrell Murder Trial*, 80–81.

7. *Terrell Murder Trial*, 81–82.

8. *Terrell Murder Trial*, 82–83.

9. *Terrell Murder Trial*, 83–84.

10. *Terrell Murder Trial*, 84.

11. *Terrell Murder Trial*, 84–85.

12. Record on Appeal, 22–38, Indiana State Archives. See also "Judge Smith's Instructions to Jury," *Bluffton Banner*, Dec. 30, 1903, 1; *Terrell Murder Trial*, 86–92.

13. "Offer to Lucy," *Bluffton Evening News*, Dec. 18, 1903, 2.

14. A search of online newspaper sources for 1903 and 1904 in Illinois does not show any information that Lucy accepted the offer and appeared at the McVicker's Theater or anywhere else in Chicago.

30. Verdict

1. "Imprisonment for Life," *Bluffton Evening News*, Dec. 20, 1903, 1.

2. Record on Appeal, 38. See also "Imprisonment for Life."

3. "Imprisonment for Life"; "Motion for New Trial Deferred," *Fort Wayne Sentinel*, Dec. 21, 1903, 1.

4. "Imprisonment for Life."

5. "Burns' Victory," *Muncie Morning Star*, Dec. 22, 1903, 5.

6. "Motion for New Trial Deferred," 1.

7. "Burns' Victory," 5.

8. "Imprisonment for Life."

9. "Imprisonment for Life."

10. "Motion for New Trial Deferred."

31. The Man Is a Lunatic

1. "One of Terrell's Attorneys Charged by Court with Fraud," *Muncie Morning Star*, Dec. 22, 1903, 1.

2. See "Terrell Attorney Subject of Charges," *Indianapolis Business Journal*, Dec. 22, 1903; "Charges against Terrell's Lawyer," *Fort Wayne Sentinel*, Dec. 21, 1903, 1.

3. "One of Terrell's Attorneys Charged by Court with Fraud."

4. "One of Terrell's Attorneys Charged by Court with Fraud."

5. "DelaCour Presents Proof of Graduation," *Indianapolis Journal*, Dec. 29, 1903, 3.

6. "DelaCour Is Formally Cleared at Bluffton," *Indianapolis Star*, Dec. 30, 1903, 5.

7. "To Fight against Terrell's Pardon," *Evansville Journal*, Dec. 24, 1903; "Terrell Must Stay In," *Muncie Daily Herald*, Dec. 24, 1903, 1.

8. "Prosecutor John Burns Upheld in His Action," *Bluffton Banner,* Jan. 6, 1904, 7.

9. A term for "an item of food, especially a choice or tasty dish." *Merriam-Webster Online Dictionary,* https://www.merriam-webster.com/dictionary/viand.

10. "Girls Send a Dinner to John W. Terrell; Employes [*sic*] of Mitten Factory Give a Substantial Exhibition of Sympathy," *Muncie Morning Star,* Dec. 24, 1903, 1.

11. Suggestion of Insanity Occurring Since Verdict, Exhibit D (Affidavit of Birt [*sic*] E. Earl), Transcript, 169–71.

12. Record on Appeal, *State of Indiana v. John W. Terrell,* Cause No. 20474, Trial Transcript, 80–158. See also "New Trial for John Terrell," *Fort-Wayne Journal Gazette,* Dec. 29, 1903, 1.

13. "Motion for Retrial in the Terrell Case," *Indianapolis Journal,* Jan. 1, 1904, 5; "Motion for New Trial Overruled," *Evansville Journal,* Jan. 2, 1904, 1.

14. "Jacob Terrell to Be Married Tomorrow Night," *Bluffton Banner,* Jan. 27, 1904, 1.

15. "John W. Terrell Sells His Jackson Township Farm," *Bluffton Banner,* Jan. 6, 1904.

16. "Terrell Sells Opera House," *Bluffton Banner,* Feb. 2, 1904, 4.

17. Suggestion of Insanity Occurring Since Verdict, Exhibit C, Affidavit of James R. Johnston, Sheriff of Wells County, Transcript, 167–68, Indiana State Archives.

18. Suggestion of Insanity Occurring Since Verdict, Exhibits A–H, Transcript, 163–78, Indiana State Archives; see also "John Terrell Raves in His Cell a Maniac," *Bluffton Banner,* Feb. 10, 1904, 1.

19. Suggestion of Insanity Occurring Since Verdict, Exhibit A, Dr. Edwin R. Horton, Transcript, 164–75, Indiana State Archives.

20. "John Terrell Raves in His Cell a Maniac"; "May Affect Terrell's Motion for New Trial," *Bluffton Banner,* Feb. 10, 1904, 1.

21. Walbert found that there was a statute providing for such an inquiry in a recent copy of Indiana Acts; however, he found that the law had never been passed by the Indiana General Assembly and was printed in law books by mistake. "Squire Has No Jurisdiction, Says Walbert," *Bluffton Banner,* Feb. 17, 1904, 3.

22. "Squire Has No Jurisdiction."

23. "Terrell Is Not Accused of Shamming," *Bluffton Banner,* Feb. 17, 1904, 8.

24. "May Affect Terrell's Motion for New Trial."

25. "Governor Durbin Wants to Get in on Terrell Case," *Bluffton Banner,* Feb. 17, 1904, 3.

26. Biennial Message of the Governor to the Sixty-Third General Assembly, 16, Messages and Documents Winfield T. Durbin, Governor of the State of Indiana (1901–5), https://www.google.com/books/edition/Messages_and_Documents_of_Winfield_T_Dur /zDsCAAAAYAAJ?hl=en&gbpv=1&dq=Governor%20Durbin%20address%20to%20gen eral%20assembly%20%22embarrassing%20condition%20at%20the%20Indiana%20Pris on%22&pg=PA16&printsec=frontcover.

27. "Governor Durbin Wants to Get in on Terrell Case."

28. "Governor Durbin Wants to Get in on Terrell Case."

29. "Notes of Interest from the Court House," *Bluffton Banner,* Feb 17, 1904, 4.

30. "Terrell Was Brought before the Court," *Bluffton Banner,* Feb. 24, 1904, 2.

31. Suggestion of Insanity Occurring Since Verdict, Exhibit A.

32. "Terrell Was Brought before the Court."

33. Special Jury Verdict, Transcript, 183.

34. "Terrell Was Brought before the Court."

35. "Pathetic Story of John Terrell," *Huntington Herald*, Feb. 19, 1904, 5.

32. Confined until Cured

1. *In re: Guardianship of John W. Terrell, Lucy Wolfe, Petitioner,* Wells County Circuit Court, No. 8066, Mar. 16, 1904, Records of Wells County Clerk. See also "Request for Guardian for John W. Terrell," *Bluffton Banner,* Mar. 16, 1904, 1.

2. "A Detective Watched Terrell at the Jail," *Bluffton Banner,* Apr. 20, 1904, 3.

3. "A Detective Watched Terrell at the Jail."

4. "A Detective Watched Terrell at the Jail."

5. One of the products of Governor Durbin's state highway initiative was that the Bluffton-Camden Pike on which John Terrell chased after the injured Melvin Wolfe to Petroleum became Indiana State Highway 1, which it remains to this day.

6. Dan Carden, "Indiana Governors, Winfield Durbin," *Northwest Indiana Times,* https://www.nwitimes.com/news/image_51f94f5a-6338–52f9-ba01–36ad0187a1b1.html. See also Linda C. Gugin and James E. St. Clair, *The Governors of Indiana: A Biographical Directory* (Indianapolis: Indiana Historical Society Press, 2006).

7. "John Terrell Sentenced by Judge Smith," *Muncie Morning Star,* Apr. 29, 1904, 1.

8. "John Terrell Sentenced by Judge Smith."

9. "John Terrell Sentenced by Judge Smith"; "Terrell Slept While Judge Pronounced Sentence," *Fort Wayne Journal-Gazette,* Apr. 29, 1904, 1; "Insane Murderer Is Sentenced to Prison," *Indianapolis Journal,* Apr. 29, 1904, 3.

10. Records of Gov. Winfield T. Durbin, Indiana State Archives.

11. "Durbin Has Hand in Terrell Case," *Fort Wayne Sentinel,* Apr. 29, 1904, 1.

12. Records of Gov. Winfield T. Durbin, Indiana State Archives. The full order to Sheriff Johnston stated:

Hon. James R. Johnston
Sheriff Wells County,
Bluffton, Indiana

Dear Sir:

I herewith enclose the necessary document authorizing you to take John W. Terrell to the Easter Indiana Hospital for the Insane, that he may be there confined until cured, and, when cured to be taken to the State Prison, unless otherwise ordered by me.

After careful consideration, I have determined to act as indicated in said instrument, because I think it the most humane course to pursue under the circumstances of this case. Terrell was convicted of murder, and, after his conviction and before sentence, it was found that he was insane, and he is now insane. He has been sentenced by the court to the State Prison for life. This action was taken by the court for the reason, no doubt, that the court believed it was the only course open to him, and that he had no power to act otherwise.

I do not believe that Terrell should be taken to the State Prison and confined therein, at this time, and for that reason I have granted what, in effect, amounts to a conditional parole, which is enclosed herewith, directing you to at once take said Terrell to the Eastern

Indiana Hospital for the Insane, and ordering that he be confined therein until cured, and when cured, to be then taken to the State Prison, unless otherwise ordered by me.

I am acting in this matter upon the advice of the Attorney General of the State. Relying upon you to faithfully carry out my directions, I have the honor to be

Very truly yours,
    Winfield T. Durbin, Governor of Indiana

13. "Governor's Power Doubted," *Fort Wayne Sentinel*, Apr. 29, 1904, 1.

14. *Jefferson Evening News*, May 2, 1904, 2.

15. "Written in Indiana," *Indianapolis Star*, Apr. 4, 1904, 4, quoting *Huntington Journal*.

16. "Terrell Declared Insane Again," *Huntington Weekly News Democrat*, May 20, 1904, 2; "Terrell Case Again an Issue," *Richmond Daily Palladium*, May 19, 1904, 8.

17. "Terrell Property in Guardian's Hands," *Muncie Morning Star*, May 24, 1904, 1.

18. "For Pardon of John Terrell a Petition Circulated in Court," *Richmond Daily Palladium*, Dec. 12, 1904, 3; "Assisting in Petition; Pardon for Terrell," *Muncie Daily Herald*, Dec. 10, 1904, 1; "An Inmate's Story; Effort to Pardon Terrell Will Be Met by Strong Opposition in Some Quarters," *Richmond Evening Item*, Dec. 24, 1904, 1; "Pardon for Terrell," *Princeton Daily Clarion*, Dec. 13, 1904, 5.

19. "Governor Refuses Pardon to Terrell," *Muncie Morning Star*, Jan. 3, 1905, 1.

20. "Governor Refuses Pardon to Terrell." See also "Gov. Durbin Has Declined; Say He Will Not Grant a Pardon to John W. Terrell," *Richmond Evening Item*, Jan. 3, 1905, 1; "No Pardon for Terrell," *Indianapolis Star*, Jan. 3, 1905, 11.

21. "J. Frank Hanly," *Encyclopedia of Indianapolis*, https://indyencyclopedia.org/j-frank-james-franklin-hanly.

33. Reversal of Fortune

1. Brooke Kroeger, *Nelly Bly: Daredevil, Reporter, Feminist* (New York: Random House, 1994); Jean Marie Lutes, *Front Page Girls: Women Journalists in American Culture and Fiction, 1890–1930* (Ithaca, NY: Cornell Univ. Press, 2006).

2. See Bhavnaa Narula, "What It Meant to Be a Mental Patient in the 19th Century?," *Medium*, https://medium.com/lessons-from-history/what-it-meant-to-be-a-mental-patient-in-the-19th-century-86340b93199b.

3. Rachel E. Sheeley, "Richmond State Hospital Celebrating 125th Year," *Richmond Palladium-Item*, Sept. 21, 2015, https://www.pal-item.com/story/news/local/2015/09/21/richmond-state-hospital-celebrating-th-year/72594846/; "Richmond State Hospital," https://www.waynet.org/waynet/spotlight/2007/070129-statehospital.htm.

4. "Richmond State Hospital"; History," Indiana Family and Social Services Administration, https://www.in.gov/fssa/dmha/state-psychiatric-hospitals/richmond-state-hospital/history/.

5. "John Terrell Is Now in the Asylum," *Bluffton Banner*, May 11, 1904, 6.

6. "Queer Tale Being Told," *Bluffton Banner*, Sept. 21, 1904, 8.

7. "Question of Sanity in Terrell Case; Is He Really Shamming?," *Muncie Morning Star*, Dec. 23, 1904, 5.

8. "Bluffton's Opera House Opened to the Public," *Bluffton Banner,* Apr. 13, 1904, 7.

9. "Files Suit for Lien Payment," *Bluffton Banner,* June 22, 1905, 1.

10. "Court to Run the House: Receiver Is Booking Shows," *Muncie Morning Star,* July 7, 1905.

11. "Sell Bluffton Opera House," *Indianapolis Star,* Oct. 1, 1905, 6. The opera house continued to operate, eventually becoming a movie theater. According to the Bluffton Public Library, after a fire, the theater was razed in about 1978. It is now a parking lot across the street from the Bluffton Public Library.

12. "Dying in the Far West," *Muncie Morning Star,* Nov. 5, 1905.

13. "Housing Lots & Land—Review," *Los Angeles Sunday Times,* Mar. 17, 1907, 22. None of the modern tools for finding death certificates, obituaries, or newspaper articles reveal any information about what happened to Charles DelaCour—where, when, or how he died or where he is buried. It seems an unfitting anonymous end for a man who, even as a lawyer, was always a showman.

14. "Case Reversed by Supreme Court," *Goshen Mid-Week News Times,* Nov. 3, 1905, 1; "Indictment Fails to Stand," *Indianapolis Star,* Nov. 3, 1905, 7; "Terrell Verdict Reversed," *Fort Wayne Evening Sentinel,* Nov. 3, 1905, 9.

15. *John W. Terrell v. State of Indiana,* 165 Ind. 443, 75 N. E. 884 (Ind. 1905).

16. "Terrell Re-Indicted," *Huntington Herald,* Nov. 28, 1905, 1.

17. "New Warrant for Terrell," *Fort Wayne Sentinel,* Nov. 29, 1905, 3.

18. "Local Brevities," *Montpelier Evening Herald,* Jan. 15, 1906, 3; "Will Remain in Asylum," *Muncie Morning Star,* Jan. 12, 1906, 9.

19. "John W. Terrell a Heavy Man," *Hartford City Telegram,* Feb. 13, 1907, 2.

20. The Twenty-Eighths [*sic*] New Judge," *Montpelier Evening Herald,* Jan. 23, 1906; "Election Results from Indiana Counties," *Indianapolis Star,* Nov. 7, 1906.

21. "Terrell Fails to Recognize His Old Friends," *Richmond Palladium-Item,* Oct. 14, 1908, 1.

22. "To Visit Terrell; Judge Erwin Will Decide Himself," *Decatur Daily Democrat,* Apr. 17, 1907, 1.

23. "To Visit Terrell."

24. "Viciously Insane," *Huntington Herald,* Oct. 5, 1907, 6; "Terrell Viciously Insane," *Muncie Morning Star,* Oct. 5, 1905, 3.

34. The Way the World Ends

1. "Causes Big Stir," *Decatur Daily Democrat,* Feb. 14, 1908, 1.

2. "Relatives Will Not Discuss Case of Terrell," *Richmond Palladium-Item,* Feb. 4, 1908, 1.

3. "Relatives Will Not Discuss Case of Terrell."

4. "Relatives Will Not Discuss Case of Terrell."

5. "John W. Terrell Visited by Gavisk of State Board," *Richmond Palladium-Item,* Feb. 6, 1908, 1.

6. Gavisk was a well-known speaker across the state. See "Talk by Catholic Priest, Rev Francis H. Gavisk to Deliver Lecture in This City," *South Bend Tribune,* Aug. 21, 1907; "Charity Meeting Tonight, Feature of Meeting Will Be Presence of Father Gavisk," *Mun-*

cie Evening Press, Nov. 20, 1908, 1; "Notables Arriving for Charity Meet; Which Opens Tonight—Gov. Hanly Speaks Tomorrow—Whittaker, Gavisk and Taylor Interviewed," *Evansville Press,* Oct. 19, 1907, 1. But Gavisk was made of sterner stuff than prayers and speaking. In 1906, a tramp became belligerent after he deemed the amount of funds (a dime) provided by Gavisk was insufficient. Gavisk responded by pummeling the tramp and throwing him out of the priest's house. "Pummeled Tramp with Fists; and Then the Doughty Priest Shoved Him into the Street," *Jackson County Banner,* Oct. 3, 1906, 6.

7. "Believes That John W. Terrell Is Insane," *Indianapolis News,* Feb. 6, 1908, 4.

8. "Says Terrell Much Better," *Richmond Morning News,* May 8, 1908; "Northern Indiana News and Gossip," *Fort Wayne Sentinel,* Sept. 21, 1908, 8; "Reported John Terrell Is Rapidly Improving," *Hartford City Telegram,* Sept. 23, 1908, 4.

9. "Father Is Sane; Says Mrs. Lucy Terrell Wolfe," *Decatur Daily Democrat,* Sept. 21, 1908, 1.

10. "Murderer Terrell Must Again Stand Trial for Crime," *Richmond Palladium-Item,* Oct. 12, 1908, 1.

11. "Is Terrell Sane?," *Decatur Daily Democrat,* Oct. 14, 1908, 1; "Terrell Again Held in Jail at Bluffton," *Muncie Morning Star,* Oct. 14, 1908, p. 1.

12. "Terrell Case Drags, Prompt Trial Unlikely," *Muncie Morning Star,* Oct. 16, 1908, 1.

13. "Terrell Refused a Nurse," *Decatur Daily Democrat,* Nov. 6, 1908, 1.

14. "Judge Erwin Declines to Act Further as Special Judge in Terrell Case," *Fort Wayne Weekly Sentinel,* Nov. 4, 1908, 24.

15. "Leffler Will Sit in Terrell Case," *Muncie Morning Star,* Dec. 29, 1908, 1.

16. "Muncie Judge Declines to Act in Terrell Case," *Muncie Morning Star,* Feb. 2, 1909, 7.

17. "Northern Indiana News and Gossip," *Fort Wayne Sentinel,* Nov. 20, 1908, 3.

18. "Jay A. Hindman Passes Away in Modesto with Flu," *Modesto Bee,* Feb. 3, 1919, 2.

19. "John W. Terrell Will Be Released; Judge Paulus Permits Him to Give Bail and Fixes Bond at $15,000," *Muncie Morning Star,* May 29, 1909, 1; "Out on Bond after Six Years; John W. Terrell, Insane Murderer, to Be Released," *Hartford City Telegram,* June 2, 1909, 2.

20. CPI Inflation Calculator, https://www.officialdata.org/us/inflation/1909?amount =15000.

21. "John Terrell's Fortune Is Swallowed by Court," *Montpelier Evening Herald,* Oct. 17, 1910, 2; "John Terrell Is Penniless," *Hartford City Telegram,* Oct. 19, 1910, 5.

22. "Murder Case Is Recalled; Jacob Wolfe Visits Bluffton—Some Think John W. Terrel [sic] Insanity Feigned," *Muncie Morning Star,* July 25, 1909, 5; "Does Not Improve; Family of John W. Terrell Sees No Change in His Condition," *Decatur Daily Democrat,* Aug. 20, 1909, 1.

23. "Insane Murderer No Better," *Hartford City Telegram,* Aug. 25, 1909, 3.

24. "Terrell in Bluffton," *Fort Wayne Sentinel,* Jan. 31, 1911, 3; "Terrell Visits Bluffton," *Muncie Morning Star,* Jan. 31, 1911, 6.

25. "John Terrell's Fortune Is Swallowed by Court"; "John Terrell Is Penniless"; "Terrell's Fortune Is Gone," *Decatur Daily Democrat,* Oct 19, 1910, 1.

26. "John W. Terrell May Be Arrested," *Hartford City Telegraph,* Dec. 13, 1911, 1.

27. "Murder Revived; John W. Terrell of Bluffton Again Becomes Wild and Assistance Called," *Decatur Daily Democrat,* Dec. 14, 1911, 6.

28. Minnie Terrell, Death Certificate No. 35205, Indiana State Board of Health, Wells County, Oct. 29, 1926.

29. Catherine Terrell, Death Certificate No. 125, Wells County, Nov. 11, 1914.

30. William Wesley Terrell, Death Certificate No. 4, Randolph County, Jan. 13, 1915.

31. William Henry Books, Death Certificate No. 17, Wells County, Dec. 23, 1914.

32. "Marriage Recalls Murder," *Fort Wayne Sentinel*, Feb. 23, 1916, 10.

33. "John W. Terrell Succumbs Here," *Muncie Morning Star*, Oct. 17, 1916, 3; "Last Chapter of Terrell Case," *Fort Wayne Journal-Gazette*, Oct. 17, 1916, 3.

34. "Funeral Notices: Terrell," *Muncie Morning Star*, Oct. 19, 1916, 6.

Selected Bibliography

Newspapers Consulted

Austin (TX) American-Statesman
Bangor (ME) Daily News
Bluffton Banner
Bluffton Evening News
Bluffton News-Banner
Boston Globe
Buffalo (NY) Enquirer
Butte (MT) Miner
Champaign (IL) Daily News
Davenport (IA) Democrat
Dayton (OH) Evening Herald
Decatur Daily Democrat
Elkhart Weekly Truth
Elwood Call-Leader
Evansville Journal
Fort Wayne Daily News
Fort Wayne Journal-Gazette
Fort Wayne News
Fort Wayne Sentinel
Garrett Weekly Clipper
Goshen Mid-Week News Times
Hamilton County Ledger
Hartford City Telegram
Huntington Daily Democrat
Huntington Herald
Huntington Weekly Herald
Huntington Weekly News Democrat
Indianapolis Business Journal
Indianapolis Journal
Indianapolis News
Indianapolis Star
Indianapolis Sunday Sentinel

Jackson County Banner
Jasper Herald
Jeffersonville Evening News
Logansport Pharos Tribune
Los Angeles Sunday Times
Marshall County Independent
Minneapolis Star-Tribune
Modesto (CA) Bee
Montpelier Evening Herald
Muncie Daily Herald
Muncie Daily Times
Muncie Evening Press
Muncie Morning Star
Nashville American
Nebraska State Journal
New Albany Public Press
New Orleans Times-Democrat
New York Times
Pittsburgh Press
Princeton Daily Clarion
Richmond Daily Palladium
Richmond Evening Item
Richmond Palladium-Item
Sioux City (IA) Journal
South Bend Tribune

Primary Sources

Affidavit for Change of Judge, *State of Indiana v. John Terrell*, Wells County Circuit Court, No. 1204, Records of Wells County Clerk.

Ben Vandergriff v. Lucinda Vandergriff, Huntington County Clerk, Divorce Proceeding, Cause No. 7609 (1899).

Benefiel v. State, 578 N. E. 2d 338 (Ind. 1991).

Biennial Message of the Governor to the Sixty-Third General Assembly, 16, Messages and Documents Winfield T. Durbin, governor of the state of Indiana (1901–5). https://www.google.com/books/edition/Messages_and_Documents_of_Winfield_T_Dur/zDsCAAAAYAAJ?hl=en&gbpv=1&dq=Governor%20Durbin%20address%20to%20general%20assembly%20%22embarrassing%20condition%20at%20the%20Indiana%20Prison%22&pg=PA16&printsec=frontcover.

Bradley v. State, 31 Ind. 492, 507 (1869).

Conway v. State, 118 Ind. 482, 21 N. E. 285 (1889).

Durbin, Winfield T., Orders No. 447 & 448, Apr. 29, 1904, Papers of Gov. Winfield T. Durbin, Indiana State Archives.

Goodwin v. State, 96 Ind. 550 (Ind. 1883).

Index of Plaintiffs and Defendants, Wells County (Ind.) Clerk (1888–1903).

Indiana Code, Sec. 35–41–3-6 (1984).

In re: Guardianship of John W. Terrell, Lucy Wolfe, Petitioner, Wells County Circuit Court, No. 8066, Mar. 16, 1904, Records of Wells County (Ind.) Clerk.

John W. Terrell v. Andrew W. Sours, Trustee of Nottingham Township, Wells County Circuit Court No. 7429, Records of Wells County (Ind.) Clerk (1901).

John W. Terrell v. Arthur L. Sharpe et al., Wells County Circuit Court No. 5497, Records of Wells County (Ind.) Clerk (1897).

John W. Terrell v. Daniel Mann et al., Wells County Circuit Court No. 5979, Records of Wells County (Ind.) Clerk (1898).

John W. Terrell v. Frank Brown, Wells County Circuit Court No. 4379, Records of Wells County (Ind.) Clerk (1894).

John W. Terrell v. John O'Brien, Wells County Circuit Court No. 5978, Records of Wells County (Ind.) Clerk (1898).

John W. Terrell v. Richard A. Waldron, Wells County Circuit Court No. 1538, Records of Wells County (Ind.) Clerk (1884).

John W. Terrell v. Robert P. Lambert, Wells Circuit Court No. 5220, Records of Wells County (Ind.) Clerk (1896).

John W. Terrell v. State of Indiana, 165 Ind. 443, 75 N. E. 884 (Ind. 1905).

John W. Terrell v. State of Indiana, Indiana Supreme Court, No. 20474, Appellants Brief, Indiana State Archives (1904).

John W. Terrell v. State of Indiana, Indiana Supreme Court, No. 20474, Appellees Brief, Indiana State Archives (1904).

John W. Terrell v. State of Indiana, Indiana Supreme Court, No. 20474, Reply Brief, Indiana State Archives (1904).

John W. Terrell v. State of Indiana, Indiana Supreme Court, No. 20474, Trial Transcript, Indiana State Archives (1904).

John W. Terrell v. William M. Park et al., Wells County Circuit Court No. 5869, Records of Wells County (Ind.) Clerk (1898).

Kahler v Kansas, Appendix, 140 S. Ct 1021, 1051 (2020).

Levi Mock, John Mock, George Mock v. John W. Terrell, Complaint on Account, Wells County Circuit Court, No. 7988, Records of Wells County (Ind.) Clerk, Nov. 6, 1903.

Official Register of the United States, Containing a List of the Officers and Employees in the Civil, Military, and Naval Service, Together with a List of Vessels Belonging to the United States, vol. 2, 1905, 110.

Plake v. State, 23 N. E. 273, 121 Ind. 433 (1890).

Sarah Vandergriff vs. Jacob Joseph Vandergriff, Wells County Circuit Court, No. 6011, Records of Well County (Ind.) Clerk (1898).

Schowgurow v. State, 213 A.2d 475 (Md. 1965).

State ex rel Lucy Wolfe v. Melvin Wolfe, Wells County Circuit Court, No. 10071, Wells County (Ind.) Clerk (1902).

Transfer Book, Nottingham Township, Wells County (Ind.) Auditor's Office (1880–83).

US Census Bureau, Wells County, Indiana, Nottingham Township, District 0152 (1900).

Secondary Sources

Amandine, Barb. "A History of Atheism, Religion, Civic Belonging, and Collective Identity in the United States," www.brewminate.com. https://brewminate.com/a-history-of-atheism-religion-civic-belonging-and-collective-identity-in-the-united-states/.

"America's First Crime Lab." *Los Angeles Almanac.* https://www.laalmanac.com/crime/cr720.php.

Ancestry.com. "Della Reed Wilson," Death Certificate No. 20904, Wells County, June 1, 1951.

——. "Hannah Louisa Lacey Wolfe," Dec. 24, 1844–Sept. 27, 1887, Brubeck Family Tree. https://www.ancestry.com/familytree/person/tree/77751850/person/30408493783/facts?_phsrc=qsr2&_phstart=successSource.

——. "Jacob Noah Wolfe," Brubeck Family Tree. https://www.ancestry.com/familytree/person/tree/77751850/person/142256617492/facts?_phsrc=qsr7&_phstart=successSource.

——. "Levi Mock," Rehn Family Tree. https://www.ancestry.com/family-tree/person/tree/72239753/person/312076138639/facts?_phsrc=qsr8&_phstart=successSource.

——. Marriage Record for Lucinda Terrell to William Books, Sept. 12, 1901, FHL Film Number 002318977.

——. Marriage Record for Sarrah [*sic*] Terrell to John Schott, Sept. 4, 1901, FHL Film Number 002318977.

——. "Mary Jane Wimer," July 12, 1843–May 15, 1915. Death Certificate No. 21, Wells County.

Appelbaum, Paul S., MD. "Kahler v. Kansas: The Constitutionality of Abolishing the Insanity Defense." *Psychiatry Online,* Nov. 10, 2020. https://doi.org/10.1176/appi.ps.202000707.

"APPL Practice Guideline for Forensic Psychiatric Evaluation of Defendants Raising the Insanity Defense." *Journal of the American Academy of Psychiatry and the Law Online* 42, no. S3–S76 (2014).

Belcher, Jonathan. "Religion Plus Speech: The Constitutionality of Juror Oaths and Affirmations under the First Amendment." *William & Mary Law Review* 34 (1940): 286–331.

"Belling Once Common Practice." Southwest Franklin County Historical Society, Grove City OH, Jan. 27, 2021. http://grovecityohhistory.org/belling-once-common-practice.

Blatchley, W. S. "The Petroleum Industry in Indiana in 1900." *Report of State Geologist* (1900): 481–527.

Campbell, Jud. "Testimonial Exclusions and Religious Freedom in Early America." *Law & History Review* 37 (2019): 431, 479.

Carden, Dan. "Indiana Governors, Winfield Durbin." *Northwest Indiana Times.* https://www.nwitimes.com/news/image_51f94f5a-6338–52f9-ba01–36ad0187a1b1.html.

"Catherine Terrell." Death Certificate No. 125, Indiana State Board of Health, Wells County, 1914.

Cep, Casey. "Why Are Americans Still Uncomfortable with Atheism?" *New Yorker,* Oct. 28, 2018.

Chandler, Craig. "The Indiana Gas Boom," Apr. 27, 2021. https://storymaps.arcgis.com/stories/87c02af2280b4f26b2320f35f038a410.

Courtright, David. *Dark Paradise: A History of Opiate Addition in America.* Cambridge, MA: Harvard Univ. Press, 2001.

CPI Inflation Calculator. https://www.officialdata.org/us/inflation/.

Crabb, George. "The Parish Register." *Monthly Review* (1808).

"Della Reed White." Death Certificate H-22, Death No. 20904, Wells County, Indiana State Board of Health, 1951.

"Drummond Terrell." Death Certificate, Indiana Department of Health, Delaware County, 1885.

Fahey, Eugene M., Laura Groschadi, and Brianna Weaver. "The Angels That Surrounded My Cradle: The History, Evolution, and Application of the Insanity Defense." *Buffalo Law Review* 68 (2020): 805–56.

"Freedom of Unbelief Denied." *Truth Seeker,* Apr. 23, 1904.

Freeman, Frank R. "The Origin of the Medical Expert Witness: The Insanity of Edward Oxford." *Journal of Legal Medicine* 22 (2001): 349, 368–73.

Garcia, Tomasula y. "The Long Tail of Indiana's Oil and Gas Boom." *Belt Magazine,* May 28, 2021. https://beltmag.com/long-tail-indiana-oil-gas-boom/.

"George C. Terrell." New Bern, Grave Marker No. 3039, North Carolina National Cemetery. https://www.findagrave.com/memorial/65165084/george-c.-terrell.

Grand Opera House, Bluffton, IN, ca. 1930, photo. https://elevation.maplogs.com/poi/linn_grove_rd_berne_in_usa.61422.html.

Gray, Elizabeth. "Losing Sorrow in Stupefaction: America's Women's Opiate Dependency before 1900." *Nursing Clio,* Aug. 18, 2022. https:nursingclio.org/2022/08/18/losing-sorrow-in-stupefication-american-womens-opiate-dependency-before-1900/.

Gruber, Rudolph J. *The Insanity Defense.* Port Washington, NY: Associated Faculty Press, 1984.

Gugin, Linda C., and James E. St. Clair. *The Governors of Indiana: A Biographical Directory.* Indianapolis: Indiana Historical Society Press, 2006.

Haimbaugh, Frank D. *History of Delaware County, Indiana in Two Volumes.* Indianapolis: Historical Publishing Press, 1924.

Hewett, Janet, ed. *The Roster of Union Soldiers, 1861–1865.* Wilmington, NC: Broadfoot, 1997.

"The History of Forensic Ballistics—Ballistic Fingerprinting." *Incognito Forensics Foundation.* https://ifflab.org/the-history-of-forensic-ballistics-ballistic-fingerprinting.

Indiana Department of Natural Resources, Division of Oil and Gas. "History of Indiana's Oil and Gas Fields." og-OilGas_in_Indiana.pdf.

"Jacob Noah Wolfe." Death Certificate No. 14348, Indiana State Board of Health, Wells County, 1936.

"Killer Breakthrough—the Day DNA Evidence First Nailed a Murderer." *Guardian,* June 7, 2016. https://www.theguardian.com/uk-news/2016/jun/07/killer-dna-evidence-genetic-profiling-criminal-investigation.

Kroeger, Brooke. *Nelly Bly: Daredevil, Reporter, Feminist,* New York: Random House, 1994.

Lapham, Lewis H. "Notebook: The Consolations of Vanity." *Harper's Magazine,* Dec. 1997.

"Leo Melvin Wolfe." Death Certificate No. 21, Indiana State Board of Health, Wells County, 1903.

Locke, John. *Letter on Toleration* (1689).

Lutes, Jean Marie. *Front Page Girls: Women Journalists in American Culture and Fiction, 1890–1930.* Ithaca, NY: Cornell Univ. Press, 2006.

"Mabel Marie Scott." Death Certificate, No. 10071, Indiana Department of Health, Adams County, 1941.

Maeder, Thomas. *Crime and Madness: The Origins and Evolution of the Insanity Defense.* New York: Harper & Row, 1985.

Merriam-Webster Online Dictionary. "Viand." https://www.merriam-webster.com/dictionary/viand.

"Minnie Terrell." Death Certificate No. 35205, Indiana State Board of Health, Wells County, 1926.

Moore, R. Laurence, and Isaac Kramnick. *Godless Citizens in a Godly Republic: Atheists in American Public Life.* New York: W. W. Norton, 2018.

Morris, Grant H. *The Insanity Defense: A Blueprint for Legislative Reform.* Lanham, MD: Lexington Books, 1975.

Narula, Bhavnaa. "What It Meant to Be a Mental Patient in the 19th Century?" *Medium,* July 21, 2021. https://medium.com/lessons-from-history/what-it-meant-to-be-a-mental-patient-in-the-19th-century-86340b93199b.

Nevius, James. "The Strange History of Opiates in America: From Morphine for Kids to Heroin for Soldiers." *Guardian,* Mar. 15, 2016. theguardian.com/commentisfree/2016/mar/16/long-opiate-use-history-america-latest-epidemic.

Nicholas, Stacey. "J. Frank Hanly." *Encyclopedia of Indianapolis* (1994, rev. 2021). https://indyencyclopedia.org/j-frank-james-franklin-hanly.

Norris, Charles, and Alexander Gettler. Crime Museum. https://www.crimemuseum.org/crime-library/forensic-investigation/charles-norris-alexander-gettler/.

Papenbrock, William A. "The Expert Witness and the Hypothetical Question." *Case Western Reserve Law Review* 13 (1962): 755–67.

Penrod, Gladys. "Father's Day Note," June 17, 1956. Courtesy of Geoffrey and Nicole Penrod.

Perkin, Michael L., and Heather Ellis Cucolo. *Mental Disability Law: Civil and Criminal.* 3rd ed. New York: Lexis/Nexis, 2017.

Petroleum, IN, Wells County Recorder's Office, 1894, plat map.

"Richmond State Hospital." https://www.waynet.org/waynet/spotlight/2007/070129-statehospital.htm.

"Richmond State Hospital, History." Indiana Family and Social Services Administration. https://www.in.gov/fssa/dmha/state-psychiatric-hospitals/richmond-state-hospital/history/.

Robyn, Alfred G. "Bye, Oh! Baby!" New York: William A. Pond, 1890.

Román, Gustavo C., MD, FACP. "Cerebral Congestion: A Vanished Disease." *Archives of Neurology* (Apr. 1987): 444–48.

Schillace, Brandy. "Forensics on Trial: America's First Blood Test Expert: The Forgotten Story of a Murdered Woman, an Ohio Chemist, and a Legal System Reluctant to Let Science into the Courtroom." *CrimeReads,* Aug. 28, 2020. https://crimereads.com/forensics-on-trial-americas-first-blood-test-expert/.

Schmidt, Leigh Eric. *Village Atheists: How America's Unbelievers Made Their Way in a Godly Nation.* Princeton, NJ: Princeton Univ. Press, 2016.

Sheeley, Rachel E. "Richmond State Hospital Celebrating 125th Year." *Richmond Palladium-Item*, Sept. 21, 2015. https://www.pal-item.com/story/news/local/2015/09/21/richmond-state-hospital-celebrating-th-year/72594846/.

Shepherd, Joshua. "Williams Wells." *Warfare History Network*, Apr. 2016. https://warfarehistorynetwork.com/article/william-wells.

Smith, Frank. *Robert Ingersoll: A Life*. Foreword by Gordon Stein. Amherst, NY: Prometheus Books, 1990.

Spencer, David R. *The Yellow Journalism: The Press and America's Emergence as a World Power*. Chicago: Northwestern Univ. Press, 2007.

State of Indiana. "Wells County." https://www.in.gov/core/mylocal/wells_county.html.

The Terrell Murder Trial: Complete History of the Crime, Trial and Conviction of John W. Terrell. Bluffton, IN: Banner Book Concern, 1904.

Trickey, Erick. "Inside the Story of America's 19th Century Opiate Addition." *Smithsonian Magazine*, Jan. 14, 2018.

Tucker, H. E. *History of Randolph County, Indiana with Illustrations and Biographical Sketches of Some of Its Prominent Men and Pioneers*. Richmond: Eastern Indiana, 1967. First published 1882 by A. L. Klingman (Chicago).

Tyndall, John W., and O. E. Lesh. *Adams and Wells Counties Indiana: An Authentic Narrative of the Past*. Chicago: Lewis, 1918.

——. *Biographical and Historical Record of Adams and Wells County, Indiana*, vol. 2.

Uenuma, Francine. "The First Criminal Trial That Used Fingerprints as Evidence." *Smithsonian Magazine*, Dec. 5, 2018. https://www.smithsonianmag.com/history/first-case-where-fingerprints-were-used-evidence-180970883/.

United States. CPI Inflation Calculator. https://www.officialdata.org/us/inflation/1909?amount=15000.

Univ. of Michigan Law Class of '86 (1886) photo.

Webster's Revised Unabridged Dictionary of the English Language. "Air line." Springfield, MA: G. & C. Merriam, 1913.

Wells County lawyers, court personnel, and sheriff, Wells County Clerk's Office, ca. 1903, photo.

Wells County Recorder, 1905, map.

White, Thomas Raeburn. "Oaths in Judicial Proceedings and Their Effect upon the Competency of Witnesses." *American Law Register* 51 (1903): 373–446.

"William Henry Books." Death Certificate No. 17, Indiana State Board of Health, Wells County, 1914.

"William Henry Eichhorn." Death Certificate No. 17087, Indiana State Board of Health, Wells County, 1948.

"William Wesley Terrell." Death Certificate No. 4, Indiana State Board of Health, Randolph County, 1915.

"Wyse Fork, Second Kinston." American Battlefield Trust. https://www.battlefields.org/learn/civil-war/battles/wyse-fork.

Index